D0914707

WORKSHOPS FOR THE WORLD

REVISED EDITION

WORKSHOPS
for the WORLD

THE UNITED NATIONS FAMILY OF AGENCIES

By Graham Beckel in collaboration with Felice Lee

*Introduction by Paul G. Hoffman, Managing Director,
United Nations Special Fund*

ABELARD-SCHUMAN
London   New York   Toronto

DEDICATED TO THE PERSONNEL OF THE

INTERNATIONAL CIVIL SERVICE

LONDON	NEW YORK	TORONTO
ABELARD-SCHUMAN	ABELARD-SCHUMAN	ABELARD-SCHUMAN
LIMITED	LIMITED	CANADA LIMITED
8 King Street	6 West 57th Street	896 Queen Street W.

Printed in the United States of America

Acknowledgments

The author wishes to express a particular indebtedness to Mrs. Bille-Brahe for permission to use her name in a chapter title, to Miss Marian Scott, Librarian, Westfield (N.J.) Senior High School, and to the personnel of the United Nations Office of Public Information.

Generally speaking, the publications resources have been those of the United Nations and of the Agency concerned. The traditions of the International Civil Service restrict the identity of authors who prepare reports, journals and releases for press and radio. It is the hope of the author that these people will recognize his appreciation of the excellence of their work as being reflected in the dedication.

The author is indebted for much secretarial aid to Mrs. Jacqueline Lamourine.

During the making of this book, its author has had the benefit of the experiences of many people. The assistance of the following merits particular appreciation: Miss Nora Jones, Dr. S. Y. Lin and Mr. John Drake (FAO); Messrs. Leon Boussard, A. O. Arnfast and S. G. Cooper (ICAO); Capt. Robert N. Buck, Mr. Kenneth S. Fletcher (TWA); Mr. Leighton Collins (*Air Facts Magazine*); Mr. Roberto Rendueles, Mr. Ronald Morse (WHO); Mrs. Patricia L. Hartwell, Miss Alison Mathers (UNICEF); Messrs. John H. Redding, John C. Allen, Cornelius Petersen and George Gibbs (*United States Post Office Department*); Dr. Fritz Hess, Mr. Fulke Radice (*International Bureau*, UPU); Messrs. Ed Allen, Snowden

Herrick, Richard Balentine and David Blanchard (ILO); Mr. Willy J. Dorchain (*American Office, International Transport Workers' Federation*); Messrs. G. Marvin Wright, Walter H. Schwaikert and Richmond B. Williams (*Long Lines Department, American Telephone and Telegraph Co.*); Mr. Soemarno (*Ministry of Information, Republic of Indonesia*); Mr. Gerald C. Gross, Mr. J. Persin (ITU); Mr. A. Salsamendi, Mrs. Betty Thomas (UNESCO); Mr. Harold N. Graves, Jr. and Miss Agnes Maher (Bank and IDA); Mrs. Beth Short (*Office of Senator Monroney, United States Senate*); Messrs. Jentry Holmes, Guiseppa Morra and Scott Seegers (IFC); Mr. Jay Reid (IMF); Mr. T. R. Brooks (*Weather Bureau, U. S. Dept. of Commerce*); Cmdr. C.E.N. Franckom, Dr. G. Swoboda, Mr. D. A. Davies (WMO); Mr. Myer Trupp (*U.S. Maritime Administration*); Mr. John Burt (IAEA); Mr. Charter Heslep (*U.S. Atomic Energy Commission*); Miss Norma Globerman (*Technical Assistance Board, United Nations*); Mr. Clint Rehling (U. N. *Special Fund*); and the personnel of the Government Room, *New York Public Library*.

PHOTOGRAPHIC CREDITS:

Chapter 2: FAO; Chapter 3: Transworld Airlines, ICAO, and Unations; Chapter 4: Unations and UNICEF; Chapter 5: U.N. Postal Administration (stamps) and Unations; Chapter 6: ILO; Chapter 7: Long Lines Division, American Telephone and Telegraph Co., and Indonesian Ministry of Information; Chapter 8: UNESCO, Unations, and UNICEF; Chapter 9: International Bank; Chapter 10: IFC; Chapter 12: IMF; Chapter 13: WMO; Chapter 14: Unations and U.S. Coast Guard; Chapter 15: Unations, IAEA, and Argonne National Laboratory; Chapter 16: Unations and UNICEF; Chapter 17: Photos of Messrs. Garner and Hoffman, Fabian Bachrach, Postmaster General Blair's photo, U.S. Post Office Department, others, Unations.

PREFACE

This new and expanded edition of WORKSHOPS FOR THE WORLD is welcomed by the United Nations Office of Public Information. Its presentation of the economic and social work of the United Nations and its family of Agencies should be helpful in developing public understanding of the international efforts now under way to achieve a better world for all people.

I am certain that these up-to-date stories will help stimulate an awareness of the relationship between United Nations activities and the lives of all of us. The United Nations belongs to all of the people of this interdependent world; as understanding and informed support of its work expand, so too will the opportunities for the less fortunate to benefit through such collective efforts.

The opinions expressed in this book are, of course, those of the authors.

Dr. Hernane Tavares de Sá
United Nations Under-Secretary for Public Information

Contents

Author's Preface

On December 17, 1903, Orville and Wilbur Wright made their first flights at Kitty Hawk, North Carolina. In the fifty-eight years that have gone by since then, the idea of one world has become a geographic fact. Cities that were not even listed in the geography books our grandfathers used are now commonplace names to all of us. Most of these cities may be reached by simply picking up your telephone transmitter and asking for the long-distance operator. A person listening to a radio in Bombay, India, will hear the words of a speaker in New York before these same words are heard by the people sitting in the lecturer's audience.

However small our world has become, if we had the good fortune to make a trip around it by air we would discover that this world is made up of series of neighborhoods. As we looked down upon these neighborhoods we would discover that some of them are vast cities linked to the surrounding countryside by an intricate pattern of highways and railways, while others are merely clearings in the jungle reached by a simple foot trail cut through the underbrush. Between these two extremes would be other neighborhoods of varying sizes. No matter how many of these neighborhoods we might visit, we would find they each have one thing in common—the people in them are dependent upon one another. Each person takes a hand in creating goods or services that are used by his fellow men.

If we were to examine more carefully this exchange of goods

11

and services in our American society, we would discover that
many of our daily transactions depend upon the goods produced
and the services performed in other neighborhoods in other lands.
Without these goods and services, we would have no tea or coffee, no important metals to mix with our ore for making steel, no
telephones, no radio or television tubes, and no automobiles. Some
thirty-eight minerals vital to our industry are either mined or in
part manufactured in neighborhoods in other lands. Without these
our life would be drab indeed.

If there is to be sharing of resources between neighborhoods
and nations, certain conditions are important. In the first place,
there must be peace. We have banded together with other nations
to create a world machine designed to solve the problem of peace.
We call this machine the United Nations. Working together
through this large organization, we hope to harmonize the neighborhoods of the world so that goods and services, people and ideas,
may flow freely among them.

But this is only part of the task. The problem of world peace
is of a general nature. In addition, there are the specific technical
problems that directly concern the people who produce the goods,
and perform the services that move goods and people from one
national neighborhood to another. These problems involve the
health of the producers, the food they eat, and the conditions under which they work. These problems also involve communication between the neighborhoods of the world—whether it be by
mail, radio, or telephone—and the safe movement of people and
goods by air, land, and sea. These problems may be concerned
with the financing of new enterprises, the exchanges of currency,
and the sharing of scientific and technical knowledge.

Problems like these require the services of experts in specialized
fields of knowledge. Long before the establishment of the United
Nations, many governments had already entered into agreements
with governments of other nations to create agencies for the purpose of bringing together specialists in some of these fields. It was
only natural that these organizations should be called *Specialized
Agencies.*

When the Charter of the United Nations was drafted, provisions were made for bringing the established agencies into working agreements with the United Nations. Besides coordinating the

work of existing Agencies, the Charter established procedures for creating new Agencies as they were needed.

The purpose of this book is to bring together in narrative form case studies of the Agencies at work. Because no two Agencies have identical membership, it would be impossible for the Agencies themselves to tell the collective story of their activities—although individual Agencies, in their own publications, have done excellent jobs of explaining their work. As a student, teacher, and member of numerous discussion groups, the author has long felt the need of some one book that would present the significant contributions of the Agencies by telling how each accomplished a specific task, and at the same time would include basic reference material for each Agency. In addition, it seems important to know how the Agencies come into being, how they team up with the United Nations, and the role that the United States plays in them.

The case study approach to the Specialized Agencies as described in this book had its origin in the author's classes in Modern World History at the Westfield (N.J.) Senior High School. We felt that the study of international cooperation and "know-how" should concern itself with situations we already knew something about. Telephones, radio, mail service, working conditions, planes, schools, doctors, food, banks, trade, and the weather were the stuff of our daily lives. As these matters were also the concern of the Specialized Agencies, a study of their operations seemed natural.

We began our study by asking ourselves a series of questions. What problems can we think of in getting a plane from the local airport to London? In making a telephone call to Indonesia? In helping the people of India rid themselves of malaria? These were typical of our self-questioning. In many instances our problems exceeded two hundred in number. We didn't find the answers to each problem then, and they won't all be found in this book. But we did make the exciting discovery that people can and do work together to solve these world neighborhood problems, even though vast differences and distances separate them one from another. We discovered that in solving the problems of goods and services man was waging peace.

Remembering the excitement of our study, I had planned to

dedicate this book to those former students. They will be happy to learn that, after meeting dozens of the people who are making the Agencies effective instruments for world peace, I decided upon my dedication to the International Civil Service. Their day is here. Your contributions are yet to be!

So many people have cooperated in making this work possible that I have acknowledged their individual contributions on the following pages.

At this point I signed the preface to the first "Workshops." The following remarks are pertinent to the new:

1. Since 1954 there has been an ever-increasing amount of Agency intercooperation under United Nations programs and auspices. This constructive development occasions the new sub-title: "The United Nations Family of Agencies."

2. Since 1954, 243 of the author's graduate students at Queens College and New York University have used "Workshops" in their own classrooms — fifth grade through twelfth. Their suggestions are incorporated in "Workshops" as new case studies geared to student interests, extensions of the reference material, and improved suggestions for classroom approaches to the study of the Agencies.

3. In 1954 Felice Lee was Liaison Officer for Specialized Agencies for the United Nations Office of Public Information. Her assistance then made the first "Workshops" possible. I welcome her as a full collaborator for the new "Workshops."

GRAHAM BECKEL

Lyme, Connecticut
1 September 1961

Introduction

Whether we know it or not, whether we like it or not, we are caught up in a vast and earth-shaking revolution, a revolution that will influence, indeed, dominate the remainder of our lives. Personal plans, national goals, international order—all hinge on the outcome of that revolution, the revolt of two-thirds of the world's people against the continued acceptance of their body-destroying and soul-destroying poverty.

These two-billion of our fellow human beings (wrap your mind around that figure) sense what we, deep inside ourselves, understand: that it is now technically possible, morally desirable and absolutely necessary to wipe mass poverty, chronic ill-health and resulting personal and national frustration off the face of the earth.

But do we recognize the size of the task of raising the standards of living in the low-income countries? Its complexity? Its urgency? We had better heed the cry for help before it is ours. For our own peace and prosperity depend upon our knowing these close neighbors, upon our comprehending their legitimate aspiration and upon our recognizing how we can and must speedily help them to achieve in decades what we and our ancestors took centuries to accomplish.

Economic and social development, the improvement of the conditions of life of so many people, is a new and a tough job.

In that effort the United Nations is playing a critically important role. The pages that follow suggest ways in which the world community, through its family of United Nations organizations, is helping to mobilize human and material resources and apply modern "know-how" to the herculean task we, all the people of the world together, must accomplish.

For practical reasons it has perhaps been necessary to divide such a huge subject, such a magnificent effort, into its vital components—fields of activity such as health, aviation and education. But I would urge the reader not to fail to put the pieces together again, to realize that the whole is, truly, much greater than the sum of its parts.

How can I best illustrate this? My work for the United Nations takes me to all parts of the world, and particularly to the less-developed countries where I seek to ascertain the most urgent needs of governments for U.N. assistance and check on ways in which our programs can be made to make a maximum impact. It is heartening on these trips to visit with our experts at their field stations—a meteorologist in the high Andes Mountains, a forestry expert in the steaming jungle, a surveyor of a mighty but astonishingly little explored river.

Yet it is when I invite the available experts to meet with me as a group in the capital of the country where they are serving that one appreciates most fully the real and comprehensive character of United Nations assistance. Recently in Addis Ababa, Ethiopia, for example, I met with several dozen experts from over a score of countries. There in one room were specialists in education, human health and animal health, in civil aviation, communications and meteorology, in agriculture, forestry, public administration and other fields. There one could appreciate the scope, the variety of combined U.N. aid to but one country, and feel the great quality, the skill and devotion of these international helpers. There one was not conscious of organizations and their initials but of a family of devoted workers brought together from all continents to assist people in their climb from poverty and its accompanying evils to more decent living standards and the opportunities for a better life which they provide.

And that is what this fine book is all about. It should stir pride in the soul of everyone who reads it, and will, I hope, make each in turn tell others of this effort of people united to help each other. Most of all, may it stimulate further study of the need to speed progress in the less-developed countries, and generate support for the larger United Nations assistance programs that are required.

by Paul G. Hoffman
MANAGING DIRECTOR OF THE
UNITED NATIONS SPECIAL FUND

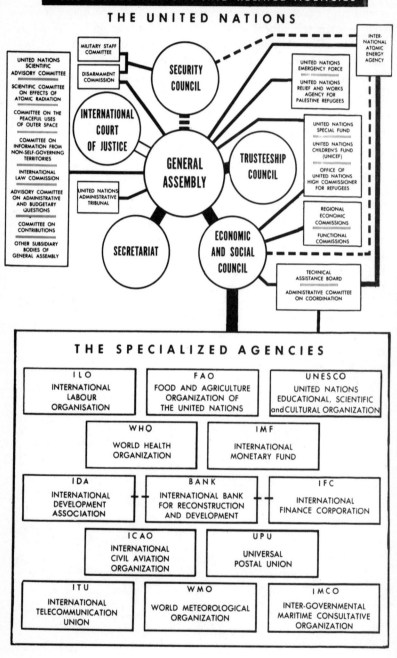

THE UNITED NATIONS AND RELATED AGENCIES

THE UNITED NATIONS

MILITARY STAFF COMMITTEE

DISARMAMENT COMMISSION

SECURITY COUNCIL

INTERNATIONAL ATOMIC ENERGY AGENCY

UNITED NATIONS EMERGENCY FORCE

UNITED NATIONS RELIEF AND WORKS AGENCY FOR PALESTINE REFUGEES

UNITED NATIONS SCIENTIFIC ADVISORY COMMITTEE

SCIENTIFIC COMMITTEE ON EFFECTS OF ATOMIC RADIATION

COMMITTEE ON THE PEACEFUL USES OF OUTER SPACE

COMMITTEE ON INFORMATION FROM NON-SELF-GOVERNING TERRITORIES

INTERNATIONAL LAW COMMISSION

ADVISORY COMMITTEE ON ADMINISTRATIVE AND BUDGETARY QUESTIONS

COMMITTEE ON CONTRIBUTIONS

OTHER SUBSIDIARY BODIES OF GENERAL ASSEMBLY

INTERNATIONAL COURT OF JUSTICE

UNITED NATIONS ADMINISTRATIVE TRIBUNAL

GENERAL ASSEMBLY

TRUSTEESHIP COUNCIL

UNITED NATIONS SPECIAL FUND

UNITED NATIONS CHILDREN'S FUND (UNICEF)

OFFICE OF UNITED NATIONS HIGH COMMISSIONER FOR REFUGEES

REGIONAL ECONOMIC COMMISSIONS

FUNCTIONAL COMMISSIONS

SECRETARIAT

ECONOMIC AND SOCIAL COUNCIL

TECHNICAL ASSISTANCE BOARD

ADMINISTRATIVE COMMITTEE ON COORDINATION

THE SPECIALIZED AGENCIES

ILO
INTERNATIONAL LABOUR ORGANISATION

FAO
FOOD AND AGRICULTURE ORGANIZATION OF THE UNITED NATIONS

UNESCO
UNITED NATIONS EDUCATIONAL, SCIENTIFIC and CULTURAL ORGANIZATION

WHO
WORLD HEALTH ORGANIZATION

IMF
INTERNATIONAL MONETARY FUND

IDA
INTERNATIONAL DEVELOPMENT ASSOCIATION

BANK
INTERNATIONAL BANK FOR RECONSTRUCTION AND DEVELOPMENT

IFC
INTERNATIONAL FINANCE CORPORATION

ICAO
INTERNATIONAL CIVIL AVIATION ORGANIZATION

UPU
UNIVERSAL POSTAL UNION

ITU
INTERNATIONAL TELECOMMUNICATION UNION

WMO
WORLD METEOROLOGICAL ORGANIZATION

IMCO
INTER-GOVERNMENTAL MARITIME CONSULTATIVE ORGANIZATION

CHAPTER ONE

The United Nations Family of Agencies

The United Nations Charter expresses man's will to peace in our day. Down through the centuries wars have been followed by plans and organizations designed to keep the peace. The people who drafted the Charter had this history of experience upon which to draw as they created their own design for peace at San Francisco in 1945.

Within the Charter they provided machinery to deal with the traditional forces making for war—militarism, nationalism, imperialism, and conflicts in ideas. They also took a giant step forward! For the first time, one of the principal organs of an international peace charter was charged with eliminating the economic and social forces that make for war.

This organ is the Economic and Social Council (ECOSOC). Its responsibilities are established in Article 55 of the Charter:

"With a view to the creation of conditions of stability and well-being which are necessary for peaceful and friendly relations among nations based on respect for the principal of equal rights and self-determination of peoples, the United Nations shall promote:

a.   higher standards of living, full employment and conditions of economic and social progress and development;

b.   solutions of international economic, social, health, and related problems; and international cultural and educational cooperation; and

c. universal respect for, and observance of human rights and
fundamental freedoms for all without distinction as to race,
sex, language, or religion."

The Charter set out a program for achieving these ends and
the framework in which they were to be pursued. First, the intergovernmental organizations already operating in the economic
and social fields were to be brought into relationship with the
United Nations. Second, the United Nations was to encourage
nations to establish new agencies for accomplishing the purposes
set forth in Article 55.

Here is the current roster of Agencies, followed by their abbre-
viated designations, the year of founding, and the year in which
they were brought into relationship with the United Nations.

Organization	Founded	Relationship with U.N.
Universal Postal Union (UPU)	1875	1948
International Labor Organization (ILO)	1919	1946
International Telecommunication Union (ITU)	1932	1949
Food and Agriculture Organization of the United Nations (FAO)	1945	1946
International Bank for Reconstruction and Development (Bank)	1945	1947
International Monetary Fund (IMF)	1945	1947
United Nations Educational, Scientific and Cultural Organization (UNESCO)	1946	1946
International Civil Aviation Organization (ICAO)	1947	1947
World Health Organization (WHO)	1948	1948
World Meteorological Organization (WMO)	1950	1951
International Finance Corporation (IFC)	1956	1957
International Atomic Energy Agency (IAEA)	1957	1957
Intergovernmental Maritime Consultative Organization (IMCO)	1958	1959
International Development Association (IDA)	1960	1961

No general account of the work of the United Nations Agencies would be complete without mention of its activities on behalf of refugees. During World War II, the Allies had established an agency, the first to bear the U.N. name, to carry out an emergency program in war-devastated areas. This agency, the United Nations Relief and Rehabilitation Administration (UNRRA), functioned until mid-1948. By that time a new United Nations agency, the International Refugee Organization (IRO), was ready to take over UNRRA's responsibilities for refugees and displaced persons. Between July, 1947, and the end of 1951, when IRO was terminated, the Agency re-established over one million persons in new homes and helped some 70,000 to return to their former homes. There remained, though, some million and a half persons who needed help. The United Nations, in December, 1950, established the Office of the United Nations High Commissioner for Refugees. This Office gives legal protection to refugees, promotes permanent solutions to their problems, and administers emergency aid. With money contributed to the United Nations Refugee Fund, the Office was able, between 1955 and 1959, to find solutions for the problems of many of these people, either in the country of residence or through resettlement. Many thousands remain, however, and "World Refugee Year," which began in mid-1959, helped to spotlight their need.

Before examining the Agencies in more detail, it is well to keep in mind certain facts concerning them:

1. Each of the Agencies is separate from the United Nations and from all the others. Each Agency has its own charter, budget, governing body, and headquarters.

2. Each of the Agencies is, like the United Nations, a freely accepted organization of governments. Not all members of the United Nations are members of all the Agencies. Some members of individual Agencies are not members of the United Nations.

Originally, the Agencies limited their activities to technical and advisory matters for their own members. But several factors have occasioned the Agencies and the United Nations increasingly to work together. At the outset there is the basic interdependence which flows from the very fact of common goals. Next, there has been a growing realization among governments that the ultimate responsibility for coordination lies with their votes in each organization. And, finally, there has been the action taken by governments to pursue a broad attack on the problems of the underdeveloped countries. This latter demands cooperation and teamwork among the Agencies. Teamwork and cooperation are the hallmarks of successful family living. Hence the phrase "Specialized Agencies" as used in the Charter has given way to the more truly descriptive "Family of United Nations Agencies."

Article 58 of the Charter authorizes recommendations for coordinating the policies and activities of the Agencies. The machinery for this consists of an Administrative Committee on Coordination, composed of the United Nations Secretary-General and the executive heads of the Agencies, reporting to the Economic and Social Council, which in turn reports to the General Assembly. This line of responsibility may be followed on the chart, p. 18.

As early as 1946, the United Nations and the Agencies began to receive requests for aid from member states. In that same year the General Assembly made the first, small appropriation for advisory social welfare services. But these activities of the U.N. Family of Agencies remained sporadic and largely uncoordinated until 1949, when technical assistance was established as a joint undertaking through the creation of the Expanded Program of Technical Assistance by the United Nations General Assembly. This action by the General Assembly was an important step towards the goals of the Charter, as it recognized the great need for specific long-range development aid to member nations and the extra effort that would be required to provide it. Thus, voluntary contributions from governments were called for to finance the program.

With the initiation of field projects in 1950, the U.N. Family formally began the new phase of operational aid. This event sharpened the need for meshing Agency and U.N. programs, and a special inter-Agency body, the Technical Assistance Board (TAB) was created by the General Assembly for the purpose. Its original members were the organizations first taking part in the Expanded Program of Technical Assistance: the U.N., ILO, FAO, UNESCO, ICAO and WHO. Later, new members of the U. N. Family, the International Telecommunications Union (ITU), the World Meteorological Organization (WMO), and the International Atomic Energy Agency (IAEA) also took part. The joint technical assistance program is directed by a twenty-four member intergovernmental body, the Technical Assistance Committee of the Economic and Social Council. Policy is carried out and operations coordinated by the Board. The International Bank and the International Monetary Fund, while performing essential functions in promoting economic development, do not receive Expanded Program funds, and thus are not members of the Technical Assistance Board.

Operations during the early years of the Expanded Program of Technical Assistance shed light on a development problem which technical assistance could not solve. This was the need for development capital. Many governments felt that the U.N. itself should be a source of long-range development capital on terms more liberal than the International Bank could provide, and proposals for a Special United Nations Fund for Economic Development (SUN-FED) were discussed in the General Assembly for some years. Such a fund has not come into existence, but several new bodies were created to deal with certain aspects of the need for capital.

The first was the International Finance Corporation (IFC), an intergovernmental agency set up in 1956 as an affiliate of the International Bank. Whereas the Bank loans money only to governments or upon government guarantee, the IFC may invest directly in private enterprise. IFC procedures also stimulate the flow of private capital to underdeveloped areas.

The second step taken to expand the movement of capital to underdeveloped regions was the establishment of the United Nations Special Fund in October, 1958. The Special Fund, a U.N. body, aims at smoothing the way for capital investment by helping countries to undertake essential preinvestment activities. Preinvestment aid prepares a country to use capital effectively. If natural resources have not been assessed, markets determined, or people trained to take part in new enterprises, capital investment is likely to be wasted. Such preparations also help to attract private foreign investment. The Special Fund therefore aids large-scale surveys of natural resources, establishment of major training schools to strengthen human resources, and applied research to determine uses of local materials and products.

Like the Expanded Program of Technical Assistance, the Special Fund depends for its operation on voluntary governmental contributions. Its investments are made in terms of expert missions, equipment and some fellowships, not in cash grants. The value of each investment is at least matched by the receiving governments. The policies and operations of the Special Fund are controlled by an eighteen-nation Governing Council, elected by the Economic and Social Council. A Consultative Board—consisting of the United Nations Secretary-General, the Executive Chairman of the Technical Assistance Board, and the President of the International Bank—advises the Fund's Managing Director. After approval of a request for aid, the Special Fund designates the appropriate member of the U.N. Family, or an outside organization, if required, as the "executing Agency" for the project.

The most recently formed organization tailored to meet the need for capital is the International Development Association (IDA). This new intergovernmental Agency came into existence in late 1960. A second affiliate of the International Bank, it begins operations with a capital fund of $1 billion, from which it will provide low-interest, long-term loans either to governments or to private enterprise. IDA will be able to make the type of loan which the Bank cannot undertake. So long as the project has a high development priority it need not be revenue-producing or directly productive. Thus such projects as water supply, sanitation or pilot housing would be eligible for IDA financing. The Agency has been given wide latitude in determining the forms or terms of its loans. For example, it may make loans repayable in foreign currencies or it may loan money to a related group of projects that form part of a development program. These are but two of many features of IDA lending which make the Agency a flexible tool for economic development.

The status of the United Nations Family of Agencies today points hopefully to the future and gives a glimpse of the possibilities which cooperation among the nations can bring to reality. With the passage of sixteen years, definition and substance have been given to the principles set forth in the United Nations Charter. Cooperation has become the taking-off point for the economic and social thinking of the United Nations. Further, from the perspective of the aided nation, U.N. Family assistance has many advantages. The very fact that it is a cooperative endeavor with a voice given to all nations and with all contributing to the cost, leads to a feeling of partnership between the country receiving assistance and the world community providing it. Again, there are no political considerations involved in U.N. aid; the sole aim is to promote economic and social progress. A third advantage lies in the fact that the U.N. and the Agencies have the whole world from which to select specialists. This has also fostered a sense of partnership, for many of the recipient nations are themselves furnishing expert help in a different field to other countries.

Many of the activities of the members of the U.N. Family of Agencies touch directly on the daily lives of individuals. Not only do they ease routine relations between nations in a world more interdependent than at any time in history, but they offer the promise of a better tomorrow to more than a billion people determined not to accept poverty, ignorance and disease as their way of life.

CHAPTER TWO

FAO

Food and Agriculture Organization

Plant an Acre of Fish

Who ever heard of *planting* fish? To most Americans the title of this chapter reads like the beginning of a whopping big *fish* story. But to millions of people throughout the world the food produced by fish farming means the difference between an adequate diet and the ugly fact of hunger. And to millions more who have the opportunity to learn the science of fish farming, malnutrition from lack of the most important of all foodstuffs, the proteins, may be a thing of the past.

In some of the world's neighborhoods the art of fish farming is an age-old practice. The ancient Romans dug ditches that carried young salt-water fish into the low areas near the coast, where they were trapped and kept until large enough to be used for food. This same practice is followed today in certain parts of France and Italy. The raising of fresh-water fish dates back many centuries, particularly in the Far East. As early as the fifteenth century, historians report that the victorious tribes of Java forced their captives to the task of building huge fish ponds. If such a large-scale industry existed in Java in the 1400's, the art of fish culture must certainly have been known much earlier to Javanese farmers.

Other neighborhoods beside ancient Rome and Java had learned the rather simple facts that make fish farming possible. In the course of a year a body of water will produce a certain amount of fish food, such as plankton and algae. These and other plants can be used directly by fish that feed on water plants, and indirectly by those that feed on smaller fish. Rice fields lend themselves admirably to the cultivation of fish, since the thin layer of water over the paddy fields produces an abundant crop of fish food. When recently hatched fish (fry) are introduced into the field, an acre of such land is sufficient to produce from 45 to 135 pounds of fish in a three-month period. It doesn't come as a surprise, therefore, to learn that fish farming has been practiced for centuries in rice-growing countries like Indonesia, Japan and Vietnam, where, in some areas, 80 per cent of the rice fields are stocked with carp and other species of fish.

Unfortunately, this knowledge has not been independently discovered by all the peoples of the world. Nearly half of the world's population, mainly in tropical countries and particularly in the

A balanced diet of fish and rice has been harvested from the pond shown in the background.

Caribbean area, suffer malnutrition from want of proteins. Yet hundreds of millions of these people live in neighborhoods where there are lakes, rivers, irrigation canals, and rice fields that could be made to yield a high production of fish. And fish are a rich source of protein! Help in spreading the "know-how" of fish farming to neighborhoods that need it is one of the services provided by the Food and Agriculture Organization.

One government making such use of FAO is the Republic of Haiti. The people of Haiti have long been faced with the fundamental problem of producing enough goods and services to provide for their steadily growing population. In 1948 the government of Haiti requested the United Nations to send a group of experts into the country to study the problem and to make suggestions for improving the life of the people. Professor Ernest F. Thompson of Yale University was the member of this mission assigned by the Food and Agriculture Organization to investigate the specific problem of food production.

In his report Professor Thompson noted, among many other things, that the fishing industry of Haiti is limited to small operations along the coast of the island. However, Haiti possesses a number of areas suitable for pond construction, and also rivers, irrigation canals, and lagoons rich in fish food. These could be utilized to raise large quantities of fish that would help solve the tragic problem of malnutrition and at the same time provide a prosperous new industry for the farmers. Professor Thompson recommended that the government of Haiti, working with the FAO, take the following action before deciding on a program of fish farming:

1. The services of a first-class fish-culture specialist familiar with practices in other countries should be employed to make an extended survey of the situation.

2. If, after the survey, the government of Haiti decided upon a program of fish farming, the services of the specialist should be retained for a number of years to guide the program.

3. At least two Haitians should be trained in the principles of fish culture to follow up the plans of the specialist.

The government of Haiti gave careful attention to Professor Thompson's report, and then requested FAO to assign a specialist for the purpose of carrying out the suggested survey. It was only natural that a person experienced in the fish-farming activities of the Far East should be chosen for this task. In June of 1950, Dr. S. Y. Lin was assigned to the fish-culture project in Haiti.

Dr. Lin was born on Hainan Island, China. Following his graduation from Yenching University in Peking, he worked with the Kwangtung Fisheries Experiment Station in Canton, China. It was here that he began the studies in fisheries biology and fish culture that finally prepared him to take charge of a fisheries investigation project in the China Sea. When the Sino-Japanese War broke out in 1937, Dr. Lin went to the British colony of Hong Kong as a refugee. The Hong Kong government made it possible for him to continue his studies, and when a Fisheries Research Station was established there in 1940 he became superintendent, a position he held until 1949, when he joined FAO as a fisheries biologist. Here was a person well trained in the modern science of fish production.

When Dr. Lin arrived in Haiti, he sought the answers to numerous questions. Were there any domestic fish that could be used for profitable farming? If not, what fish might be imported? Did the fresh-water systems, such as rivers, lend themselves to fish farming? What land area might be used for the construction of fish ponds? Might the rice fields be used? What kind of fish food was available? Was the climate of Haiti suitable for fish farming? Could the farmers be interested in raising fish? Could the skills and techniques of fish farming be easily learned?

After careful consideration of these matters, Dr. Lin was convinced that Professor Thompson had been correct in his suggestion that fish farming might be a part of the solution to Haiti's food problem. After consultation with officials of the Haitian government, Dr. Lin forwarded the results of his survey to the Fisheries Division at FAO Headquarters in Rome. Here other fisheries experts appraised the report and drafted a tentative plan for action. This plan was then submitted to the Inter-Divisional Group, which is composed of representatives of the major Divisions of FAO. This afforded an opportunity to get a many-sided view of the project based upon experiences gathered from all parts of the globe. After modifications had been made, the Fisheries Division drew up a formal working agreement for submission to the government of Haiti.

Under this first agreement the Haitian government was to provide a 1950-51 budget of 50,000 *gourdes* ($10,000) to cover expenses in Haiti, such as the building of ponds, the purchase of equipment, and travel costs within the country. Dr. Lin's salary, allowances, and traveling expenses outside Haiti were to be paid by FAO from United Nations Technical Assistance Program funds. This mutual program was approved by the government of Haiti, thus beginning the second part of the action suggested by Professor Thompson in 1948.

Dr. Lin then set about constructing a fish-farming program in three steps. In the first place, it was necessary to build a fish-fry nursery with a few experimental ponds to determine what fish would offer most in the way of production. After a supply of fish fry was established, he planned to develop demonstration and extension centers throughout Haiti where farmers could be schooled in fish culture. Lastly, attention was to be given to the marketing and use of fish, so that farmers might be offered an incentive to engage in fish farming.

By early 1951, enough experimental ponds had been established so that Dr. Lin and his assistant could determine what fish would be best suited to Haitian waters. In February and September, 1951, a total of 420 carp fingerlings was introduced into the ponds from a hatchery in Alabama. In July of the same year 103 *Tilapia* were imported from Jamaica in the BritishWest Indies. Both types of fish have shown remarkable growth, and their offspring are even now furnishing food for the people of Haiti. But if planting an acre of fish seemed to indicate the beginning of an American-style fish tale, this is nothing when compared with the story of how the *Tilapia* came to arrive in Haiti!

Back in 1939, Mr. W. H. Schuster, later of FAO, was visiting a fish farm in Indonesia. The farmer was pointing out some fingerlings he had raised in his fish pond. Although Mr. Schuster had spent many years in fishery work in Indonesia, he had never seen anything quite like them. While he was observing them, one of the fish released young fry from its mouth, as did several others that had been placed in a bucket by the farmer. Mr. Schuster realized that these must be mouth-breeding fish, a type of fish which protects eggs and young by guarding them in the mouth during the incubation period and moments of danger. But no fish

Workmen are shown deepening an already existing pond in Haiti.

of this type were known in Indonesia! Research determined that these were *Tilapia*, and of the type native to the inland waters of Mozambique, East Africa! The farmer declared he had found them in a small lagoon. No others were ever found. To this day there is no explanation of how these fish happened to be found thousands of miles from their home waters.

Whatever the *Tilapia* mystery might be, the important thing was that here were fish ideally suited to pond farming. Many freshwater fish will spawn only in running water, in lakes, or in special breeding ponds. This means that fish ponds must be stocked each year from fry caught in natural waters or raised in hatcheries, a time-consuming and expensive process. Not so the

Tilapia! They will breed in stagnant pond water as well as in free-running streams.

Fry from the original types were introduced into other ponds in Indonesia. They soon became the most popular pond fish. It wasn't long before the *Tilapia* were being raised on fish farms in Malaya, and it was from this latter region that they were brought to Jamaica in 1950 and then on to Haiti in 1951.

Having discovered several types of fish that would thrive in Haiti, Dr. Lin then turned to demonstrating methods of fish culture to the farmers of the island. An example of one farmer's interest is best expressed in Dr. Lin's own words:

"For instance, there is a farmer in Damien who was inspired by the ponds I built there and the fish raised in them. He asked me in April 1951 to advise him how to build a small pond in his farm, which I did. He immediately began work, but it took him almost fourteen months to complete that little pond of 1,200 square feet in area and two feet deep in water. It is now stocked with *Tilapia*, which are very prolific and easy to raise. Though the yield of the small pond will not be large, yet the zeal and effort made by the farmer is admirable."

However small the yield may be, this farmer will always have a convenient, fresh supply of high-protein fish to supplement his diet. The will and stamina of this one farmer is indicative of the way in which people help themselves when human goodness and example point the way.

By the middle of 1951 it became apparent that fish farming in Haiti was well started. Equally important, however, to the long-range program was the training of Haitian citizens themselves in fish culture, as suggested in Professor Thompson's report.

In 1951 and 1952 two Haitian fisheries officials received FAO fellowships, one for study of pond and rice-field culture in Java and the other for study of fish culture in Brazil and Surinam. The knowledge gained through these fellowships made it possible for the Haitians to take over the project in 1954—and to run it efficiently ever since. But meanwhile, Dr. Lin was succeeded by another FAO expert, Shimon Tal, of Israel. Mr. Tal introduced another variety of carp from Israel. Descendants of these carp, reared in Haiti, were later taken to Mexico to serve as a basis for a fish-culture industry there!

Dr. Lin supervises the transporting of carp and "Tilapia" fingerlings in five-gallon cans.

Haiti now has scores of large fish ponds as well as many small ponds run simply to augment family food supplies. In addition, the Haitian rivers which had hardly any fish ten years ago are now well-stocked.

Other neighborhoods throughout the world are taking advantage of this typical way in which FAO helps people to help themselves. Fish-farming projects are in operation in such widely separated places as Thailand, India, Morocco, Iraq and Syria. In Syria the drainage of a large marshy area in the Ghab did away with valuable freshwater fish resources. To replace this source of food, a number of artificial fish ponds were constructed on the advice of an FAO expert. In just a year, the yield has shown excellent results, and it is expected that soon these new ponds will produce twice as much as was obtained from the Ghab marshes.

Another neighborhood that has taken advantage of FAO's fish-farming expertise may come as a surprise: it is the United States. It would not be expected that one of the world's largest food-producing nations would ask for the services of an FAO expert. However, in 1959, at the request of the U.S. government, FAO sent Dr. Shao-Wen Ling on a three-month assignment to the U.S. Fish and Wildlife Service to advise on the establishment of a research station in Arkansas to investigate fish-farming possibilities in the U.S. Individual rice farmers in Arkansas had already experimented with fish farming, but the results had been disappointing. Dr. Ling's experience has been in the coordination of all the biological sciences necessary to make fish farming a success, and it is this highly specialized skill that he shared with U.S. scientists. It has been estimated that more than a half million acres in rice-growing areas in Arkansas would be suitable for a commercial fish-farming industry.

To return to Haiti, the interest of the Haitians in developing fisheries received further help from FAO from 1955-1960 when another expert, Martin Routh, of England, helped establish the first commercial fishing industry. Mr. Routh plotted the location of tuna fishing grounds, taught the fishermen how to fit out a motorized fishing boat, store fish under refrigeration and, eventually, saw the project through to the establishment of new, sanitary fish shops in Port-au-Prince, the capital. The new company is already bringing in 3,500 pounds of fish a week and is exporting

"Tilapia" fingerlings imported from Jamaica are placed in ponds in Haiti.

1,000 pounds of crawfish to the United States each fortnight.

In lands in every part of the globe FAO is showing the advantages that can come from combining traditional experience with laboratory knowledge and applied science; is proving that the skill of one neighborhood can be extended to another; and is illustrating that "know-how" is not a monopoly of the more highly developed neighborhoods of the world.

Planting acres of fish is a skill now known to the many rather than the few. While this is but a small part of FAO's work, it demonstrates that, by harmonizing the will of people, the intelligence of governments, and the facilities of international organizations, neighborhoods can do something about that most persistent of all stumbling blocks to peace—hunger.

FOOD AND AGRICULTURE ORGANIZATION OF THE UNITED NATIONS: FAO
International Headquarters: Viale delle Terme di Caracalla, Rome, Italy

ORIGIN
In May 1943 a United Nations Conference on Food and Agriculture met at Hot Springs, Virginia. Forty-four nations had accepted President Franklin D. Roosevelt's invitation to send representatives to this meeting. The delegates found themselves in agreement on certain basic points that later became the basis of FAO policy. Some of these were:

• The world has never had enough to eat. At least two-thirds of its people are ill-nourished in spite of the fact that two-thirds of the world's people are farmers.

• The modern science of nutrition proves beyond doubt that if all people could get enough of the right kinds of foods, the average level of health and well-being could be raised much higher than it is now.

• The modern science of production shows that it is entirely possible to produce enough of the right kinds of foods.

• But production alone is not enough. Foods must be so distributed that the levels of consumption of those who do not 'have enough are progressively raised.

Sure that no danger threatens, a "Tilapia" releases the amazing number of young fish it has been guarding in its mouth.

· This implies an expanding world economy, in which each nation will play its own part, but all will act together.

The Hot Springs Conference recommended the establishment of the United Nations Interim Commission on Food and Agriculture to draft the plans for a permanent international organization whose purpose would be to work for the common objectives outlined above. The Interim Commission was set up in Washington, D.C., where a Constitution was drafted. After twenty of the forty-five nations eligible for original membership had informed the Interim Commission of their intention of joining a permanent organization, the first session of the FAO Conference was convened at Quebec, Canada, in October, 1945.

Forty-two nations became charter members of FAO, which was the first of the new Specialized Agencies created after the end of World War II. Seldom before had so many nations joined together in a common effort to improve the lot of peoples throughout the world.

PURPOSE

The purpose of the FAO is stated in the Preamble to the Constitution, which reads as follows:

The Nations accepting this Constitution, being determined to

promote the common welfare by furthering separate and collective action on their part for the purposes of
• raising levels of nutrition and standards of living of the peoples under their respective jurisdictions,
• securing improvements in the efficiency of the production and distribution of all food and agricultural products,
• bettering the condition of rural populations,
• and thus contributing toward an expanding world economy, hereby establish the Food and Agriculture Organization of the United Nations, hereinafter referred to as the "Organization," through which the Members will report to one another on the measures taken and the progress achieved in the fields of action set forth above.

FUNCTIONS

Article 1 of the Constitution describes the functions of FAO as follows:

1. The Organization shall collect, analyze, interpret, and disseminate information relating to nutrition, food, and agriculture. In this Constitution, the term "agriculture" and its derivatives include fisheries, marine products, forestry and primary forestry products.

2. The Organization shall promote and, where appropriate, shall recommend national and international action with respect to

a. scientific, technological, social, and economic research relating to nutrition, food, and agriculture;

b. the improvement of education and administration relating to nutrition, food, and agriculture, and the spread of public knowledge of nutritional and agricultural science and practice;

c. the conservation of natural resources and the adoption of improved methods of agricultural production;

d. the improvement of the processing, marketing, and distribution of food and agricultural products;

e. the adoption of policies for the provision of adequate agricultural credit, national and international;

f. the adoption of international policies with respect to agricultural commodity arrangements.

3. It shall also be the function of the Organization

a.   to furnish such technical assistance as governments may request;

b.   to organize, in cooperation with the governments concerned, such missions as may be needed to assist them to fulfill the obligations arising from their acceptance of the recommendations of the United Nations Conference on Food and Agriculture and of this Constitution; and

c.   generally to take all necessary and appropriate action to implement the purposes of the Organization as set forth in the Preamble.

MEMBERSHIP

New members may be admitted to FAO by a two-thirds majority of the Conference, provided that a majority of the membership of the Organization is present. By February 1, 1961 there were eighty-two members and six associate members of FAO. A listing of members appears in the Appendix.

Upon joining FAO, member nations assume certain obligations to the Organization. Among these are the submitting of reports and information relating to the purposes of the Organization; contributing to the budget as determined by the Conference; according immunities to staff members in so far as necessary to facilitate their work; maintaining membership for at least four years before giving notice of withdrawal from the Organization, which becomes effective a year following notification of intention to withdraw to the Director-General.

STRUCTURE AND ORGANIZATION

FAO is operated by a Conference, a Council of the Food and Agriculture Organization, and the Director-General and his staff.

The Conference

The Conference is the policy-making body of FAO, and is composed of one representative from each member nation. Each nation has one vote in the Conference, which provides means for member governments to get together biennially to review the world situation in food and agriculture, forestry and fisheries, discuss common problems, and agree on common action.

The Council

Between sessions of the Conference, the twenty-five-nation

FAO expert working with the fisheries officers of Bangkhen Fisheries Station on the selection of breeders. Fish shown is the common carp, a popular pond fish.

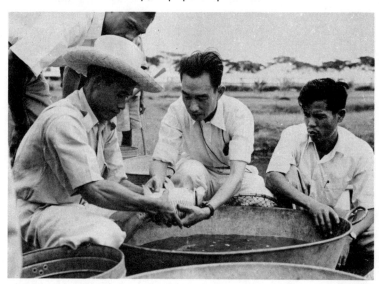

Council of FAO keeps the world food and agriculture situation under constant review and makes whatever recommendations it considers necessary to member governments, international commodity authorities, and other specialized international agencies.

The Secretariat

The working staff of FAO is headed by a Director-General chosen by the Conference. Subject to the general supervision of the Conference and the Council, the Director-General has full power to direct the work of the Organization.

Two major departments carry on FAO's substantive program. The Technical Department comprises divisions working in the fields of land and water development, plant production and protection, animal production and health, rural institutions and services, fisheries, forestry and forestry products, and nutrition. The Economics Department has divisions concerned with agricultural commodities, statistics and economic analysis. An Administrative Division provides services to the other divisions on budget, personnel and similar matters.

Regional offices for Asia and the Far East, for Latin America, for the Near East and for North America serve as centers for the exchange of information, technical assistance and encouragement to governments to act together to solve special problems of their regions.

ACTIVITIES

FAO's program aims at the fullest and wisest exploitation of the basic soil and water resources of the world, with special emphasis on the underdeveloped countries. In carrying out its program, the Agency works in three different fashions.

First, it analyzes and defines the world food problem. This includes the collection and publication of statistics concerning agriculture, fisheries, forests, food distribution; the determination of trends in the agricultural economy, such as the patterns of demand for various commodities; and the preparation and publication of technical studies summing up world knowledge in the many fields related to agriculture.

Second, FAO promotes cooperative action to solve food and agricultural problems. This may be done in one country, in a region, or among a number of countries which face similar problems. An example is the campaign against the desert locust in which all the countries concerned have joined together in a program of research and action to prevent the costly damage inflicted on crops by this destructive pest. (The UN Special Fund has recently allocated over $3.8 million to further this campaign; twenty countries are currently taking part.)

Another example of the FAO method for stimulating action is found in the study group or commission. The International Rice Commission, for instance, brings together production experts from many parts of the world. One of the programs of this Commission is the development of new strains of rice which will give higher yields than the varieties presently grown in tropical areas. A different phase of the world food problem is dealt with by the Committee on Commodity Problems, where experts representing twenty-four governments deal with problems of agricultural trade, such as the disposal of agricultural surpluses in a manner which will not disrupt trade patterns.

Third, and not less important, FAO gives technical aid to individual countries or to groups of countries on the many facets of developing basic agricultural resources. This part of the program is financed by funds from the U.N. Expanded Technical Assistance Program. For some years, agricultural programs have headed the list of Expanded Technical Assistance Program allocations; FAO has already aided more than sixty countries.

Such a wide-ranging program of technical assistance may best be illustrated with examples which indicate the types of aid given.

Animal and plant diseases take a heavy toll in many parts of the world. FAO is coordinating the fight against African horse sickness, which recently spread into the Near East and has killed tens of thousands of horses. Rinderpest, a deadly cattle disease, is being controlled in African and Asian countries; in Ethiopia and Afghanistan, to name two, it has now been eliminated. Poultry diseases have been checked; and, in Israel, for example, there has been a fifty-per cent increase in egg production as the result of better feeding and housing methods taught by an FAO expert. A virologist was recently sent to the Philippines to deal with a coconut disease know as cadang-cadang. FAO has worked for several years on methods of combatting sunnpest, a cereal disease found in the Middle East.

Forestry experts have advised the government of Indonesia on forest management with the goal of cultivating fast-growing softwood trees to serve as the basis of new paper and textile industries. Other FAO specialists are helping to train Liberia's first professional foresters, while in the Sudan, uncharted forests were mapped by an FAO expert and an inventory was made of mixed tropical forests.

In Central America, the advice of an FAO expert has led to striking improvement in the cultivation of cotton: the total crop has been raised by twenty per cent to date. In Guatemala, which only produced enough cotton to meet six per cent of its needs a few years ago, production now is sufficient to export cotton valued at $4 million a year. In Argentina, a specialist has helped improve the growing and processing of tea; the country has already expanded planting to 75,000 acres.

Milk production and processing is being stepped up in dozens of countries: Iraq, India, Spain, El Salvador, Iran, and Ethiopia, to name only a few. FAO and UNICEF work together on most of the projects which aim at improving the nutrition of mothers and children. These nutrition programs include aid to educational campaigns, training programs, research, and surveys of food needs, as well as all phases of dairying.

Wise use of water resources and conservation of soil are equally important to expand agricultural production. In the Sudan, an FAO expert was responsible for the digging of small reservoirs all across the country. These are being used to water cattle during dry seasons. In West Pakistan and Tunisia, other FAO experts have shown how to reduce the salinity of the soil, thus reclaiming the land. Irrigation schemes, reforestation projects, soil testing and mapping are gradually bringing more and more land into the area of production.

Fisheries experts are helping to increase food production in many parts of the world besides Haiti. This type of aid must often include educational campaigns. Fish is not always a popular food with those who should eat it.

Grain storage and transport is another phase of food production receiving FAO aid. About ten per cent of the world's grain crops are lost annually in storage to insects, rats and mold. Within the last few years, FAO has conducted courses on safe storage and transport in Turkey and Latin America, in addition to sending experts to individual countries. Still another aspect of the world's agricultural problem is land reform. In Latin America an FAO advisory team has been working with governments to draw up such reform programs, while in Ruanda-Urundi and Tanganyika, an FAO expert has conducted a land-tenure study for the government.

A recent FAO project well exemplifies the many ways in which this agency can help. Known as the Mediterranean Development Project, it is a study of the land problems of all the countries of the Mediterranean Basin. Some of this land has been worked for six or seven thousand years and is now virtually useless. FAO undertook a two-year, country-by-country study of means to improve crop lands, to anchor the soil and to upgrade the land in other ways. Specific recommendations were made for each country of the region. Turkey and Greece are already carrying out parts of the project. U.N. Special Fund allocations have been made for implementing several of the recommendations, and in future years, technical assistance experts will be requested as the vast project of making this land fruitful once again gets underway.

Thus FAO's activities range all the way from the little fish pond built by Dr. Lin's friend in Haiti to plans for the agricultural development of an entire region. But whether the projects be great or small, each is devoted to helping the neighborhoods of the world help themselves to a just share of the world's resources.

THE FREEDOM FROM HUNGER CAMPAIGN

"Millions still go hungry . . . And there are 140,000 new mouths to feed every day."

This quotation, from an FAO announcement, sums up the thinking which led FAO to propose a five-year special effort, above and beyond all current development programs, to make food production everywhere adequate to the needs of men everywhere.

All the programs of the postwar era, national, bilateral, and international, have not made a great difference to the world food situation. While food production has increased, population has increased by a greater degree. Man's numbers have doubled in the past sixty years, and it is expected that they will double again— to six billion—in fewer than forty years. FAO feels, however, that the problem does not lie in the numbers of people to be fed, but in the fact that farmers in underdeveloped countries do not have the skill and resources to make the most of their land. Agricultural research in the well-fed countries has suggested that physical limits on production are receding; the land may be able to give us much more than it does now. The solution, therefore, lies in bringing to the underdeveloped countries the techniques that have brought prosperity to the highly developed nations.

The Freedom from Hunger Campaign is being financed by voluntary contributions. Proposed by FAO's Director-General, Binay Ranjan Sen, it runs from 1960 to 1965 and will include a World Food Congress in 1963. The campaign features information and education programs to spread knowledge of the scale of the world food problem and the possibilities for solving it, research projects to enlarge knowledge of means to improve the food situation, and "national action programs" which are the heart of the campaign. These are demonstration and pilot projects in underdeveloped areas, showing how more food may be produced and distributed with greater efficiency. Seventy-six key projects have been suggested by FAO in relation to the general needs of undernourished nations; these projects provide a practical means to carry out the goal of the campaign. Funds raised in the campaign will be used to finance the "national action" projects. FAO looks to contributions from governments, individuals, foundations and non-governmental organization to make the campaign a success. In many countries National Committees have been established both to raise funds and to carry out the programs of the campaign.

Complementary to the Freedom from Hunger Campaign is FAO's World Seed Campaign. This campaign aims directly at increasing production. FAO's experience in advising countries on better or more suitable seed has shown that dramatic results may be obtained in a relatively short time. Better seed is easily distributed, can be used without great capital investment, and calls for only slight changes in farming systems. Direct individual and group participation in this campaign may be undertaken through the UNESCO Gift Coupon Plan. Contributions may be made for the purchase of seed, technical equipment or teaching equipment, such as visual instruction aids. As the needs are unlimited, contribution amounts are not specified, and even a small amount has a far-reaching effect in the fight against hunger and malnutrition.

NATIONAL FAO COMMITTEES

Realizing that the action necessary to achieve the aims of FAO must be taken in member countries, the Director-General has invited member governments to establish FAO National Committees. Although each government must determine for itself whether such a Committee will be established, and, if so, what its functions will be, there has been general agreement that the following services are appropriate to such a Committee:

1. Preparation of the annual progress and program report;
2. Provision of answers to inquiries made by FAO;
3. Preparation of material for the national delegation to FAO conferences and meetings;
4. Liaison with non-governmental national organizations and institutions concerned with the work of FAO;
5. Dissemination of information about FAO;
6. Reception of and assistance to technical missions and indi-

vidual officers sent to the country by FAO;

7.   Assisting FAO to establish contact with scientific workers and technical experts;

8.   Insuring that the government makes the fullest possible use of the services of FAO and furnishes the Organization with any available material that may be useful for its work.

The United States has formed what is known as the FAO Interagency Committee to meet the needs outlined above. This Committee has its Headquarters in the Office of Foreign Agricultural Relations at the Department of Agriculture in Washington.

CHAPTER THREE

ICAO
International Civil Aviation Organization

Flight Seven Hundred

The first commercial international air service was established between London and Paris in 1919. This was but a scant sixteen years after the Wright brothers had made their first historic flights at Kitty Hawk, North Carolina. It was only natural that, because of the short distances between important trading centers of different countries in Europe, international air services should have had their beginning there. This system gradually expanded as airlines sought to link the countries of Europe with their colonies, and as they saw business opportunity in transferring people and goods from one neighborhood to another.

By the late 1920's and early 1930's, British airlines were operating out of London down to the Middle East, from whence they branched either toward South Africa or on east to Australia. French air service linked Paris to Indo-China in the Far East and to Dakar in Africa. From this latter point the French lines crossed the Atlantic to Brazil. KLM (Royal Dutch) Airlines was providing like services to the Dutch colonies. In the same era Deutsche Lufthansa (German Airlines) was flying commercial planes through Africa and across the South Atlantic to Argentina. The first major United States concern to engage in international transport was Pan American Airways, which began a service in the Caribbean area in 1927.

By 1939 there were more than half a million miles of international air routes linking the major regions of the world. Although

Giant TWA jet is fueled and loaded for transatlantic flight.

this marked a rapid advance in aircraft communication, the carrying of passengers and freight by air was but a small fraction of total international transport. World War II, which began in this same year, had a terrific impact upon air transport. Large military networks were built up around the civilian services. During six years of war, 27,000 aircraft were flown from North America to the combat areas of the world by the Royal Air Force Transport Command alone!

While the Royal Air Force Transport Command was the first such organization to be established, it was soon followed by the United States Army Air Transport Command and the United States Navy Air Transport Service. Together these services created a trail of air routes and landing fields across the globe. Much of the success enjoyed by these organizations can be traced to the skills acquired through civilian operations before the war.

These military operations not only made air transport a major factor in the exchange of goods and services throughout the world in wartime; they showed the enormous potential of air transport in a peacetime economy. This potential is being realized. The volume of air passenger traffic in 1960 was more than six times that of 1946, and is going up each year by about fifteen per cent. In the same period, world air cargo traffic has increased about sixteen times and is now a major part of world-wide commercial air transportation.

Obviously this rapid development of international flying presents some very real problems. First are the technical problems of developing uniform operating procedures. Airlines of nineteen different nations have scheduled flights to and from the New York International Airport at Idlewild. One can well imagine the confusion and danger that would exist without international cooperation to standardize operations! Less obvious, but equally important, are the economic and political problems that must be solved in regulating the movements of peoples, goods and services between neighborhoods.

To solve these specialized problems, eighty-four nations have banded themselves together in the International Civil Aviation Organization (ICAO) with headquarters in Montreal, Canada. Although not all nations in which airlines operate are members of ICAO, member nations account for over ninety-five per cent of all commercial international air transport. Some of the problems which ICAO has solved by gaining the cooperative consent of member nations become apparent when one looks behind the

A jet is airborne fifty-five seconds
after start of the take-off run.

scenes as Trans World Airlines Flight Seven Hundred is completed from the New York International Airport to London.

Flight Seven Hundred, a Boeing intercontinental jet, leaves New York at 7:30 p.m. daily and flies nonstop to arrive in London at 7:00 the next morning (2:00 a.m. New York time). To many passengers this is a routine way of getting between neighborhoods; they give as little thought to how the plane gets to London as most of us do to the route of the train that takes us to visit relatives. But back of this flight is a very real example of teamwork — involving individuals, companies, governments and, in each phase, ICAO.

The pilot arrives at the airport two hours before flight time. He is joined there by the nine other members of the crew: two copilots, the flight engineer, the navigator and five cabin crew members — pursers and stewardesses. Each member of the crew is a specialist in a particular field. Each has met licensing standards, established by ICAO. These specify the requirements as to training, experience and physical condition that all members of the flight crew must meet. Requirements have also been set for those people engaged in ground occupations connected with aircraft maintenance and operations.

After checking in the crew, the pilot, with his copilots, engineer and navigator, confers with the TWA dispatcher. The dispatcher gives the pilot a preliminary flight plan, showing gross weight, fuel and route plus copies of weather maps including wind analysis charts at the higher levels of altitude. The flight plan was figured out on a Minimum Time Route (MTR) basis — the track considering winds which would get the flight to London in the least time. In this case it was somewhat south of a great circle course. After preparing an analysis of the preliminary flight plan, the pilot turns it over to his first officer and the navigator to work out the final plan. The complications of jet fuel consumption at different altitudes and temperatures, weather and winds at desirable cruising altitudes, and the routines of figuring compass headings and times made these calculations take almost an hour. Meanwhile the pilot was at TWA's weather bureau questioning the meteorologists about the upper air wind analysis. With all pre-flight work completed the crew goes to the terminal where the airplane has previously been towed to its assigned location. Here the food for the

Each member of the crew is a specialist in a particular field.

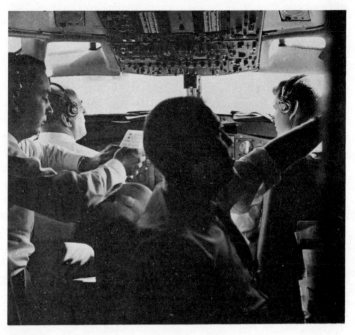

trip is placed aboard and the plane fueled.

On this particular flight, 17,700 gallons of kerosene jet fuel have been allowed. Under normal conditions, a TWA Boeing jet will use 14,250 gallons of fuel on the New York-London flight. As a safety measure sufficient additional fuel is carried to insure an adequate reserve if the plane is forced to fly beyond its destination because of bad weather conditions. In this case, the extra 3,450 gallons means that Flight Seven Hundred has almost two hours reserve flying time to reach an alternate destination.

In the meantime the pilot has been going over the plane's equipment. He checks the fire extinguishers, the life rafts, the hand-powered radio, the evacuation chute, the emergency lights, and dozens of other items specified by ICAO's "*Standards on Search and Rescue*." These not only enumerate the items a plane must carry, but also set up procedures that are to be used should the plane be forced down en route. Detailed plans based upon the experience of many years in coping with disasters are published in manuals known to ship captains as well as to pilots. They include instructions for reporting difficulties, techniques for ditching and open-sea landing, search plans for both aircraft and rescue boats, suggestions for locating survivors, instructions for survivors, details on dropping supplies, and the training of rescue crews.

Unaware of these elaborate precautions being taken to insure air safety, the passengers have been boarding the plane. Before joining them, the pilot signs out with the customs, immigration, and public health officials assigned to the airport. In recent years ICAO has had considerable success getting national governments to cut down on the number of forms that must be completed before a plane may clear an international airport. Agreements now in effect among certain ICAO members lay down the maximum number of formalities that any country may require, thus simplifying the paper work which airlines and airline crews must go through, and cutting down the waiting time for passengers.

Boarding the plane, the pilot and his operating crew double check a long list of items as a final precaution. Shortly before 7:30, the pilot receives permission from the control tower to taxi the plane to the head of the runway. There full power is turned into the engines as pilots and engineer search the instrument panels for the slightest indication of trouble. Sensing no difficulties they are all set to receive final clearance from the tower: "TWA Seven Hundred cleared to London Airport via the outer marker, Fire Island, Hampton, Nantucket, Cod Intersection, then Minimum Time Route to London." The power is increased as the big plane moves down the runway and at an exactly calculated speed takes off. A jet won't take off by itself as there is no lift to the wing structure, and the pilot must take it off by pulling back on "the stick." The entire takeoff run takes fifty-five seconds and Flight Seven Hundred is airborne at 7:35 p.m. New York time.

From this point on, all references to time will be that of "Z" time, figured on the twenty-four-hour clock to coincide with the time at the Greenwich meridian. Because of the vast number of time zones and the large number of dimensional units in use throughout the world, care must be taken so that there will be no confusion in air-to-ground communications. One of the dimensional units specified by ICAO is Greenwich mean time. "Z" time is five hours ahead of Eastern Standard Time; thus the official take-off time was 0035Z.

Twenty-five minutes after takeoff, the plane reaches its cruising altitude of 33,000 feet. The plane is capable of reaching this altitude much more quickly but the pilot had to restrict power to comply with the noise-abatement procedures in force at the airport. Airways traffic control and area traffic control are regulated by standards established by ICAO. Both horizontal and vertical flight lanes are set up. Planes flying from New York to London travel at the odd-numbered thousands of feet; those flying in the opposite direction, from London to New York, use the even-numbered levels. Only by such controls on the "superhighway of the air" can the constant flow of traffic between America and Europe be maintained safely and economically.

Jets are difficult to fly manually. The plane's reactions are so delicate that a human being almost can't respond fast enough, and most of the flying in cruise is done by automatic pilot. The captain never leaves the controls in a jet, as there is too much happening when traveling at such a great speed. The automatic pilot and the flight instrments are constantly monitored by the captain and first officer in turn. Every member of the crew is constantly busy with his specific duties. All the way to London, the flight is in constant touch with ground and ocean stations by voice. An aircraft is never alone in the sky. Even during its trip through the stratosphere, Flight Seven Hundred talks at any time to the stations whose job it is to make air travel safe. The telecommunications network that keeps aircraft in touch with these stations and with other aircraft is the creation of ICAO. Working with the International Telecommunication Union (*Chapter 7*) ICAO assigns wave lengths for both mobile and fixed aeronautical radio services. ICAO is also responsible for arrangements made to broadcast weather information by special codes, and cooperates with the World Meteorological Organization (*Chapter 13*) in coordinating the reports received from thousands of weather-reporting facilities both on land and at sea.

Each time the plane crosses an imaginary line marking another ten degrees of longitude on the chart, position reports are made to land and ocean stations so that air traffic can be regulated — and so that rescue units will have this information for their operations if the plane stops checking in. In addition, pilots report when they are over designated spots established by air traffic controllers as check points through which all planes must enter and leave. These check points are indicated on the New York-London flight map at the intersections of certain agreed-upon degrees and minutes north, and degrees and minutes west. Flight Seven Hundred checks in over "Shark" intersection, located 49° 40′ N and 51°30′ W. As a further safety precaution, twice each hour the radio is tuned in at 500 kilocycles for three minutes. This is the international distress frequency to which all ships and planes throughout the world are tuned at the same time, with their operators listening for S O S — three dots, three dashes, three dots — the international distress signal.

Over the three thousand miles of water between North America and Europe, Flight Seven Hundred must have constant reports on the weather. The North Atlantic is one of the most unpredictable weather areas on earth, and without accurate information as to winds and storms, air travel over the New York-to-London route would be extremely dangerous. ICAO has solved this problem through the establishment of a network of nine ocean weather stations jointly maintained and financed by eighteen nations whose planes cross this much-traveled region.

The U.S. Coast Guard Cutter "Spencer" is a 2300-ton turbine-powered vessel, built for patrolling and assigned to ICAO North Atlantic weather ship duty.

As trans-Atlantic planes approach the "Spencer" the radar operator traces their courses on the twin screens.

Five of these nine stations are manned continuously by ten European vessels in rotation, averaging two vessels per station. Four stations in the western part are manned continuously by eleven U.S. vessels, the larger number of vessels per station being required because of the greater distance from the station to the home port. Latitude 52° 45′ N and longitude 30′ W marks the weather station "C for Coca," a U.S. station, one of several that serve Flight Seven Hundred. Hour after hour, for weeks at a time, a United States Coast Guard ship cruises about in a few square miles of North Atlantic water. Every three hours the weather men record the surface weather conditions, and every six hours they make upper air observations. This latter is accomplished by releasing a helium-filled balloon to a height of 60,000 feet. Delicate instruments attached to the balloon record the temperature, pressure, and humidity of the air through which it passes. These observations must be made in daylight and darkness and in all kinds of weather — tasks that demand the best in seamanship, courage, and skill.

The reports from the ocean weather stations make it possible to forecast weather conditions more accurately, and by so doing make travel across the Atlantic safer and more profitable. If an airline dispatcher knows the weather conditions, he can plot a course to take advantage of the wind; and, when it is favorable, he can reduce the fuel load and increase the passenger and freight load.

"Ocean Station Coca" has duties other than reporting weather conditions. The navigator aboard Flight Seven Hundred keeps his ADF (Automatic Direction Finder) tuned to Coca during the flight over Coca's area in order to check his course. Four times an hour for five minutes the homing facility (radio directional signal) operates from equipment aboard Coca and serves as a navigational check point. The navigator may ask Coca for a "radar fix." This means he wants the radar operator aboard Coca to pick up the plane on his radar screen and to figure the plane's distance from the ship. This gives the navigator an opportunity to check his own calculations as to the plane's position.

"Spencer" radioman relays weather and navigational information to pilot of passing plane.

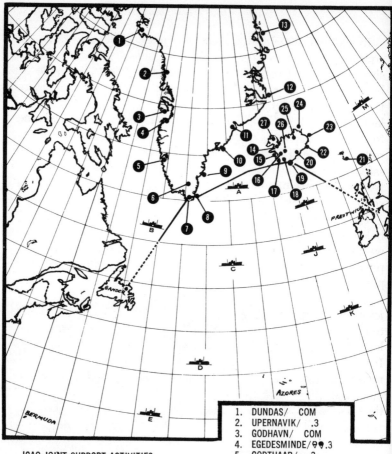

ICAO JOINT SUPPORT ACTIVITIES
IN THE NORTH ATLANTIC.

North Atlantic Ocean Station

Area Control   ACC

Main Meteorological Office   MMO

Surface Observation Station   .6 .3 or .1 Hourly

Radiosonde Station   ϙ

Radiowind Station   ♥

Communication Station   COM

Loran   LORAN

Non-Directional Radiobeacon   NDB

Jointly financed voice and duplex
teletypewriter circuits in
undersea cable

1. DUNDAS/   COM
2. UPERNAVIK/   .3
3. GODHAVN/   COM
4. EGEDESMINDE/ϙ♥.3
5. GODTHAAB/   .3
6. NARSSARSSUAQ/ϙ♥.3
7. FREDERIKSDAL/   LORAN
8. PRINS CHRISTIANS SUND/
        .3.1 COM—NDB
9. TINGMIARMIUT/   .1
10. ANGMAGSSALIK/ϙ♥.1 COM
11. APUTITEQ/   .3
12. KAP TOBIN/ϙ♥.3
13. DANMARKSHAVN/ϙ♥.3
14. STYKKISHOLMUR/   .3
15. KEFLAVIK/ϙ♥.3, 1 MMO
16. REYKJAVIK/   .3 ACC
17. GRINDAVIK/   COM
18. RJUPNAHAED/   COM
19. VESTMANNAEYJAR/   .3
20. VIK/   LORAN
21. SKUVANES/   LORAN
22. HOLAR/   .3
23. DELATANGI/   .3
24. RAUFARHOFN/   .3
25. AKUREYRI/   .3
26. GUFUNES/   COM
27. GALTARVITI/   .3

In addition, the crew aboard Coca, and other weather ships, is equipped and trained to provide search and rescue assistance should a plane get into difficulties. Several years ago the flying boat *Bermuda Sky Queen*, bound from Ireland to Newfoundland, ran short of fuel and was forced to "ditch" in the North Atlantic. Following Coca's radio beacon, the large plane was able to come into the ocean almost beside the station. In spite of a high, rolling sea the crew and passengers, numbering sixty-nine, were safely taken off the plane. A few weeks later the crew of a sinking Norwegian freighter was rescued by another weather ship operated by the British.

The passengers of Flight Seven Hundred may be sleeping, but below them in the night, the small speck of white that is the weather ship continues its ceaseless plodding back and forth, providing unseen but unceasing service to the safety of the people above.

In addition to the weather ships, ICAO is responsible for other joint support operations in the North Atlantic. These include meteorological and communications centers maintained in Greenland and Iceland, and air traffic control (area control center) in Iceland. Safety for North Atlantic crossings makes the establishment of these services essential. But it would not be fair to ask the citizens of these lands to support financially a service from which they derive but slight benefit. As a result ICAO has worked out agreements whereby the maintenance of these installations is jointly financed by the governments whose airlines use the facilities.

This same joint support applies to the three LORAN (long range) stations in Iceland, Greenland and the Faroe Islands that provide long-range radio navigational aids for aircraft operating along the North Atlantic route. These LORAN stations provide a fixed point of absolute dependability for navigators. Under ordinary conditions the navigator can best determine his exact position by a sextant shot of the sun during the day or of the stars at night. During rough weather these aids are, of course, not available, although it is then that positional readings are most important. While the weather ships can be used to advantage as fixing points, their position is never *exactly* known, and during gales and storms they may actually be off their station and not know too accurately where they are themselves.

Throughout the flight the navigator combines his own technical knowledge and the practical experience of many years with ICAO-planned services to keep the giant jet on its proper track. In contact with "Ocean Station Julliet" he again obtains a "radar fix" and ADF bearing. After this contact, Flight Seven Hundred is 350 miles from the Irish coast. The navigator relays this information to the captain. As the weather reports indicate all stations ahead are clear, the plane continues past the southern tip of Ireland, winging toward London airport at a ten-mile-a-minute clip.

Forty-five minutes out of London the jet streaks past an ocean liner Liverpool-bound and not due to dock for another twenty-four hours. From a check point on the southwest tip of England, Flight Seven Hundred receives clearance to begin its descent. Several minutes before crossing the check point the pilot closes the throttles to reduce the plane's speed. Even with throttles closed, it will take three minutes flying at a level altitude to bring the speed down to a point where the landing gear could be lowered. The plane starts down at the rate of three, sometimes four thousand feet per minute and is soon picked up by London radar control which "talks" Flight Seven Hundred in.

Whether the aircraft is landing by night or day, in fair weather or under conditions of very bad visibility, ICAO regulations make for perfect coordination between the pilot and the ground air traffic control. ICAO international standards on aerodromes specify the layout and design of airports and of approach lights. Agreement has been reached as to the pattern of high-intensity approach lights to guide an aircraft coming to the airport on an instrument-landing-system beam (ILS) or ground-controlled approach (GCA).

The London Director has lined up Flight Seven Hundred for a landing on Runway Ten, right. The pilot goes over his check list with other members of the crew and then orders the landing gear down. The great plane sinks lower and lower, and finally crosses over the approach lights. Suddenly the cement runway is reached, and the wheels touch down on London Airport just six hours and eight minutes from New York!

Certainly Flight Seven Hundred can be viewed as a lesson in international cooperation. The International Civil Aviation Organization has played an important role in this flight. ICAO will play an ever more vital role in the orderly movement of people and goods between the neighborhoods of the world as peoples and governments work toward the ideals expressed in the "Five Freedoms of the Air":

1. The privilege of an airline of one country to fly across the territory of another country, without landing, en route to its final destination.

2. The privilege of an airline of one country to land in another country's territory for non-traffic purposes, such as refueling or engine repairs.

3. The privilege of an airline of one country to carry passengers, freight, and mail from a foreign country to its own.

4. The privilege of carrying passengers, freight, and mail from its own country to a foreign one.

5. The privilege of an airline of one country to carry passengers, freight, and mail between the airports of two foreign countries.

INTERNATIONAL CIVIL AVIATION ORGANIZATION: ICAO

International Headquarters: International Aviation Building, Montreal, Canada

ORIGIN

The first international meeting to reach agreements on air flight was the Paris Peace Conference of 1919. The rapid advance in aircraft development during World War I had made possible the establishment of commercial air service. As has been noted, the first regularly scheduled air run between London and Paris was established in 1919, and focused the attention of the peacemakers upon this new method of international transportation.

Out of the Paris Conference came two important decisions. The first of these was the acknowledgment that the air space over each nation was owned by that nation. This meant that other nations wishing to fly planes into or over any other nation must first get permission. The second agreement led to the establishment of the International Commission for Air Navigation (ICAN), an organization open to nations who wished to share in the technical im-

ICAO has helped the Central American republics to improve their air services. Here, an airplane is being signaled in at Toncontin Airport, Tegucigalpa, Honduras.

provement of aviation. Some of the major powers, including the United States, did not join ICAN. Nevertheless, ICAN was an important influence in the expansion of commercial air travel that took place between the two world wars.

The rapid development of air transport during World War II raised new technical, political, and economic problems that had to be solved for peacetime aviation. Realizing that the limited influence of ICAN would not be sufficient to cope with these new problems, the government of the United States extended invitations to fifty-five allied and neutral nations to meet in Chicago in November 1944 to discuss international air affairs.

For seven weeks the delegates of the fifty-two nations that accepted invitations to the Chicago Conference considered the problems of international civil aviation. Their decisions mark a great milestone in man's attempt to facilitate the exchange of goods and services between the neighborhoods of the world.

The delegates reaffirmed the Paris Peace Conference principle that each nation had absolute control of the air space over its territory. Upon this principle they drafted a Convention on International Civil Aviation consisting of ninety-six articles. This provided for the establishment of an International Civil Aviation Organization that was to come into existence thirty days after a minimum of twenty-six nations had ratified the Convention. The provisions of ratification stated that the governments concerned must approve the Convention as a treaty. As this is a time-consuming task, the Conference drafted an Interim Agreement on International Civil Aviation which established a temporary body known as the Provisional International Civil Aviation Organization (PICAO), with limited powers, to serve as an advisory group until the Convention might be approved.

By June, 1945, twenty-six nations had signed the Interim Agreement, and PICAO was established in Montreal, Canada. For the twenty months of its existence, PICAO laid the foundations for an international organization designed to improve, facilitate, and coordinate air flight over national boundaries. Much of PICAO's work consisted in the drafting of recommendations for standards, practices, and procedures to achieve safe and efficient international flight. PICAO did its task well, and when, on April 4, 1947, thirty days after the twenty-sixth nation had ratified the Convention, ICAO came into being, it inherited a going organization.

PURPOSES

The purposes of the ICAO are clearly laid down in the Preamble to the Convention on International Civil Aviation:

· Whereas the future development of international civil aviation can greatly help to create and preserve friendship and understanding among the nations and peoples of the world, yet its abuse can become a threat to the general security; and

· Whereas it is desirable to avoid friction and to promote that cooperation between nations and peoples upon which the peace of the world depends;

· Therefore, the undersigned governments having agreed on certain principles and arrangements in order that international civil aviation may be developed in a safe and orderly manner

and that international air transport services may be established on the basis of equality of opportunity and operated soundly and economically;
• Have accordingly concluded this Convention to that end.

FUNCTIONS

ICAO's responsibilities are established in the Convention as follows:
• Develop the principles and techniques of international air navigation and foster the planning and development of international air transport so as to:
• Insure the safe and orderly growth of international civil aviation throughout the world;
• Encourage the arts of aircraft design and operation for peaceful purposes;
• Encourage the development of airways, airports, and air navigation facilities for international civil aviation;
• Meet the needs of the peoples of the world for safe, regular, efficient, and economical air transport;
• Prevent economic waste caused by unreasonable competition;
• Insure that the rights of contracting states are fully respected and that every contracting state has a fair opportunity to operate international airlines;
• Avoid discrimination between contracting states;
• Promote safety of flight in international air navigation;
• Promote generally the development of all aspects of international civil aeronautics.

MEMBERSHIP

As of February 1, 1961, eighty-four nations were members of ICAO. A listing of members appears in the Appendix.

Although the Chicago Conference that drafted the Convention met during the height of World War II, provisions were made for the later admission of Axis nations. These provisions called for an affirmative four-fifths vote of the Assembly and the approval of any member nation that had been invaded or attacked during the war by the state seeking admission. Under these provisions, Italy, Germany and Japan have become members of ICAO and are at present members of its governing Council.

STRUCTURE AND ORGANIZATION

ICAO is governed by an Assembly that in turn elects a Council to serve as the executive body. The administrative functions of the Organization are performed by the Secretariat, which makes up the third principal organ of ICAO.

The Assembly

The ICAO Assembly governs the activities of the Organization. Each member nation has representation in the Assembly and each nation has one vote. Article 49 of the Convention established the powers and duties of the Assembly as follows:

a) elect at each meeting its President and other officers; b) elect the contracting states to be represented on the Council; c) examine and take appropriate action on the report of the Council and decide on any matter referred to it by the Council; d) determine its own rules of procedure and establish such subsidiary

Trainees learn functioning of aircraft fuel system at a new civil aviation training school at Collique, Peru, established by the government with the aid of ICAO experts.

commissions as it may consider to be necessary or desirable; e) vote an annual budget and determine the financial arrangement of the Organization; f) review expenditures and approve the accounts of the Organization; g) refer, at its discretion, to the Council, to subsidiary commissions, or to any other body any matter within its sphere of action; h) delegate to the Council the powers and authority necessary or desirable for the discharge of the duties of the Organization and revoke or modify the delegations of authority at any time; i) consider proposals for the modification or amendment of the provisions of this Convention and, if it approves of the proposals, recommend them to the contracting states; j) deal with any matter within the sphere of action of the Organization not specifically assigned to the Council.

On October 30, 1947, following Assembly approval, ICAO formally entered into working relationship with the United Nations.

The Council

The ICAO Council is a permanent body composed of twenty-one member nations elected by the Assembly for a term of three years and responsible to the Assembly. In order to insure more adequate representation of all member states, an increase in the membership of the Council to twenty-seven states has been recommended by various governments. Council decisions require a majority vote. Member states not members of the Council may participate in Council proceedings (without voting) when the matter under discussion concerns the member's interest. Article 54 of the Convention lays down the following functions for the Council:

a) submit annual reports to the Assembly; b) carry out the directions of the Assembly and discharge the duties and obligations which are laid on it by the Convention; c) determine its organization and rules of procedure; d) appoint and define the duties of an Air Transport Committee, which shall be chosen from among the representatives of the members of the Council, and which shall be responsible to it; e) administer the finances of the Organization; f) determine the emoluments of the President of the Council; g) appoint a chief executive officer who shall be called the Secretary-General, and make provision for the appointment of such other personnel as may be necessary; h) request, collect, examine, and publish information relating to the advancement of air navigation and the operation of international air services, including information about the costs of operation and particulars of subsidies paid to airlines from public funds; i) report to contracting states any infractions of the Convention, as well as any failure to carry out recommendations or determinations of the Council; j) report to the Assembly any infraction of the Convention where a contracting state has failed to take appropriate action within a reasonable time after notice of the infraction; k) adopt international standards and recommended practices, and notify all contracting states of the action taken; l) consider recommendations of the Air Navigation Commission for amendment of the Annexes; m) consider any matter relating to the Convention which any contracting state refers to it.

Assisting the Council in carrying out its functions are special advisory bodies. The Air Navigation Commission makes recommendations concerning technical matters. This twelve-member body has drafted Annexes to the Convention on such matters as personnel licensing, rules of the air, and search and rescue, which the Council in turn has submitted to member nations for their guidance. The Air Transport Committee advises the Council on economic matters of importance to international flight, such as commercial rights, air mail, payments for airport facilities, and statistical reporting. The Committee on Joint Support of Air Navigation Services studies and reports to the Council on joint operations such as the ocean weather stations. The Legal Committee provides advice on public and private air law and drafts international agreements for ICAO.

The Secretariat

The administrative functions of ICAO are performed by the Secretariat under the direction of the Secretary-General, who is chosen by the Council. Made up of five bureaus (Air Navigation, Air Transport, Technical Assistance, Legal, Administration and Services) the Secretariat supplies technical and administrative aid to the various committees and divisions of the Council.

Personnel for the Secretariat are recruited on a wide geographical basis. Opportunities are provided to member nations so that they may send selected young men to the ICAO Secretariat for a period of training. Following this study, the trainees return to the employment of their governments and airlines better equipped to contribute to safe and efficient air transport in their own lands and with a realistic understanding of ICAO's spirit and purpose.

ACTIVITIES

The activities of the International Civil Aviation Organization are as far-flung as the airways they help service. The ICAO world map is subdivided into ten major regions. On this map are pinpointed some 40,000 future facilities to be located or services to be rendered as they have been drafted at regional meetings. ICAO carries on constant study leading to the ways in which governments may be encouraged and helped to fill these gaps. Record books are kept that reflect the day-by-day progress that is being made toward fulfilling these world-wide plans.

Specific problems are brought to the attention of ICAO by organizations such as the International Air Transport Association. One such problem concerned the need for better coordination of civil and military air traffic in much-traveled Western Europe. Following a proposal of investigation submitted to ICAO by the Netherlands, the Council worked out plans for a special meeting to be held in Paris on this subject. With the cooperation of governments, airlines, and ICAO, agreements were reached that led to an improved, hence safer and more efficient, European airways system.

The wide use of jet-propelled aircraft and the increase in helicopter service create new problems in the fields of aerodrome construction and operating conditions. Many problems that were new several years ago have been solved and are matters of record in Annexes to the Convention. These include: standardization of radio aids to navigation, codifying instrument flight rules, and many communication procedures. Although ICAO actions are not binding upon any member government until that government formally adopts them, the wide use of ICAO's publications and the small number of rejections of parts of Annexes attest to the wide acceptance of ICAO decisions.

The increased use of voice communications raises serious problems, since pilots and control personnel must often use a language other than their own. ICAO has developed a new phonetic alphabet that can be pronounced by airmen of almost every nationality.

ICAO technicians take part in United Nations civilian aid to the Congo. While performing technical tasks on an emergency basis, they train Congolese staff. Photo shows flight information center manned by ICAO technician at Leopoldville civil airport.

The Alfa-Bravo-Coca alphabet is coming into wide acceptance and lessens the danger of misinterpretation, resulting in greater safety. Ocean Station Coca was known as "Charlie" under the old alphabet.

One of the most difficult fields of operation for ICAO has been that of simplifying the rules and regulations involved in clearing an aircraft and its load across international boundaries. Over the last ten or twelve years the time that passengers must spend in being cleared at an international airport has been greatly reduced. Although much remains to be done to speed procedure and reduce documentation, ICAO-recommended standards concerning baggage, customs inspections, travel visas, landing cards, and passport controls, etc. have proved their worth when used by member governments. Even more pressing are the economic and political problems connected with "the privilege of an airline of one country to carry passengers, freight, and mail between the airports of two foreign countries" — the "fifth freedom." Thus far, nations have not been able to agree upon solutions to these problems. ICAO's Council has made recommendations on the subject and stands ready to call future conferences when member governments so desire.

ICAO takes part in the United Nations Expanded Program of Technical Assistance. A major contribution of ICAO has been the training of local personnel in such fields as air transport control, communications, and aeronautical meteorology, when governments have so requested. Without this training, safe and efficient civil air operations are an impossibility.

A wide variety of other technical assistance programs has been undertaken: Commercial pilot training, instruction in maintenance and repair of aircraft, organizing and operating airlines, preparing air laws and regulations, advice on airport construction; in fact, every phase of aviation with the exception of aircraft construction. Twenty-nine countries received expert aid in 1960, and regional training centers have been assisted for a number of years in Latin America and Central America. Fellowships and scholarships are another important aspect of ICAO's technical assistance program, both to train supervisory staff and to make basic training possible for students who have no facilities in their own countries.

Under the program of the United Nations Special Fund, a number of civil aviation research and training centers have been approved. ICAO will carry out these Special Fund projects in the United Arab Republic, Thailand, India, Mexico, Morocco and Tunisia. The aid to Mexico will help the established Center expand its training to meet the problems arising from jet transportation. In Morocco and Tunisia, separate schools will handle complementary aspects of training and will be open to students from other African countries.

Dr. Edward Warner, former President of the Council of ICAO, has summarized the purpose behind ICAO'S activities in the following words:

"ICAO is an association of national governments which have recognized the need for working together for the good of civil aviation and for the healthy development of international relationships. No one nation acting within its own territory and with its own resources could make its civil aviation as safe, as reliable, as economical, or as useful as it could be if that nation worked together with its neighbors. Not even the most powerful government on earth, sovereign over the widest territories, could do that. Recognition for the need of constant cooperation has brought most of the world into the ICAO membership."

CHAPTER FOUR

WHO/UNICEF
World Health Organization
United Nations Children's Fund

The Diary
of Mrs. Bille-Brahe

February 4: *Went along the main road to Edakkara, then turned left along a sandy path. Jeep was able to take us only two miles. From there we had to walk. The houses here are very scattered, often as much as a mile apart.*

If one had to identify the writer of these lines unaided, it would prove quite difficult. Perhaps the extract is from the diary of a military commander visiting his outposts at the front? Or these might be the notes of a surveyor on a field trip to spot the route for a new highway. A fisherman seeking for out-of-the-way streams in which to try his luck might record these words at the end of the day's sport. One would never guess that this is actually part of a diary kept by an attractive flaxen-haired young Danish woman who was reporting a routine part of her duties as a nurse from deep in the south of India!

The story of how the author of this diary, Mrs. Inga Bille-Brahe, happened to be walking along a remote trail thousands of miles from her native city of Copenhagen is one that involves governments, international organizations, and people of skill, patience and good will.

The 438 million people of India comprise one-sixth of the world's population. Since 1947 India has been a free and independent nation. Working through their democratic institutions, the people of India are resolved to seek a better future for themselves by attacking the allied problems of poverty, disease, and hunger.

Malaria is a wasting disease that has intensified hunger and hardship in India. Although it strikes people of all ages, it is particularly hard on children, who run a high fever and become too listless to play or study. Sometimes their stomachs become horribly swollen, while the rest of the body shrinks to extreme thinness. Aside from the suffering which is directly attributable to malaria, the disease adds to India's constant threat of famine; malaria-weakened farmers produce less food for themselves and others.

Government leaders in the new state of India realized that Western scientists and doctors had knowledge that could lead to the elimination of this scourge. Further, their government was a participating member in international organizations set up to tackle problems of this very nature. Accordingly, India petitioned for help in the form of World Health Organization and United Nations Children's Fund (WHO/UNICEF) malaria-control teams.

For these teams WHO provided the technical personnel, while UNICEF furnished the supplies, equipment, and transport. The government of India assigned an understudy team of its own citizens and provided labor squads, foremen, mechanics, and chauffeurs.

WHO secured the services of Mrs. Bille-Brahe as the public health nurse for one of these teams. A citizen of Denmark, she was a graduate of a nursing school, where she had specialized in surgical training. After registering with the Danish National Health Service in 1942, she continued her studies, this time concentrating on epidemic diseases and pediatrics. In 1949 she completed a public health nurse's course, and in September of that year joined WHO. Her technical training made her an excellent choice for the WHO/UNICEF assignment; and, in addition, she possessed those qualities of patience, perseverance, and good will so essential for winning the confidence and cooperation of others.

After a period of training with a WHO/UNICEF malaria-control team already at work in Mysore State, Mrs. Bille-Brahe was assigned to join team-leader Dr. L. Mara, of Italy, who was opening an operation in India's Malabar District. The team's headquarters was in the city of Nilambur, from which it was to service a 236-square-mile area in which were hundreds of small villages.

Mrs. Bille-Brahe begins health records for village mothers and children in WHO-UNICEF team's area in India.

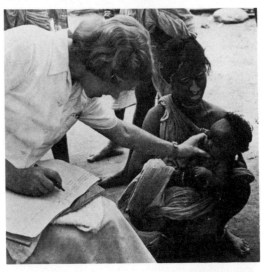

Transportation to the villages presented some very real problems, as the following three entries in Mrs. Bille-Brahe's diary indicate:

February 2: Karakod is the farthest hamlet in Nilambur Taluk. The place can be reached only by walking for about two miles through the paddies. Altogether there are only seven houses in the village.

February 8: These three villages we reached by walking through the forest. Once we lost our way and spent two hours wandering about until we finally came across the houses that we were looking for.

February 28: Visited the hamlets of Meppad, Manthoni, and Punjoola. After crossing several streams the jeep was unable to go farther. These villages are situated just below the hills, and the houses are very scattered. The people are chiefly from the hill-tribes and some of them live only in tiny huts made of leaves. Oddly enough they were not shy or afraid, but came forward and talked frankly about their problems.

Many times on the first visit to the villages the people were quite

frightened of meeting such queerly dressed strangers. The head-
man in each village had to be convinced of the reasoning behind
the visit. Team members had to make the village leader understand
that the mosquito is the carrier of malaria, and that DDT sprayed
on the walls of the hut will kill the mosquito but will not harm
the members of the family. It is the custom among some of the
Mohammedans living in this area to whitewash the inside of their
huts after a baby has been born. The mosquito will not die if the
walls are whitewashed after the application of DDT. Getting the
villagers to forego this important custom required many long hours
of persuasion. But soon the teams were known throughout the
area, and on the day of their expected arrival in a village people
would walk for miles to greet them.

While the homes were sprayed and the malariologists and en-
tomologists went about their tasks of examining patients, collecting and dissecting mosquitoes and larvae, and maintaining their
scientific records, Mrs. Bille-Brahe made contact with the village
people. She gave drugs to malaria sufferers, treated minor ill-
nesses, and above all helped care for the health of the mothers
and children.

. . . Of course, at the same time we inquire about the health of
the family and give suggestions on cleanliness, food, etc. We
always ask about the food of the baby and try to help mothers

An enlarged spleen marks this child as a malaria victim.

understand the importance of carrying out a few simple rules concerning its feeding. The mothers are often ignorant about what kind of solid food is suitable for a child. The baby's resistance is thus likely to be reduced and it becomes an easy prey to different infectious diseases. It is difficult to find a way of getting improvement in health through better food. Even a mother who is expecting a baby can't be expected to buy milk and eggs. These products are very expensive. The price of a goat, for instance, is much too high even for a schoolmaster. Unfortunately, even vegetables are difficult to get, and only a few families will have a kitchen garden.

The teams realized that many diseases were due to malnutrition. They taught mothers the value of using limes in the family menu and convinced many of them that spinach can be fed to babies. Milk powder and cod-liver oil received from UNICEF through the government proved a blessing to many mothers, infants, and children.

When the parents proved reluctant toward the planting of kitchen gardens, Mrs. Bille-Brahe took her educational campaign into the schools.

March 6: Saw the headmaster of the school at Etekkare village. He promosed to let the children make a kitchen garden near the school as soon as the rainy season starts. The schoolteachers everywhere are very kind and a good help. The children are sweet and attentive and very eager to carry out the small bits of advice that we give them. The older children were asked to draw the plan for a kitchen garden. They found out what was best to sow in it. Some went to the market to find out the price of seed. Many have interested their parents in these projects.

The schools also provided a wonderful opportunity for valuable public health work.

March 7: Gave lesson No. 11 to the school children. Explained to the headmaster that we were going to start a laboratory examination for evidences of intestinal worms. He immediately promised all the help we wanted. On the way back we visited Tharisil village and gave a lesson on malaria in Manbata school.

Short, very simple talks for the small children. We draw a

picture of a fly on the blackboard to count how many legs a fly has. So many flies with so many unwashed legs (a fly never washes its legs as an Indian child does!) come in from outside and sit on the food. What to do about it? The children find out themselves. "Cover the food with banana leaves!"

In addition to the village leaders and the schools, it proved very important to get the cooperation of the village midwives. These women care for mothers who are expecting new babies and safeguard the children at the very start of their life. They always have the confidence of the entire village, and if they can be convinced

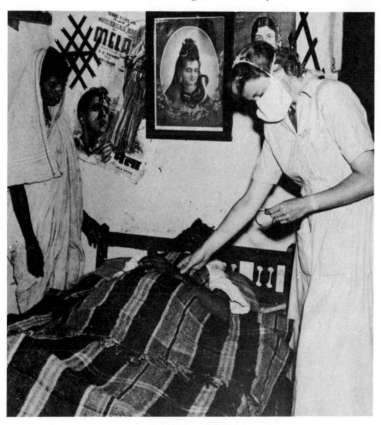

Here is Nurse Bille-Brahe at bedside of a village plague victim.

of the value of the WHO/UNICEF program the other residents can be won.

March 10: Many home visits were made, and due to the interest shown by the midwife we are expecting an improvement of antenatal and postnatal care in the future. We discussed the following items with this midwife: (1) keeping as a help for herself a brief diary which would make it easier for her to remember the questions she would like to talk over with us and to see whether advice given had been acted upon, etc.; (2) marking up the maternal cards more carefully.

By the end of March Mrs. Bille-Brahe had paid seven visits to the Kalikavu midwife, and the results are clearly reflected in her report for that month.

... We are happy to state that she is not at all sorry for our visits even if it does mean that she has more work. She is eager to learn and her work has improved in many ways.

Trained midwives are few in number. To encourage their interest and improve their service, UNICEF has assembled medical kits for distribution to those in training and those in practice. Some 68,000 have been distributed during the past ten years to midwives who have completed training courses.

Work of this kind is not without its humor. After a few visits to the villages with the team, the Danish nurse and her native public health assistant, "the wonderful, sweet" Josephine Devasahayam, would return alone. The Indian women who had long wondered how it was possible for women to travel by themselves decided that Josephine was her daughter. As Mrs. Bille-Brahe was some ten years younger than her assistant, this didn't make her too happy. When she asked the village women how they discovered this relationship, they said innocently: "Why, little mother — you have white hair and so many wrinkles!"

The people in the villages had difficulty in pronouncing Mrs. Bille-Brahe's name, but she soon learned that her given name, Inga, was easily enunciated. She became affectionately known as "Mrs. Inga" to thousands of residents in the Malabar District. With her Indian assistant, "Mrs. Inga" visited nearly a hundred villages during the month of February alone.

Not every day was spent in the villages. During the month of

March there are brief entries in the diary such as these: "Holiday; office work," or "Jeep under repair; office work," or "Office work — lack of petrol; a large number of patients came to the office for treatment." Near the end of the month a more detailed entry appears.

March 30:   Office work. A great number of dressings were made out of old rags, washed and boiled. They also have produced a great number of children's diapers, etc. We never fail to tell mothers how they themselves can prepare these things; but, of course, many will not be able to spare even old rags. It's then that we are happy to have our little stock.

Mrs. Bille-Brahe didn't mention the conditions under which she lived at the headquarters. Dr. Cecily Williams of the WHO Re-

In Indian villages workers spray with DDT solution to kill mosquitoes that carry malaria. India's anti-malaria campaign aims eventually to wipe out this disease.

gional Office in New Delhi included the following comments after a visit to the WHO/UNICEF team: drinking water and all other water had to be carried from a well some distance away, and be boiled; there was no modern plumbing; no electricity, so that it was impossible to use fans even though the temperature went above one hundred; team members could not sleep outside, as many people do, because tigers had been seen prowling around not far from the bungalow!

Dr. Williams also recorded her observations of the results of the work performed by the public health nurses. Each village and school that had been regularly visited showed great improvement. The villages were neater and the housekeeping more efficient. The residents had a better knowledge of hygiene and were aware of its importance for themselves and for their families. The confidence of the village people had been won, and with it the first step in the battle against malaria.

The work of the WHO/UNICEF team of which Mrs. Bille-Brahe was a member laid the foundations for many of the programs of aid to mothers and children which WHO and UNICEF help governments to carry out. The battle against malaria no longer aims at control, but at completely wiping out the disease. Training was and continues to be an integral facet of all aid, so that Mrs. Bille-Brahe and her fellow nurses of that time have in some eight years largely been replaced by Indian, Burmese, Indonesian, and Chilean, public health nurses. Nationals now staff the thousands of maternal and child welfare centers which have been established with UNICEF equipment and WHO technical advice. India is now producing DDT for use in the battle against malaria, reducing the need for imported supplies. UNICEF helped to equip the DDT factories and WHO assisted in training the technical staff. Midwife training and nutrition education, including school gardens, are but two of the aspects of Mrs. Bille-Brahe's work which have grown to full-fledged programs, not only in India, but throughout Asia, the Middle East, Africa and Latin America.

The importance of the contributions made by this and other WHO/UNICEF teams and their devoted members is reflected in the new hopes in the minds of people. Strong, healthy, and happy people will maintain and strengthen their democratic institutions. Their cause is the cause of freedom.

WORLD HEALTH ORGANIZATION:
WHO

International Headquarters: Palais des Nations, Geneva, Switzerland

ORIGIN

The origin of the World Health Organization may be said to date from the proposal of the Brazilian delegation at the San Francisco Conference that the word "health" be included in the United Nations Charter. The subsequent decision of the Conference is included in Article 55 of the Charter, which states that the United Nations shall promote *health* as one of the "conditions of stability and well-being which are necessary for peaceful and friendly relations among nations . . . " To insure cooperative future action, Brazil and China jointly appealed the Conference to provide for an international health conference.

This plea was met with dispatch by the Economic and Social Council at its first meeting in February, 1946. ECOSOC named a Technical Preparatory Committee of sixteen experts who drafted an agenda and certain proposals for the first international health conference, which convened in New York City on June 19, 1946.

There the Constitution of the new World Health Organization was drafted and signed at its conclusion, July 22, 1946, by the representatives of sixty-one nations. On this same date these representatives signed an agreement setting up an Interim Commission of eighteen members charged with the responsibility of making preparations for the first Health Assembly, to be convened within six months after the twenty-sixth nation had formally approved the Constitution. Accordingly, on June 24, 1948, the representatives of most of the countries on earth met at Geneva, Switzerland, for the initial World Health Assembly. For the first time in history a single organization was mobilized to attack international problems of health.

PURPOSES

The purposes of the World Health Organization are set forth in the Preamble to its Constitution, the provisions of which ring sturdy challenges to the peoples and governments of the world.

• Health is a state of complete physical, mental and social well-being and not merely the absence of disease or infirmity.

• The enjoyment of the highest attainable standard of health is one of the fundamental rights of every human being without distinction of race, religion, political belief, economic or social condition.

• The health of all peoples is fundamental to the attainment of peace and security and is dependent upon the fullest cooperation of individuals and States.

• The achievement of any State in the promotion and protection of health is of value to all.

• Unequal development in different countries in the promotion of health and control of disease, especially communicable disease, is a common danger.

• Healthy development of the child is of basic importance; the ability to live harmoniously in a changing total environment is essential to such development.

• The extension to all peoples of the benefits of medical, psychological and related knowledge is essential to the fullest attainment of health.

• Informed opinion and active cooperation on the part of the public are of the utmost importance in the improvement of the health of the people.

• Governments have a responsibility for the health of their peoples which can be fulfilled only by the provision of adequate health and social measures.

FUNCTIONS

The functions of the World Health Organization are established in Chapter II of the Constitution. Those functions pertinent to the carrying out of such objectives as India's request for aid in eradicating malaria are as follows:

• to act as the directing and coordinating authority on international health work;

• to establish and maintain effective collaboration with the United Nations, specialized agencies, governmental health administrations, professional groups and such other organizations as may be deemed appropriate;

• to assist governments, upon request, in strengthening health services;

• to furnish appropriate technical assistance and, in emergencies, necessary aid upon the request or acceptance of governments; . . .

• to stimulate and advance work to eradicate epidemic, endemic and other diseases; . . .

• to promote, in cooperation with other specialized agencies where necessary, the improvement of nutrition, housing, sanitation, recreation, economic or working conditions and other aspects of environmental hygiene; . . .

• to promote maternal and child health and welfare and to foster the ability to live harmoniously in a changing total environment; . . .

• to promote improved standards of teaching and training in the health, medical and related professions; . . .

• to assist in developing an informed public opinion among all peoples on matters of health.

MEMBERSHIP

Membership in WHO is open to all nations. Members of the United Nations may join by accepting the Constitution. Other nations may be admitted when their application has been approved by a simple majority of the Health Assembly. An interesting provision of the Constitution provides for the admission as associate members of territories not responsible for the conduct of their own international affairs, provided that their representatives are qualified by technical competence and that they come from the native population.

As of February 1, 1961, there were 104 members of WHO and two associate members. A detailed listing of WHO membership appears in the Appendix.

In joining WHO, each member assumes certain responsibilities of reporting to the Organization. These obligations are enumerated in Chapter XIV of the Constitution.

• Each Member shall report annually to the Organization on the action taken and progress achieved in improving the health of its people.

· Each Member shall report annually on the action taken with respect to recommendations made to it by the Organization and with respect to conventions, agreements and regulations.

· Each Member shall communicate promptly to the Organization important laws, regulations, official reports and statistics pertaining to health which have been published in the State concerned.

· Each Member shall provide statistical and epidemiological reports in a manner to be determined by the Health Assembly.

· Each Member shall transmit upon the request of the Board such additional information pertaining to health as may be practicable.

STRUCTURE AND ORGANIZATION

The policies of WHO are determined by the World Health Assembly. The Executive Board serves as the organ for carrying out the policies agreed to by the Assembly. The administative work of the Organization is accomplished by the Secretariat.

The World Health Assembly

The World Health Assembly meets annually and is composed of delegates from member states, each of which has one vote. The Assembly is empowered to adopt regulations necessary to carrying out the functions previously enumerated as necessary to attain the objectives of the Organization. The Assembly appoints the Director-General and names the members entitled to designate a person for the Executive Board. It also reviews and approves the WHO budget.

The Executive Board

The Executive Board consists of eighteen persons designated by as many member nations and chosen by the Assembly with due regard for geographical distribution. The Twelfth Assembly voted to enlarge the membership of the Board from eighteen to twenty-four. For this constitutional change to become effective, it has to be formally ratified by two-thirds of WHO member states. The Constitution requires that the Board meet at least twice a year, and empowers the Board to elect its own chairman. Members serve for three years and may be re-elected. In addition to carrying out the policies of the Assembly and serving as its adviser, the Board is given authority to take emergency measures

Nurse Nalina Parulkar shows Indian mothers how to wash a child with skin disease. WHO-UNICEF aid helps India expand nurse training programs and set up new health centers.

within the financial capacity of the Organization in case of epidemics and calamities.

The Secretariat

The Secretariat comprises the Director-General and whatever technical and administrative staff may be required. In addition to his duties as chief technical and administrative office, the Director-General appoints members of committees chosen from panels of experts who advise WHO on technical and scientific matters.

ACTIVITIES

The activities of WHO fall into two main groups: advisory services and technical services. The work being carried on by the malaria control team of which Mrs. Bille-Brahe was a member is a good example of WHO advisory service. What this team was doing was applying the "know-how" that had been gained in other parts of the world to a specific problem in India. Such an exchange of knowledge and techniques among world neighborhoods has produced dramatic results.

In early 1961 WHO reported that out of a total population of 1,136 million people in currently or formerly malarious areas, 298 million are now living in areas from which the disease has been eradicated, while more than 612 million are covered by eradication programs now in progress.

It is hoped that, through international cooperation, malaria will eventually disappear from the earth. Towards that end, and to finance its share of the campaigns, WHO has established a Malaria Eradication Special Account, to be voluntarily financed by governments, organizations, foundations, associations, and individuals. The Account has a target of $50 million to cover operations over several years.

WHO's principal task is to assist governments to strengthen their health services. One method is to provide specialists and technicians to show how to combat diseases, such as tuberculosis, leprosy or yaws, how to set up public health services or to put into effect the minimum standards of sanitation which are a keystone of public health. The other method — which goes hand in hand with advisory work — is training. Almost everywhere there is a serious shortage of health personnel and unless their numbers are expanded governments cannot take over and extend the services which WHO has helped them to establish. Fellowships provide for advanced study abroad, while, within the countries aided, training programs guided by WHO prepare other health workers to staff the new services.

WHO's technical services include the developing of international standards for vaccines and drugs. Another important service keeps the world informed of outbreaks of diseases such as cholera and smallpox. Facts and figures on epidemics are broadcast throughout the world by radio transmitters. Plagues have been kept from spreading because WHO served as an organization through which many governments could help the peoples of a stricken area. WHO carries on special research projects on diseases such as influenza and poliomyelitis. In addition, WHO issues technical bulletins and publications that are used by medical scientists and public health officials throughout the world.

It is important to understand that the World Health Organization is *not* a "world sickness organization." No organization within itself could ever dare hope to administer to the health needs of the almost three billion people on earth. Nor is this the purpose of WHO. WHO is a workshop dedicated to helping the neighborhoods of the world to help themselves, not only toward the eradication of disease but to "a state of complete physical, mental and social well-being" without which international good will cannot flourish.

THE UNITED NATIONS CHILDREN'S FUND: UNICEF
Headquarters: United Nations, New York, N.Y.

ORIGIN
UNICEF is *not* a Specialized Agency of the United Nations. The United Nations International Children's Emergency Fund was created by unanimous vote of the United Nations General Assembly on December 11, 1946. On that date UNICEF became an integral part of the United Nations.

PURPOSE
UNICEF was established for the purpose of bringing assistance to children of war-devastated countries and raising the level of child health conditions. In December 1950 the General Assembly directed UNICEF to shift its emphasis from emergency relief to aid for long-range child care programs, particularly in underdeveloped countries. Emergency aid is also given children suffering from catastrophes such as earthquakes and floods, as well as those suffering from the dislocations of war. In 1953, the Assembly voted unanimously to continue UNICEF on a permanent basis and changed its name to the United Nations Children's Fund, but kept the well-known symbol "UNICEF."

To accomplish its purpose UNICEF, within its financial limitations, provides governments with the equipment they need to start mass campaigns to control diseases, to build health services and to improve nutrition for their children and to carry these on permanently with local people and local facilities after UNICEF aid ceases. Each dollar that UNICEF contributes to a program *must be matched by at least* an equal amount by the government receiving assistance. This policy underscores UNICEF's belief that the primary responsibility for the care of children is that of the individual country concerned.

The importance of clean hands is impressed on youngsters through thousands of health centers, community and school programs in Asian countries. Teaching sanitation is an important step in improving health.

STRUCTURE AND ORGANIZATION

UNICEF is governed by an Executive Board of thirty members designated by the Economic and Social Council of the United Nations. The Executive Board meets regularly for the purpose of deciding upon allocations for UNICEF programs and to review progress and policies. The Executive Board is responsible to the Economic and Social Council, which in turn is responsible to the General Assembly of the United Nations.

The policies of the Executive Board are carried out by the Executive Director, who is appointed by the Secretary-General of the United Nations in consultation with the Executive Board. The Executive Director has a staff of approximately 550, all of whom are members of the United Nations Secretariat.

ACTIVITIES

We have seen how Mrs. Bille-Brahe and the malaria-control team were dependent upon UNICEF for DDT, maternity kits for midwives and powdered milk. This is but one of thousands of UNICEF activities that are going on.

There are some 1 billion children in the world. About three-fourths of them — 750 million — live in the less developed countries, which are the principal areas of UNICEF assistance. Currently, UNICEF aid is reaching about 55 million of these children directly. Disease control programs aim at the five major killers and cripplers of children: malaria, tuberculosis, leprosy, yaws and trachoma.

Forty-seven countries are now helped in campaigns against malaria. Tuberculosis control programs have tested some 306 million persons: 118 million of them have been vaccinated. Yaws, a tropical disease which causes painful, crippling sores can be cured with one shot of penicillin. So far more than 80 million have been examined and 30 million treated. In Haiti, where one in three had yaws in 1950, a house-to-house campaign has wiped out the disease.

Leprosy control is now underway in twenty-six countries. In the trachoma campaigns, about seven million afflicted children have been saved from possible blindness through treatment with UNICEF antibiotics.

While UNICEF continues to provide powdered milk for supplementary feeding, the emphasis is on helping governments to develop their own sources of protein-rich food. One hundred fifty-four new plants producing dried or fluid milk are already in operation. These and other plants now authorized benefit millions of children, who receive much of the milk free or at low cost. In areas where milk is scarce, research aided by UNICEF and FAO is developing new protein foods from locally available supplies. These include peanut flour, saridele (a soybean mixture), and fish flour. Nutrition education is another vital aspect of the campaign against child hunger, since ignorance of the child's need for protein is by itself responsible for much malnutrition and illness.

Health services include the programs for maternal and child welfare under which equipment for mother-child centers has gone to seventy-two countries, the training courses for midwives, nurses and other child-care workers, and also assistance to help villages secure water and waste disposal systems.

All of this and more, without bombast, without table thumping, without heated debate. Just thousands of dedicated people, backed up by the financial support and understanding of most of the nations in the world, all helping to put into practice the principle set forth in the United Nations Declaration of the Rights of the Child:

"Mankind owes to the child the best it has to give."

FINANCES

UNICEF is supported entirely by the *voluntary* contributions of the peoples and governments of nearly a hundred countries. It has aided a total of 127 countries and territories. In early 1961, the figure stood at 104. Recipient countries have recently matched each UNICEF dollar with $2.00 to $2.50 of their own, and most of these countries also contribute to UNICEF.

As realization of the urgent need for UNICEF help has grown, so the number of governments contributing to UNICEF has steadily increased. In 1950 they numbered 30. In 1960, 98 governments contributed. Annual contributions from governments averaged $11.9 million for the period 1951-54. For 1957-59, they averaged $19.5 million.

Although governments have contributed the great bulk of funds to UNICEF, the organization's files attest to the fact that UNICEF purpose and spirit have reached people everywhere. A ninety-two-year-old woman of Mrs. Bille-Brahe's home town of Copenhagen, Denmark, contributed 1,000 crowns ($145) of her hard-earned savings from working days with the message: "I give this money to UNICEF where it will help a little child." Each year recently in the United States, in some 10,000 communities, youngsters have turned the traditional "Trick or Treat" of Hallowe'en into "Trick or Treat for UNICEF." In 1961, these youngsters collected $2,000,000. This amount would enable UNICEF to equip about 20,000 small maternal and child welfare centers or to provide DDT protection against malaria for some 20,000,000 children for a year. "Trick or Treat for UNICEF" also resulted in the smallest gift ever received by the organization: three pennies, wrapped in an old handkerchief, addressed "To the World's Children" from "Jimmy."

UNICEF holiday greeting cards issued to stimulate public interest in the Fund's work have been widely accepted. Sales of over 21.5 million cards in about 100 countries in 1961 provided another welcome source of revenue to UNICEF.

National Committees for UNICEF, formed by private citizens and interested organizations, help to further public understanding of the Fund's work. In the United States, the "Trick or Treat" program is but one project of the National Committee.

THE FUTURE

Though UNICEF aid is small in terms of the need, it has a decisive impact because it helps countries to establish their own permanent services to look after their own children and to train national personnel to run these services. In a five-year "forward appraisal" prepared for the Economic and Social Council in 1959, the UNICEF Executive Board foresaw an increase of eleven per cent in the child population of the countries receiving UNICEF aid. Permanent health services, nutrition, and family and child welfare services would be especially needed in those countries. This will call for a larger number of professional staff than do disease control campaigns and, hence, the Executive Board expected that more UNICEF assistance will go for training facilities within each country.

It has been increasingly recognized that the needs of children arising from illness, hunger and ignorance are closely related; each is part cause and part effect. Governments are beginning to plan their services for children with the goal of improving these inter-related conditions in a comprehensive program. UNICEF aid will help them turn these plans into the reality which promises a healthier, happier future for hundreds of millions of children.

CHAPTER FIVE

Postmarked
"United Nations, New York"

On October 24, 1951, the United Nations issued *international* postage stamps. For the first time in history an organization of nations produced stamps for world-wide circulation. This date marked an important milestone in international cooperation as well as in philately. The first day of issue was an appropriate commemoration of the U.N.'s fifth year of dedication to world peace.

These new international symbols had their origin on November 16, 1950, when the General Assembly unanimously adopted a resolution establishing the United Nations Postal Administration and authorizing it to issue United Nations postage stamps. With this authority, the Secretary-General of the United Nations began negotiations with the government of the United States which led to the special United Nations-United States Postal Agreement that was signed March 28, 1951.

Under the provisions of this agreement, the United Nations was to issue and use its own postage stamps. A United Nations post office station was to be opened on the date of issue of U.N. stamps, with services and personnel provided by the United States Post Office Department. All mail postmarked "United Nations, New York" was to be stamped with United Nations stamps which were to be valid for postal purposes only in the United Nations Headquarters' post office. The U. S. Post Office was to be reimbursed for all postage used for mail dispatched from UN Headquarters. In 1960 alone, the reimbursement was over $450,000.

By the beginning of 1961, about 274 million United Nations stamps and other postal items, such as stamped postcards, had been printed. United Nations stamps have been very popular with collectors all over the world, and gross revenue from philatelic sales had reached almost $10 million by this date, making a significant contribution to the financial support of the organization.

Far more important than monetary profit is the fact that the United Nations postage stamps have carried word of the organization to the far corners of the globe. The stamps are designed to show the aims, work, and activities of the United Nations and its related organizations. The organization that makes it possible for these messages of peace, justice, and security to be transmitted to the neighborhoods of the world is the Universal Postal Union (UPU), a Specialized Agency of the United Nations.

Members of the Universal Postal Union include the postal administrations of ninety-four nations and eight territories. UPU's basic principle is that, for postal purposes, all member states form a single territory. A partial glimpse of UPU's many activities may be had by following a letter postmarked "United Nations, New York" and addressed to Moscow, U.S.S.R.

The purchase price of a stamp for a letter weighing an ounce or less from the United States to the Soviet Union is eight cents.

On October 24, 1951, the United Nations issued the first international Postage stamps.

One of a series dedicated to U.N. agencies, this 1961 commemorative stamp honors the International Monetary Fund.

New thirty-cent stamp meets airmail and special delivery rates.

The Universal Postal Union stamp design was chosen by an international jury of five experts appointed by the Secretary-General of the United Nations.

This same postage rate applies to all letters destined to most postal services throughout the world, thus underscoring the UPU's successful drive toward a single postal territory. Exceptions to this letter rate apply to mail intended for delivery by the postal services of the United States, Canada and Mexico. Currently the rate from the United States to these countries is four cents — subject to change should the Congress pass, and the President approve, a law to raise the postage rates. Such arrangements are authorized by the provisions of the Universal Postal Union Conventions.

A customer might purchase any one of the United Nations eight-cent postage stamps for this letter. The money received from the sale of this stamp is retained by the United States Post Office Department. The members of UPU have agreed that each country is to keep all of the postage it collects. Prior to this decision a state of chaos existed, since postage collections for international mail were shared by the various postal administrations through which the mail passed in proportion to the services each country was supposed to have rendered. This division of postage money made for a very elaborate and costly system of accounting in each post office. While some senders might have enjoyed the game of determining what was the least costly route over which their mail might be sent, in the main there was intolerable confusion in the international postal service. Now, under UPU, each country keeps the postage it collects, and settles with other countries for their services on the basis of *weight* rather than *rates*.

Mail from the United Nations post office is taken by truck to the main post office in New York City. Here the postal officials whose responsibility it is to dispatch international mail have access to dozens of services provided by UPU agreements. While the processing of a letter directed to Moscow is a routine matter for these experienced people, there are times when UPU publications must be consulted. The International Bureau of the UPU provides member nations with such data as: complete information on the airmail services of all UPU members, including a list of airports, showing ownership and geographical location; maps showing the routes of some six hundred airlines; a directory of post offices throughout the world; statements of rates; lists of prohibited articles; regulations governing the classification of mail into such categories as letters, commercial papers, post cards, samples and the like; a world map of surface communication routes, including railway, road, river, and sea facilities, capitals, frontier offices of exchange, ports, and postal centers.

Based upon this latter information, the port of destination is determined; in this case Helsinki, Finland. The mail for Moscow is kept open until shortly before ship departure time and then is placed in United States Mail pouches, weighed, and labeled. The ship upon which this letter will be forwarded is designated by United States postal officials, and poundage rates are paid the shipping company as provided by United States Postal Laws and Regulations.

Upon arrival at Helsinki, one of the most important of UPU's principles becomes operative. This is that every country is obliged to let foreign mail matter circulate within its territory on the same basis as its own, and for a just and reasonable compensation to forward it to its destination by the most rapid means available under its classification. This principle applies as the pouch is forwarded by rail across the border of the U.S.S.R. to Moscow.

The mail is received at the Central Telephone and Telegraph Building in Moscow. Article 172 of the UPU Regulations of Execution of the Convention of Ottawa provides that the United States Mail pouch shall be returned empty, by the next mail, to this country. Other UPU regulations affect the delivery of mail; articles addressed to persons who have submitted notices of change of address are to be forwarded, unless the letter bears instructions to the contrary in the language of the country of destination, after delivery has been unsuccessfully attempted; the special-delivery indication on special-delivery articles may be stricken out; and many others.

By much the same procedure, mail from Moscow reaches the United States. The postage rate for a letter mailed from Moscow to St. Louis is sixty kopecks, a sum equal to about eight cents in United States currency. The mail may follow the same return route or be forwarded to Cherbourg and Havre, France. By UPU regulation the postal administration forwarding the mail determines the shipping lines to be used. Vessels of the Cunard, Holland-America, French, and United States lines are used.

The United States government becomes responsible for such mail upon delivery of same to the United States Post Office by the conveying vessel. The average transit time for mails from Moscow to the United States is seventeen days, depending upon shipping schedules. Between February 1 and May 1, 1960, mails were received from the U.S.S.R. on eleven occasions. Twenty dispatches of mail were sent from the United States during this same period.

The Universal Postal Union has designated its International Bureau as a clearing house for the settlement of accounts among member nations who may want to take advantage of this service. Although the United States Post Office Department settles all accounts direct with the postal authorities concerned, its figures attest to the magnitude of international mail service. In the year ending June 30, 1959, the United States paid $11,478,755 to other Administrations and received $12,093,938. In addition to this amount $7,168,894 was received on behalf of United States air carriers for the conveyance of mails of other countries.

Letter communication between the neighborhoods of the world has become such a simple, everyday affair that most of us take it for granted. But behind the modern efficiency of letter post are centuries of struggle on the part of the human community. No more vital contribution than that of the Universal Postal Union exists in postal history. Today the members of the UPU handle over 108 billion articles in the letter post a year. The UPU purpose has never been more clearly stated than in the words of Mr. Gunner F. E. Lager, formerly Assistant Director of Posts in Sweden and Dean of the Thirteenth Universal Postal Congress. He addressed its opening session as follows:

"The purpose of our Union is clearly defined: organize and improve the postal service. Its only concern is to facilitate spiritual and material intercourse between men and nations. In that task, it takes no account of geographical frontiers, nor of barriers erected by differences in ideology, race or religion. In its province, it has made true that ancient dream which is always alive in minds of men of good will: make the World one."

UNIVERSAL POSTAL UNION:
UPU
International Headquarters: Schosshaldenstrasse 46, Berne 15, Switzerland

ORIGIN

The suggestion for the establishment of an international organization to handle postal matters originated in the United States. In 1862, Mr. Montgomery Blair, then Postmaster General of the United States, communicated with postal officials throughout the world urging that an international postal conference be held for the purpose of exchanging ideas that might bring some order out of the chaos then existing in the international postal service. It is interesting to note that Postmaster General Blair's suggestion was made at a time when his own country was engaged in the great internal struggle of the Civil War.

In 1863, the representatives of fifteen nations met at Paris for the first international postal conference. They adopted thirty-one articles of "general principles of such a nature as to facilitate relations among peoples, through the postal service, capable of being used as a basis for international conventions governing such relations." While no international organization was created at this meeting, the possibility of doing so at a future date was discussed by the delegates.

At the suggestion of Heinrich von Stephan, then Director-General of Posts of the North German Confederation, the first Postal Congress met at Berne, Switzerland, in 1874. After deliberating less

This five-cent stamp is dedicated to the United Nations Children's Fund.

A commemorative stamp marks the work of the International Bank.

than a month the delegates signed a "Treaty Concerning the Creation of a General Postal Union," subject to the ratification of their governments. This latter was accomplished on May 3, 1875, and brought about great and constructive changes in the international postal services.

The second Postal Congress, held at Paris in 1878, changed the name of the General Postal Union to the Universal Postal Union. The Twelfth Congress of the Universal Postal Union met at Paris in 1947, and adopted a proposition that established the UPU as a Specialized Agency of the United Nations. The Thirteenth Universal Postal Congress met at Brussels in May, 1952; the Fourteenth at Ottawa in August, 1957.

PURPOSE

Article I of the Universal Postal Convention says the aim of the Universal Postal Union "is to secure the organization and improvement of the various international postal services, and to promote the development of international collaboration in this sphere." To attain this goal, the countries which concluded the Convention form a single postal territory for the reciprocal exchange of correspondence.

FUNCTIONS

All members of the UPU agree to follow the provisions of the Convention regulating the transmission of eight types of letter post: letters, single and reply-paid post cards, commercial papers, printed matter, raised print for the blind, samples of merchandise, small packets, and phonopost articles (such as phonograph records). Further provisions fix international maximum and minimum rates, weight limits, and dimensions for this type of mail. Under the provisions of Article II of the Final Protocol of the Convention, each country can increase the basic rates laid down in the Convention by sixty per cent as a maximum, or reduce them by twenty per cent as a maximum.

By agreements supplementing the Convention, and binding only for those members that adhere to them, the UPU regulates certain other postal services: insured letters and boxes, parcel post, money orders, postal transfers, collection orders, savings bonds, subscriptions to newspapers and periodicals, and cash-on-delivery articles.

MEMBERSHIP

The UPU with 102 members is one of the largest of the Specialized Agencies. A complete list of members appears in the Appendix.

The Universal Postal Union is an organization without any political ramifications whatever. Its work is purely administrative and technical.

STRUCTURE AND ORGANIZATION

The Universal Postal Union is composed of the Universal Postal Congress, the Executive and Liaison Committee, the Consultative Committee for Postal Studies, and the International Bureau of the UPU.

The Universal Postal Congress

The Universal Postal Congress, or legislative body, is composed of representatives of all members of the Union. It usually meets every five years to review the Convention and its subsidiary agreements on the basis of proposals submitted by the members.

The Executive and Liaison Committee

The Permanent Executive and Liaison Committee consists of twenty members elected on a geographical basis by each Congress. The Committee normally meets once a year in Berne. Its functions include the maintenance of relations with member nations, the study of questions relating to the international postal service, and the establishment and maintenance of working relations with the United Nations and other international organizations. The Committee also controls the activities of the International Bureau and on the recommendation of the Swiss government appoints its Director.

The Consultative Committee for Postal Studies

All the members of the Union are automatically members of the Consultative Committee for Postal Studies. It generally meets in plenary assembly prior to the Congress. It elects within itself a Management Council of twenty members divided into three sec-

The first day of issue of a new stamp draws crowds to sales counter at United Nations Headquarters.

tions: technical, operational and economic. The Committee's task consists of carrying out studies and giving advice on technical, operational and economic questions concerning the postal service. To help governments modernize and speed up mailing procedures, the Committee seeks such information as the latest developments in mechanization and automation in sorting operations, automatic machines for selling stamps and the most efficient methods of organizing post offices.

The International Bureau

The International Bureau is the administrative organ of the UPU. It assembles, coordinates, publishes, and distributes information of all kinds essential to the various postal administrations. The Bureau serves postal administrations as a clearing house for accounts if they so request. The Bureau makes preparations for Congresses and performs other functions assigned to it by the Convention.

ACTIVITIES

In addition to the activities previously mentioned, the UPU provides other services to its members through the International Bureau. These include giving opinions on disagreements arising on postal questions; distribution to other members of stamps of all types used by each member; supplying members with international reply coupons to cover the cost of return postage; exchanging information on postal equipment; and the exchange of films on postal subjects.

It has long been a function of UPU to encourage mutual technical assistance between postal administrations. In addition, UPU cooperates with the Technical Assistance Office of the United Nations providing advice and locating experts when an individual country seeks help in solving postal problems. Some of the countries to which such help has been given are the Republic of Korea, Paraguay, Iran and Lebanon.

CHAPTER SIX

ILO

International Labor Organization

Boatmen on the Rhine

The Rhine River has from early times been one of the chief waterways of Europe. Rising in Switzerland, the Rhine flows in a northerly direction, touching upon neighborhoods in the German Federal Republic, France, and the Netherlands, and is linked by canals to Belgium. These neighborhoods are rich in mineral resources, and produce goods that are shipped to all parts of the world from the great ports of Rotterdam, Antwerp, and Amsterdam.

Nearly eight thousand freighters, passenger boats, tugs and lighters constantly ply the 550 navigable miles of the Rhine, providing trading facilities essential to the economic life of the regions they serve. Forty-five thousand people, the Rhine boatmen and their families, live and work on the river. The average barge carries a crew of two or three in addition to the skipper and his family.

Life is both hazardous and hard for the Rhine boatmen. Handling heavy bulk cargoes such as fuel, coal, sugar, and cereals is a difficult task. Routine chores aboard ship, such as painting, cleaning the smokestacks, and maintaining steam engines, have their dangerous moments. The hours are long. For the crew members this is a lonely life, since it may mean being away from home for weeks at a time.

While the work to be done does not vary much from one craft to another, the same cannot be said for labor conditions. The river

Life is hazardous and hard for the Rhine boatman. Here a disabled boatman works an
anchor hoist.

boats are owned by individuals and companies of five different
nations. This means that there are five different standards of employment regarding wages, hours of work, vacations, and the like.

Until June of 1953 the same confusion and hardship existed in
medical care and social security protection. Before this date, if a
Rhine boatman became ill or was injured, he did not qualify for
free medical care or accident allowance under the social security
laws of his own or other countries. Too, the Rhine boatman found
it difficult to qualify for a pension after his working days were
over, as there was no system for coordinating retirement payments.

The story of how the Rhine boatmen came to have social security protection without regard to national boundaries is a story of cooperation and good will by owners, unions, and governments working through the International Labor Organization (ILO), a Specialized Agency of the United Nations.

Labor problems resulting from situations where more than one nation used a common waterway had long been the concern of ILO. As early as 1920 the Organization had recommended that owners, workers, and governments sharing common waterways should standardize on an eight-hour day and a forty-eight-hour week. Prior to the outbreak of World War II, the International Labor Organization had made many studies regarding particular problems connected with inland transport of all types. Following the war, ILO established an Inland Transport Committee as a permanent group charged with the responsibility of furthering ILO's purposes by bringing together employer, worker, and government representatives who were experts in this field. This Committee recognized the special problems of the boatmen on the Rhine and on the canals of the Rhine basin.

Many of the owners of Rhine craft were aware of the inequalities of the social security protection afforded their employees. In February of 1947 the Committee of French Owners of Rhine Shipping adopted a resolution suggesting that a social insurance system for workers in Rhine navigation should be dealt with in an international convention between governments represented on the Central Commission for Rhine Navigation. This latter organization was set up under the provisions of the Congress of Vienna in 1815. Although modified by subsequent treaties, the major purpose of the Commission has remained the same since that date — to insure that the navigation of the Rhine and its mouths shall be free to vessels and people of all nations for the transportation of goods and persons.

It remained for Rhine boatmen to take the initiative in this matter. Through their union, they appealed to the International Transportworkers' Federation with which they were affiliated, and which represents some 5,500,000 workers in over forty different countries. The ITF decided to convene a Rhine Navigation Conference to discuss working conditions in Rhine shipping. This Conference, held in 1946, adopted a provisional program for conditions of employment for the Rhine boatmen. It also authorized a committee to approach the International Labor Organization with a view to promoting agreements on social insurance for Rhine navigation workers.

The International Transportworkers' Federation subsequently stated the case for the Rhine boatmen in a letter sent to the Director-General of ILO at Geneva, Switzerland, on March 14, 1947, and signed by the General-Secretary of the ITF, Mr. J. H. Oldenbroek. This letter advised the Director-General that ITF planned to raise these matters in behalf of the Rhine boatmen at the next meeting of the Inland Transport Committee of the ILO. The ITF suggested that since any agreements would involve German workers, it would be advisable to invite representatives from the United States and the United Kingdom, two of the three powers then occupying Western Germany; the third was France, a country directly concerned in its own right.

Mr. Oldenbroek's letter stated a particular case for social security. He noted that workers living in one country forfeited their social security claims in that country when working on a vessel of another nationality. The ITF suggested as a basis for discussion at the Inland Transport Committee meeting that, for medical aid and sickness benefits the boatman should be treated as a national of the country for which he was working; but for incapacity or retirement, as a national of his own country. With this letter the ITF submitted a list of minimum claims of the Rhine shipping workers as to hours of work, rest periods, minimum wages, overtime, and annual vacations, plus some other items.

The Director-General of ILO circulated the communication from the ITF among the government, employer, and worker delegates to the Inland Transport Committee, as well as to its general membership. This gave the delegates adequate time to prepare for discussion of this matter before the meeting of the Inland Transport Committee held at Geneva in May, 1947. The ITC established a Subcommittee on Rhine Navigation, consisting of eighteen members representing Belgium, France, Netherlands, Switzerland, United Kingdom, and the United States, and balanced so that six members represented the governments, six the workers, and six the employers.

The Subcommittee on Rhine Navigation met at Geneva in May, 1947. The members unanimously adopted a resolution that rec-

Dutch Captain M. van Dam, owner of the Rhine boat "God mit Uns," with his wife in their living quarters.

ognized the hardships that existed for the Rhine boatmen because of differences in laws and regulations as well as differences in collective agreements in the various countries, and recommended that the governments concerned should hold a special tripartite (government-employer-worker) conference to consider drafting conventions to correct conditions. The Subcommittee further charged the International Labor Organization to provide detailed reports and all documentation necessary for such a conference.

Acting upon this authority, the International Labor Office accomplished the background research. The Director-General of ILO handled the exchange of views of the governments concerned, and when all had signified their acceptance of the Subcommittee's resolution the ILO planned the Special Tripartite Conference concerning Rhine boatmen which opened at Geneva October 31, 1949. A delegation of the new German Federal Republic attended the Conference with representatives of the High Commissioners in Germany. This was the first meeting of a United Nations agency to which the German Federal Republic had sent representatives.

The International Labor Organization had been the first to admit a German delegation after World War I — at the Washington Conference of 1919.

Basing its work upon drafts prepared by the International Labor Office, the Geneva Conference completed its work on December 14, 1949. After disagreements had been resolved harmoniously, the texts of two agreements were adopted unanimously. One concerned social security and the other dealt with working conditions. Under the draft agreement on social security, the insurance protection was to be granted by the country in which the head office of the employer was located. A boatman was to be insured for sickness and other benefits. If a boatman had social insurance benefits resulting from illness or injury outside the country that afforded his protection, the country in which his disability occurred was to provide the necessary services and was entitled to repayment by the insurance institution of the responsible country. Pension payments were to be made by each country in proportion to the time the boatman had been employed. The second agreement fixed minimum hours, holidays, and other working conditions. Some of the latter, such as limited time off to cover family responsibilities, were new in ILO history.

The draft agreements, with suggestions for their implementation, were submitted to the ILO Governing Body. After having approved the work of the Geneva Confernence, the Governing Body convened a conference of government representatives at Paris in July, 1950, for the purpose of approval in final form. This was accomplished with the further stipulation that the acceptances of the countries concerned were to be entrusted to the Director-General of ILO, who in turn would register them with the United Nations. The agreements were to become effective on the first day of the third month following deposit of ratification instruments by the governments of Switzerland, France, Belgium, the Federal Republic of Germany, and the Netherlands.

On March 4, 1953, when Belgium deposited its ratification, Director-General David A. Morse of the ILO announced that the Agreement on Social Security would become effective on June 1. This notable achievement proved, however, to be but a first step in providing the Rhine boatmen with social security protection. Experience in administering the Agreement and the desire to extend to the boatmen the advantages which had been incorporated in newer social security legislation led to a call by several governments for revision of the Agreement. A preparatory meeting held in March, 1960, agreed on new provisions drafted by the ILO at the request of the signatory governments. A special meeting of chiefs of delegations held at Geneva in January, 1961, then was followed by a formal governmental conference held at ILO headquarters, February 7-13, 1961.

In addition to the original signatory governments, Austria and Luxembourg and a representative of the long-established Central Commission for the Navigation of the Rhine signed the Final Act of the Conference. Indicative of the progress made in European economic and social cooperation in the past eight years was the presence also at the conferences of observers from the Commission

Seaman's wife hangs laundry on the deck of the "Richebourg."

Boarding school for children of the Rhine boatmen on a remodelled barge in Rotterdam harbor.

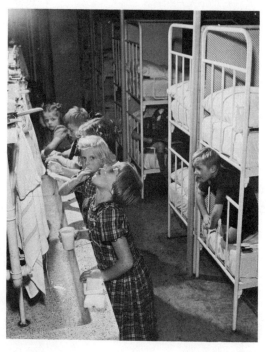

of the European Economic Community and the United Nations European Economic Commission.

The revisions to the Agreement bring it into harmony with multilateral or bilateral social security conventions binding upon parties to the Agreement, notably regulations of the European Economic Community. The revised text also contains detailed provisions concerning unemployment compensation and daily allowances not included in the 1950 Agreement. The revised Agreement was opened to signature and ratification by Luxembourg and also, under certain conditions, to other countries. It will come into effect on the first day of the third month following deposit of ratification instruments by the countries bordering on the Rhine and by Belgium. Meanwhile, the 1950 Agreement remains in force.

The Agreement concerning the Conditions of Employment was amended at another special tripartite conference before it had been adopted by all of the countries concerned. The modified text was signed at Geneva on May 21, 1954. The Netherlands and Switzerland ratified the Agreement in 1955, and France and the Federal Republic of Germany in 1957. On September 18, 1959, the ILO Director-General registered the ratification by Belgium of the Agreement, which then became effective on December 1, 1959.

As a result of these international agreements, the conditions of life and labor have been improved for the Rhine boatmen and their families. The ILO's contribution to the solution of this human problem was one of seeking an exchange of experiences upon which actions could be harmonized and international treaties written if the nations concerned so desired. By making it possible for governments, workers, and employers to resolve problems through democratic discussion and free decision, the ILO is contributing toward building a lasting peace.

INTERNATIONAL LABOR ORGANIZATION: ILO
International Headquarters: Geneva, Switzerland

ORIGIN

The International Labor Organization was established on April 11, 1919, as an autonomous organization associated with the League of Nations. Samuel Gompers, who represented the United States on the Commission on International Labor Legislation at the Versailles Peace Conference, and who was subsequently named Chairman of the Commission, was one of the leading advocates of this international organization dedicated to improving living and working conditions throughout the world. Although the United States did not join ILO until 1934, the First International Labor Conference, held at Washington, D.C., in October 1919 unanimously invited Gompers to participate in its deliberations.

The twenty-sixth session of the General Conference of the International Labor Organization met at Philadelphia in 1944 and adopted a Declaration of aims and purposes. This Declaration redefined the original aims and purposes of ILO's Constitution, which had formed a part of the Treaty of Versailles and other treaties. Subsequent sessions of the General Conference have amended the Constitution.

In 1946 the ILO became associated with the United Nations as a Specialized Agency under the terms of an agreement which recognized the responsibility of the ILO in the field of labor and social conditions.

PURPOSE

The ILO purpose is stated in Article II of the Declaration of Philadelphia.

Believing that experience has fully demonstrated the truth of the Statement in the Constitution of the International Labor Organization that lasting peace can be established only if it is

Grocery boat serves boatmen in Duisburg harbor.

based on social justice,.the Conference affirms that:

a.   all human beings, irrespective of race, creed or sex, have the right to pursue both their material well-being and their spiritual development in conditions of freedom and dignity, of economic security and equal opportunity;

b.   the attainment of the conditions in which this shall be possible must constitute the central aim of national and international policy;

c.   all national and international policies and measures, in particular those of an economic and financial character, should be judged in this light and accepted only in so far as they may be held to promote and not hinder the achievement of this fundamental objective;

d.   it is a responsibility of the International Labor Organization to examine and consider all international economic and financial policies and measures in the light of this fundamental objective;

e.   in discharging the tasks entrusted to it the International Labor Organization, having considered all relevant economic and financial factors, may include in its decisions and recommendations any provisions which it considers appropriate.

FUNCTIONS

The ILO is charged with the following functions as established in Article III of the Declaration of Philadelphia:

The Conference recognizes the solemn obligation of the International Labor Organization to further among the nations of the world programs which will achieve:

a.   full employment and the raising of standards of living;

b.   the employment of workers in the occupations in which they can have the satisfaction of giving the fullest measure of their skill and attainments and make their greatest contribution to the common well-being;

c.   the provision, as a means to the attainment of this end and under adequate guarantees for all concerned, of facilities for training and the transfer of labor, including migration for employment and settlement;

d.   policies in regard to wages and earnings, hours and other conditions of work calculated to ensure a just share of the fruits

STRUCTURE OF THE ILO

EACH GOVERNMENT
SENDS 4 DELEGATES

2
Government

1
Employer

1
Worker

to the annual

INTERNATIONAL LABOUR CONFERENCE

which examines social problems and adopts conventions and
recommendations for submission to governments

The conference elects the

GOVERNING BODY

10 Workers

20 Governments

10 Employers

which supervises the work of the

INTERNATIONAL LABOUR OFFICE

Research

Investigations

Technical
assistance

Publications

of progress to all, and a minimum living wage to all employed and in need of such protection;

e.   the effective recognition of the right of collective bargaining, the cooperation of management and labor in continuous improvement of productive efficiency, and the collaboration of workers and employers in the preparation and application of social and economic measures;

f.   the extension of social security measures to provide a basic income to all in need of such protection and comprehensive medical care;

g.   adequate protection for the life and health of workers in all occupations;

h.   provision for child welfare and maternity protection;

i.   the provision of adequate nutrition, housing and facilities for recreation and culture. . . .

MEMBERSHIP

As of February 1, 1961, ILO had ninety-six members. A complete list of members is included in the Appendix.

Any member of the United Nations may become a member of ILO by accepting the obligations of membership. The admission of non-members of the U.N. must be approved by the General Conference.

Each nation assumes the responsibility of submitting Conventions approved by the ILO General Conference to its competent national authority to be considered for ratification. When a government ratifies a Convention, it submits annual reports to ILO on the steps taken to make the Convention effective.

Recommendations adopted by the ILO General Conference need not be submitted for ratification, but members are under obligation to consider giving effect to their provisions.

Members report periodically to ILO on the position of their law and practice regarding unratified Conventions and Recommendations.

STRUCTURE AND ORGANIZATION

The ILO has three principal organs: the General Conference, (International Labour Conference) the Governing Body, and the International Labor Office.

The General Conference

The General Conference is composed of two government delegates, one worker delegate, and one employer delegate from each member nation. The worker and employer delegates are chosen by the member nations after consultation with the most representative worker and employer organizations of the country.

The primary function of the General Conferences is the formulation of international minimum standards of working and living conditions. A two-thirds vote of the delegates present is necessary to adopt these standards, which then become Conventions or Recommendations. Collectively these are known as the International Labor Code. ILO agreements become operative only in those member countries whose governments ratify them.

Other responsibilities charged to the General Conference at its annual sessions include: electing members of the Governing Body, adoption of the annual budget, and the review of reports from member states regarding the implementation of Conventions and Recommendations.

The Governing Body

The Governing Body is composed of the representatives of twenty governments, ten workers, and ten employers. Ten of the government seats are allocated to the countries of greatest industrial importance, and the other ten filled by election.

The Governing Body acts as the executive organ for ILO. It supervises various committees and commissions, drafts proposals for the budget, appoints the Director-General, and supervises the work of the International Labor Office.

International Labor Office

The International Labor Office is the permanent secretariat of the ILO. Its responsibilities include the following: preparing documents for ILO meetings; publishing periodicals, studies, and reports on social and economic matters; giving advice and assistance to governments and worker and employer groups when requested to do so; providing machinery for making the Conventions effective.

The Director-General is responsible for the functioning of the International Labor Office.

Supplementary Committees, Commissions, and Conferences

Numerous committees, commissions, and conferences are essential to carrying out ILO's purposes. The Inland Transport Committee that created the Subcommittee on Rhine Navigation, and the Special Tripartite Conference that formally considered recommendations concerning the Rhine boatmen, are examples of such supplementary organizations.

ACTIVITIES

The ILO employs a wide variety of methods in seeking to fulfill its purposes. The way in which its machinery may be utilized to solve problems brought to its attention by member governments, workers and employers has been described in the case of the Rhine boatmen. A résumé of some technical assistance projects sponsored by ILO gives further evidence of the widespread activities of the Organization.

Vocational training centers are one of the foremost means by which ILO helps countries to develop the skills needed to produce goods and services. These schools cover a great range of jobs and deal with the most simple as well as highly technical operations. In Haiti, the need was for quite basic training — how to make the broad knives used to cut sugar cane, how to make wheels and windmills. In Yugoslavia, on the other hand, specialists and technicians have been given advanced training and also an opportunity to learn in the factories of highly industrialized countries. Nations of seven Asian countries with inland water routes have learned diesel mechanics at a regional school in Rangoon, Burma. They will teach others on returning home. The Training School in Libya literally started from an abandoned barracks without furniture or equipment when that country became independent in 1951. The success of this school may be measured by the fact that Libyan instructors have now taken over the teaching from ILO. Ecuador, Venezuela, Brazil, Sudan, Ghana, Lebanon, and Tunisia are a few of the other countries with such training schools. Under U.N. Special Fund projects, ILO will set up instructor training centers in India, Israel, the United Arab Republic and Colombia, and management training courses in Poland.

ILO projects to increase productivity have put more buses on the streets of New Delhi as training courses have improved the efficiency of the repair shops; production has increased by fifty per cent in Pakistani textile mills visited by an ILO team. In Israel a Productivity Institute set up with ILO aid has already trained more than six thousand persons. Similarly, an ILO productivity mission at work in Egypt since 1954 has given more than fifty courses to employees and executives of some forty firms. Other experts are teaching better methods and introducing new tools to workers in Bolivia, Ceylon, Colombia, Indonesia and the Central American Republics. Not infrequently, these experts are nationals of a country which is itself receiving technical aid. Like other U.N. Agencies, ILO has found that a developing country which has solved a particular problem may be in a better position to aid a neighbor than a highly industrialized country.

Social security schemes are gradually being extended to all parts of the world with the advice and help of ILO. In Burma, ILO experts, at the government's request, wrote a social security law, and then trained the administrators. Eighty thousand Burmese workers are already protected by the new law. India has greatly extended social security coverage; Turkey, Iran, Guatemala, Malaya, Vietnam, Iraq, Morocco, and Libya are some of the other countries which are advancing in this field with the support of ILO's expert knowledge.

Occupational safety and health programs are more effective in Turkey and Venezuela because of specific ILO technical aid. In all appropriate technical assistance projects, ILO experts introduce standards of occupational safety and health. One of the more recent concerns of the Organization has been the preparation of an international Convention and Recommendation to protect workers against radiation hazards.

Labor codes to set out the rights of a nation's workers have been drafted, manpower needs surveyed, the problems of migratory workers tackled, inspection and statistical systems taught. The interchange between governments, workers and employers which ILO promotes and the movement of skills between neighborhoods which it arranges are an important element in providing the firm ground on which a lasting peace may be built.

CHAPTER SEVEN

ITU
International Telecommunication Union

"New York Calling Djakarta"

From earliest times neighborhoods of the world have had systems of distance communication. For thousands of years primitive man transmitted his messages by smoke signals, drums, and fire towers. Later the development of written languages enabled peoples to communicate through messages carried by pigeons and by riders on horseback. The Romans developed this latter system into a highly efficient postal service operating over the imperial roads. Caesar's letters written to Cicero from Britain were delivered in Rome within twenty-six days.

For many centuries there was no improvement over the Roman post that Caesar used in the first century B. C. A message transmitted from London to Rome in 1800 was seldom delivered within thirty days! But in the early years of this same century discoveries were being made that revolutionized communications over long distances. Pioneers such as Samuel F. B. Morse in the United States brought together knowledge that led to the development of the electromagnetic telegraph. In the 1840's Morse was granted $30,000 by Congress to construct an experimental telegraph line between Baltimore and Washington. In that same decade countries in Europe were being linked with signals transmitted by wire.

Side by side with improvements in overland telegraphy came inventions that made submarine telegraphy possible. In 1851 a cable was laid between Dover, England and Calais, France. Within the next few years other submarine telegraph cables were laid from England to other shores, between Denmark and Sweden, and between various points in the Mediterranean Sea. After two unsuccessful attempts a telegraph cable was laid under the Atlantic Ocean in 1866 that linked Valentia, Ireland, with Heart's Content, Newfoundland. In 1882 cable contact was established between the United States and countries in Central and South America. In 1906 a trans-Pacific telegraph cable was laid. This linked the United States with Shanghai by way of Hawaii, Midway Island, Guam, and the Philippines. With these developments it became possible to flash signals between the neighborhoods of the world in a matter of minutes.

Other inventions, beginning with those of Guglielmo Marconi in the 1890's, soon made it practicable to send telegraphy messages by radio. The first transocean radiotelegraph service was established in 1912 between San Francisco and Honolulu. This was followed in 1920 by the opening of a direct service from the United States to England. Servies of this kind were gradually expanded until now it is possible for a person to send a radiotelegram to almost any place in the world.

During the latter part of the nineteenth century events were taking place that led to more intimate communication among peoples. On March 10, 1876, Alexander Graham Bell transmitted the first complete sentence heard over a wire, and the telephone became a reality. Beginning in 1877 with the first regular telephone line between Boston and Somerville, Massachusetts, service was gradually expanded until today a telephone subscriber in New York can be connected with over 66,600,000 telephones in the United States.

After Marconi had successfully accomplished the transmission of telegraph signals by radio, other scientists began experimenting with telephone transmission by the same means. In 1915 speech was successfully transmitted from Arlington, Virginia, to Paris. On January 7, 1927, New York and London were first connected for commercial telephone service. This Bell System service extended to other countries, and on April 25, 1935, the first round-the-world telephone circuit was established over a combination of radio and land-line facilities. By 1960 it was possible for any subscriber in the domestic telephone system to be connected with ninety-seven per cent of all the telephones in the world.

Typical of such a call is one between New York City and Djakarta, Indonesia. Most of the calls made between these two points are placed from New York between the hours of 9:30 a.m. to 10:30 a.m. and between 6:30 p.m. and 9:00 p.m. Because of the time differential these calls are received at Djakarta between 10:00 p.m. and 11:00 p.m. the same day and between 7:00 a.m. and 9:30 a.m. the following day.

When the subscriber informs the long distance operator that he wants to place a call to Djakarta, she switches his call to the operator handling calls to Indonesia at the Oakland, California overseas office. At Oakland the call is relayed by radio transmitter across the Pacific Ocean to the Indonesian radio terminal station at Bandung. From this point the call goes by land wire to the central switchboard in Djakarta, where the operator uses the regular telephone system to reach the person for whom the call is intended. If there are no calls ahead of that placed by the customer, and if atmospheric difficulties do not interfere, the connection is completed in a matter of minutes.

At Oakland, California, overseas operators handle calls to the Pacific area.

While English is the language used by the operators handling this call, the customers may converse in the language of their choice. If at any time during the conversation the radiotelephone circuit is subject to static, noise, or fading, it is expected that the customer will flash the operator. The weekday rate for a three-minute message between New York and Djakarta is twelve dollars.

In settling accounts on this call the Bell System deals directly with the Indonesian Post, Telegraph and Telephone organization. Divisions of revenue are independent of the point of origin of the call. A moderate deduction is made by the Bell System because the land line service between New York and Oakland is longer than that between Bandung and Djakarta, and the remainder of the toll charge is divided between the two telephone systems.

Calls between New York and Djakarta are as important to the daily business of the world's neighborhoods as those we place through the local switchboard are to our own communities. The exporters use this service to speed the movement of the tobacco products, cotton goods, machinery, buses and trucks that we sell to the people of Indonesia. Importers utilize the overseas telephone service to regulate the flow of oil, rubber and hard fibers that we buy from the Indonesians. Government delegates to meetings at the United Nations are able to communicate with officials at Djakarta when matters of importance require decisions from the capital of Indonesia. The radiotelephone service is used for on-the-spot news broadcasts to keep the peoples of the world informed of international affairs. Communications over vast distances have become so commonplace that this service may be looked upon as an intercontinental speech path linking our neighborhood with all parts of the world.

The development of radiotelegraphy and radiotelephony has led to many other important developments in the field of communications. Ships and aircraft are linked to shore points and to one another through both these services. The importance of these services is well illustrated by an Associated Press report carried by the papers on the date this was being written:

"A weak distress signal sputtered for more than two hours today from the sea lane between Wake Island and Hawaii, raising hopes for the persons on board the transocean airliner.

The Navy shifted its massive air and surface search closer to the Hawaiian end of the Wake-Honolulu run. It estimated that the sender was 300 to 800 miles west of Honolulu.

The signal was so weak that ships and planes were unable to get an accurate bearing.

But the distress call was heard continuously for more than two hours starting at 3 p.m., the Navy said. The signal was on an international wave band reserved for distress calls."

The reserving of the international distress frequency at 500 kilocycles is illustrative of the work of the International Telecommunication Union (ITU), a Specialized Agency of the United Nations. As has already been noted in Chapter Three, twice each hour radio operators on ships and planes the world over turn for a period of three minutes to this frequency, reserved for their fellow men who may be in distress.

The recording of frequency assignments is a function of the International Frequency Registration Board (IFRB), an integral part of ITU. Signals sent from place to place by radio are carried on a radio wave. The number of waves that pass a fixed point in a second determines the frequency of a wave. No two messages transmitted from stations in the same general locality can use the same frequency without jamming each other. As these radio highways have become more crowded, nations have joined together through the ITU so that each nation can use a particular group of radio frequencies without fear of its messages being jammed by the radio services of its neighbors. The development of radar and television and their utilization of high-frequency waves have posed new problems for the IFRB.

As international telecommunication becomes of increasing importance to the industry, government, trade, finance, and social affairs of neighborhoods throughout the world, the finding of a common basis for the orderly and efficient transmission of signals between them will require both technical ingenuity and mutual cooperation and good will. In the ITU the nations of the world will find a workshop devoted to helping them solve their common telecommunication problems.

INTERNATIONAL TELECOMMUNICATION UNION: ITU

International Headquarters: Palais Wilson, Geneva, Switzerland

ORIGIN

In 1838 electrical telegraphy came into use in Europe. In the years that followed, various European nations concluded agreements that standardized operations and the collection of telegraph rates. These earlier agreements were followed by regional covenants involving nations in both Eastern and Western Europe. In 1865 twenty countries ratified a treaty signed at Paris that created the International Telegraph Union. This treaty was amended in 1885 to include the first provisions for international telegraph service.

By 1906 radiotelegraphy had become so generally used that twenty-seven countries realized international agreements were necessary in this field. As a result, these nations banded together to form the International Radiotelegraph Union under a convention signed in Berlin.

The International Telecommunication Union formally came in-

Technical operator maintains radiotelephone circuit at Oakland office.

to being on January 1, 1934. The ITU resulted from the merger of the International Telegraph Union and the International Radio-telegraph Union, following a conference held in Madrid in 1932.

The International Telecommunication Convention was completely redrafted in 1947 by the Plenipotentiary and International Radio Conferences held at Atlantic City, New Jersey. By an agreement approved by the General Assembly of the United Nations in 1947 and annexed to the Atlantic City Convention, the ITU in its new form became a Specialized Agency related to the United Nations. Modifications to the Convention were made at conferences in Buenos Aires in 1952 and Geneva in 1959.

PURPOSES
The purposes of the International Telecommunication Union are established in the Atlantic City Convention as follows:

a.   to maintain and extend international cooperation for the improvement and rational use of telecommunication of all kinds;

b.   to promote the development of technical facilities and their most efficient operation with a view to improving the efficiency of telecommunication services, increasing their usefulness and making them, so far as possible, generally available to the public;

c.   to harmonize the actions of nations in the attainment of those common ends.

FUNCTIONS
To accomplish these purposes, the Geneva Convention, 1959, charges ITU with these particular functions:

a.   effect allocation of the radio frequency spectrum and registration of radio frequency assignments in order to avoid harmful interference between radio stations of different countries;

b.   coordinate efforts to eliminate harmful interference between radio stations of different countries and to improve the the use made of the radio frequency spectrum;

c.   foster collaboration among its Members and Associate Members with a view to the establishment of rates at levels as low as possible consistent with an efficient service and taking into account the necessity for maintaining independent financial administration of telecommunication on a sound basis;

d. foster the creation, development and improvement of tele-communication equipment and networks in new or developing countries by every means at its disposal, especially its participation in the appropriate programs of the United Nations;

e. promote the adoption of measures for assuring the safety of life through the cooperation of telecommunication services;

f. undertake studies, formulate recommendations and opinions and collect and publish information concerning telecommunication matters for the benefit of all Members and Associate Members.

MEMBERSHIP

As of February 1, 1961, ITU had 105 members and five associate members. A complete list of members appears in the Appendix.

Non-members of the United Nations may become members of ITU if their applications are approved by two-thirds of the members of the Union. Each member has one vote at all ITU conferences and meetings of ITU organizations in which it participates. Any trust territory or group of territories not entirely responsible for the conduct of its own international affairs may be admitted as an associate member of ITU, without vote.

STRUCTURE AND ORGANIZATION

The structure of the ITU consists of a Plenipotentiary Conference, Administrative Conferences, the Administrative Council, and the permanent organs of the Union: the General Secretariat, the International Frequency Registration Board, the International Telegraph and Telephone Consultative Committee, and the International Radio Consultative Committee.

Plenipotentiary Conference

It determines the general policies for fulfilling the purposes of the Union; considers the reports of the Administrative Council; establishes the basis of the ITU budget for a five-year period; elects members of the Union which are to serve on the Administrative Council; elects the Secretary-General and the Deputy Secretary-General; revises the Convention when necessary; concludes or revises, if necessary, agreements between the Union and other international organizations; deals with such other telecommunication questions as may be necessary. On decisions other than those relating to the admission of new members, all action is by majority vote.

Administrative Conferences

All members and associate members may be represented at Administrative Conferences. The Administrative Telegraph and Telephone Conference and the Administrative Radio Conference revise the Administrative Regulations in these fields. Although Administrative Conferences generally meet at the same time and place as the Plenipotentiary Conference, special sessions may be convened if twenty nations so indicate their desire, or upon proposal of the Administrative Council.

Administrative Council

The Administrative Council is composed of twenty-five members elected by the Plenipotentiary Conference. The Council supervises ITU administrative affairs between meetings of the Plenipotentiary Conference, reviews and approves the annual budget, and coordinates the work of the Union with other international organizations. The Council normally meets once a year, but can be convened in special session at the request of the majority of its members.

General Secretariat

Under the direction of the Secretary-General of ITU, the General Secretariat carries out the administrative work of the Union. It carries out the work preparatory to and following meetings within the Union; it publishes recommendations and reports of the permanent organs of the Union; it issues other information of importance to members, such as international or regional telecommunication agreements. The General Secretariat also prepares the annual budget for submission to the Administrative Council.

International Frequency Registration Board

The IFRB consists of eleven members, elected on a regional basis by the Administrative Radio Conference. Members serve, not as members of their countries, or of a region, but "as custodians of an international public trust." The IFRB records all frequency assignments and furnishes advice to members of ITU with a view to the operation of the maximum number of radio channels.

Consultative Committees

Two international Consultative Committees, one for radio and one for telegraph and telephone, have been created for the purpose of studying technical and operating questions in these fields and issuing recommendations to the respective Administrative Conferences.

ACTIVITIES

Scientific and technological advances in the field of telecommunications, plus the ever-increasing use of these facilities

Indonesian overseas operators receive New York calls at Bandung radio terminal station.

throughout the world, have posed exacting and difficult problems for the ITU.

One continuing activity has been the preparation of a new worldwide radio frequency allocation table. This undertaking began with a series of conferences between countries using maritime, aeronautical, and broadcasting facilities in the several regions of the world. At each conference plans were drawn up whereby each station or group of stations would be assigned one or more frequencies on which to carry out its transmission.

The Cairo Conference of 1938 had provided for such a table, ranging from 10 kilocycles per second (kc/s) to 200,000 kc/s. The impact of scientific advance in this field can be best appreciated by the decision of the Atlantic City Radio Conference of 1947 that the new table extend from 10 kc/s to 10,500,000 kc/s! Add to this the understandable desire of nations and services to further their own effectiveness by utilizing the most effective channels, and one begins to realize the difficulties confronting ITU.

At the Radio Conference of Geneva, in 1959, the radio frequency spectrum was re-apportioned up to 40,000 megacycles per second (Mc/s) according to the needs envisaged for the various services: Fixed, Broadcasting, Aeronautical Mobile, Land Mobile, Maritime Mobile, Radionavigation, Radio-location, Space, Earth-Space, Radio Astronomy, Meteorological Aids, Amateur, Standard-Frequency and Time Signal Services. It was considered that beyond 40,000 Mc/s it is not feasible to apportion the radio frequency spectrum.

ITU provides many services without which international telecommunication would be impossible. It provides members with an international listing of telegraph offices and of radio frequencies. These become working documents in the offices of governmental and private companies, as well as in all kinds of stations: ship, aircraft, and land. Every two weeks ITU supplies current information on new or closed circuits, new rates and charges, and services temporarily suspended or reopened.

Technical studies and recommendations on such questions as television, protection of telephone lines, signaling and switching, letter and graphic symbols connected with telephony, tests and measurements of commercial telephone systems, and the like, are regular contributions made by ITU to its membership.

At Djakarta switchboard the
final connection is made,
only minutes after the call is
placed in New York.

The work of the Consultative Committees and of the International Frequency Registration Board is a form of technical assistance to Members of the ITU. The Union also participates in the Expanded Programme of Technical Assistance and the Special Fund of the United Nations, working out programs in the field of telecommunications, supervising the activities of experts, organizing fellowship groups.

Economic development creates the need for communications, for telegraph and telephone services not only for domestic use, but also to improve connections with the outer world. The ITU is asked to help in the planning of trunk lines connecting isolated areas; in improving existing services and developing new services; in maintaining and modernizing equipment. Lack of skilled labor and operating specialists is one of the principal handicaps to developing telecommunication services, and the ITU concentrates on training in its technical assistance work. For example, the ITU has provided a director and lecturers for the Ethiopian Telecommunications Institute, where some 500 telecommunication employees have already been trained.

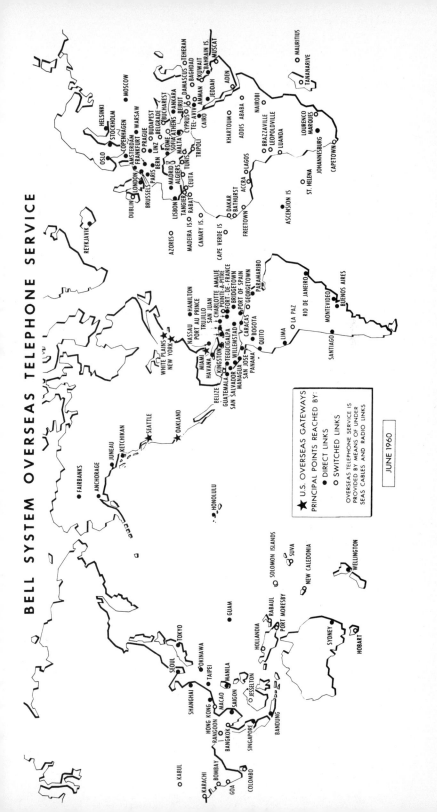

BELL SYSTEM OVERSEAS TELEPHONE SERVICE

U.S. OVERSEAS GATEWAYS

PRINCIPAL POINTS REACHED BY:

★ DIRECT LINKS

○ SWITCHED LINKS

OVERSEAS TELEPHONE SERVICE IS PROVIDED BY MEANS OF UNDER SEAS CABLES AND RADIO LINKS

JUNE 1960

With the expansion of ITU's technical aid program twenty-some countries have been assisted each year either with fellowships for specialized study abroad or by experts helping on the spot. This help has resulted, among other things, in a new radio link between Paraguay and New York City, the first local automatic telephone exchange in Kabul, Afghanistan, thousands of miles of new telephone lines in Iran and new telegraph circuits in Pakistan. Burma, Guinea, Korea, Malay and Tunisia are a few of the other countries where ITU has helped the growth of telecommunications in recent years.

For nearly a century now the International Telecommunication Union has, link by link, sponsored a network of telecommunications among the neighborhoods of the world. The ITU has survived two world wars and has emerged from each a stronger instrument for world peace. No nation has ever withdrawn from this workshop for the world. No workshop has contributed more to the cause of internationalism.

CHAPTER EIGHT

UNESCO
United Nations Educational, Scientific and Cultural Organization

250,000,000 Absent Today!

"Nearly half the world's children of school age do not attend a school of any kind."
(Preamble to resolution adopted by Eleventh General Conference of UNESCO.)

Nearly half the world's children — 250 million — receive no education! This startling estimate of the world's situation in 1960 was revealed in surveys made by the United Nations Educational, Scientific and Cultural Organization (UNESCO) for its member nations.

Unanimously, UNESCO's General Conference, representing ninety-eight nations, decided that top priority must be given to those denied an elementary school education. Despite immense efforts made in the last ten years, the developing nations have been able to raise the school enrollment rate by only a small percentage, and as the birth rate continues to rise, the problem becomes greater. UNESCO's General Conference urged that all international assistance programs give the same consideration to educational programs as to economic development. Unless today's children are educated, half of tomorrow's adults will still be illiterates.

The problem is a staggering one. Cost estimates are huge, teacher-training facilities inadequate or non-existent. Only the greatest determination and bold imagination would inspire hope for universal elementary school education within the next twenty years.

Determination and imagination are not lacking among the leaders who aspire to a better life for their fellow men. This is strikingly evidenced in the continent-spanning Latin American program to give an adequate education to every school-age child by 1968. Four years under way, this program, officially called "Extension and Improvement of Primary Education in Latin America," has achieved some results which excite hope that the job *could* be done for all the world's children.

UNESCO has played a significant role in the Latin American project from its beginning at a conference in Lima, Peru in 1956. Convened jointly by UNESCO and the Organization of American States (OAS), the conference assessed the problem and laid down the goals.

The population of Latin America was nearing the 200 million mark and estimated to pass 300 million by 1975. In 1956 out of a total of 40 million children then of school-going age, only 19 million were attending school and less then 20 per cent of these finished eighth grade. Nearly 50 per cent of the classroom teachers were untrained, and 500,000 more were needed. There were great shortages of buildings, books, and equipment.

Among the goals which the conference set were:
  • extension of primary education so that by 1968 every school-age child could have an adequate education;
  • systematic planning of education in Latin American countries;
  • improvement of teacher-training systems;
  • improvement of the economic and social level of the teaching profession;
  • training of a nucleus of educational leaders capable of guiding reforms for each Latin American country.

Within that same year, UNESCO's General Conference decided that the organization should give special assistance to this plan, and it became a major UNESCO project.

Neither UNESCO nor any other international organization could provide the money required for a program of this kind. Nor was it expected to do so. Each Latin American nation bears the cost of extending education in its own national budget—often at the sacrifice of other pressing needs.

UNESCO has concentrated on key areas of the plan; specifical-

None of the six children in this Honduran family attend schools, as their parents do not think education is important. One phase of the Latin-American program to extend elementary education is to interest rural families in schooling.

ly, helping to prepare educational programs and training leaders and specialists capable of training others and carrying out national educational plans.

At the Universities of Santiago, Chile, and Sao Paulo, Brazil, UNESCO-appointed experts have organized and are teaching courses for educational leaders, administrators, supervisors and other specialists who attend on fellowships. Another of the major training centers is the Inter-American Rural Educational Center at Rubio, Venezuela, founded by the Organization of American States and supported by the Venezuelan government. This center prepares directors for rural school systems and staff members of rural teacher-training schools. UNESCO has supplied instructors for the faculty and granted fellowships to enable more educators to study at Rubio. In the first two years of the program, over 270 educators received advanced training in these three institutions.

Five normal schools for the improvement of teacher training have been established in Honduras, Ecuador, Colombia and Nicaragua, which has two. Each training school has a resident UNESCO expert who is aided by a group of experts who visit the schools in rotation. UNESCO also makes grants to these schools for the purchase of books and teaching equipment. These "Associated Normal Schools," as they are called, are pilot schools not only for teacher training, but for the improvement of teaching methods and curriculum guides. They are not expected to solve the teacher shortage, but to help all Latin American countries develop better teacher-training methods.

UNESCO has worked out a system of reporting on all the phases of the program in order that other nations of Latin America may

Children learn to count with stones in a village in Ecuador. Elementary school teaching in Latin-American nations is hampered by lack of equipment.

benefit from the experiments or new methods used in any one. A continuing series of specialized meetings and seminars, sponsored by UNESCO, is another tool to advance educational training.

Fellowships are of special importance to the success of the project. UNESCO has been able to provide most significant help. In the first three years, 580 fellowships were granted.

At the end of three years, each Latin American nation reported on its progress to a meeting of the Advisory Committee for the project. The reports showed that four million more children — an increase of about 18 per cent — were now in school. Ninety thousand new teacher's jobs had been created. Considerable increase had been made in national budget appropriations for education. All tangible evidence of progress.

Some of the noteworthy achievements were singled out in the Advisory Committee's report.

Colombia had doubled its educational budget.

Brazil and Mexico, whose populations represent nearly half the total population of Latin America, had trebled the number of children enrolled in schools.

Argentina had adopted a Teacher's Charter giving them security of tenure.

Venezuela had enrolled 450,000 new pupils in two years, built new classrooms for 250,000 children and increased the education budget by 150 per cent.

Bolivia had raised its education budget to 32 per cent of the national total, increased school enrollments by 22 per cent and the number of teachers by 27 per cent.

Mexico had launched a nationwide eleven-year education plan, developed inexpensive, prefabricated school buildings and established social benefits for teachers.

While expressing satisfaction with these initial results, the Latin American nations also took a hard look at the problems still ahead. The major problem, they felt, lay in improving the quality of teaching. In this respect they looked for a solution to the groups of educational leaders and specialists who are being trained in the UNESCO-aided institutions. A related problem is the difficulty of recruiting teachers. This, they felt, called for national action to improve the economic and social status of teachers and intensified efforts were urged. Systematic educational planning to take care of population increases was a third problem area calling for increased attention.

The Latin American nations have set a high goal in this project and are demonstrating their firm determination to make that goal a reality. UNESCO has devised a plan whereby the people of the world may share in their efforts — and in similar efforts in other regions. Through the UNESCO Gift Coupon Plan, groups or individuals can aid designated projects directly. The contribution of a UNESCO gift coupon can provide such items as classroom equipment, textbooks, even pencils and paper for children who have never had them.

This Latin American program has a significance which goes beyond the practical. Here twenty nations have joined together to make a reality of one of the fundamental rights of man as set forth in the Universal Declaration of Human Rights:

"Everyone has the right to education."

UNITED NATIONS EDUCATIONAL, SCIENTIFIC AND CULTURAL ORGANIZATION: UNESCO
International Headquarters: 7 Place Fontenoy, Paris, France

ORIGIN

The Conference for the Establishment of an Educational, Scientific and Cultural Organization was convened by the government of the United Kingdom in association with the government of France. Such a conference had been suggested at several meetings of the Conference of Allied Ministers of Education held in London during the war, and was further recommended at the Conference at San Francisco that drafted the United Nations Charter. The Conference met at London from November 1 to 16, 1945.

Discussions were based upon a draft constitution prepared by the Allied Ministers of Education. The Conference, at which the governments of forty-three members of the United Nations were represented, drafted and adopted the United Nations Educational, Scientific and Cultural Organization (UNESCO) Constitution. The Constitution became effective on November 4, 1946. An agreement between the United Nations and UNESCO recognized the latter as a specialized agency on December 14, 1946.

PURPOSE

UNESCO's purpose is stated in Article I of its Constitution. The purpose of the Organization is to contribute to peace and security by promoting collaboration among the nations through education, science and culture in order to further universal respect for justice, for the rule of law and for the human rights and fundamental freedoms which are affirmed for the peoples of the world, without distinction of race, sex, language or religion, by the Charter of the United Nations.

FUNCTIONS

To realize its purpose, UNESCO is charged with the following responsibilities:

a.   Collaborate in the work of advancing the mutual knowl-

Pencils and paper were provided these Bolivian youngsters through UNESCO Gift Coupon Program. In the last three years Bolivia has raised its education budget to one-third of the national total. These children are now housed in a new school building.

edge and understanding of peoples, through all means of mass communication and to that end recommend such international agreements as may be necessary to promote the free flow of ideas by word and image;

b. Give fresh impulse to popular education and to the spread of culture;

• by collaborating with Members, at their request, in the development of educational activities;

• by instituting collaboration among the nations to advance the ideal of equality of educational opportunity without regard to race, sex or any distinctions, economic or social;

• by suggesting educational methods best suited to prepare the children of the world for the responsibilities of freedom;

c. Maintain, increase, and diffuse knowledge;

• by assuring the conservation and protection of the world's inheritance of books, works of art and monuments of history and science, and recommending to the nations concerned the necessary international convention; by encouraging cooperation among the nations in all branches of intellectual activity, including the international exchange of persons active in the fields of education, science and culture and the exchange of publications, objects of artistic and scientific interest and other materials of information;

• by initiating methods of international cooperation calculated to give the people of all countries access to the printed and published materials produced by any of them.

Article I concludes with an important reservation concerning the implementation of UNESCO's purpose.

With a view to preserving the independence, integrity and fruitful diversity of the cultures and educational systems of the States members of this Organization, the Organization is prohibited from intervening in matters which are essentially within their domestic jurisdiction.

MEMBERSHIP

As of April 1, 1961, ninety-nine nations were members of UNESCO. Associate members numbered six. A complete list of members appears in the Appendix.

Membership in the United Nations carries with it the right to membership in UNESCO. States not members of the U.N. may be admitted to UNESCO upon recommendation of the Executive Board and by a two-thirds majority vote of the General Conference. Members who are suspended by the United Nations may, upon U.N. request, be suspended from UNESCO. Members expelled by the U.N. automatically cease to be members of UNESCO.

Article VII of UNESCO's Constitution obligates members to make arrangements for the purpose of bringing its own groups interested in educational, scientific, and cultural matters into association with UNESCO. A joint resolution of the Congress, approved July 30, 1946, provided for United States membership in UNESCO and authorized the establishment of a U.S. National Commission for UNESCO.

Recommendations and international conventions adopted by the General Conference of UNESCO are inoperative in any member state unless approved by appropriate authority. However, such recommendations and international conventions are to be sub-

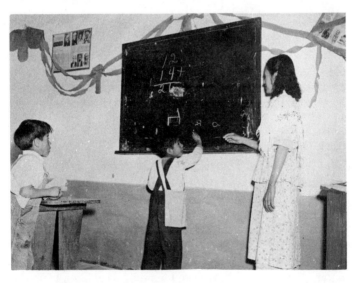

More and better-trained teachers are major goals of Latin-American project to bring education to all youngsters. This Mexican teacher now receives social benefits in a program aimed at bettering teachers' status.

mitted to such appropriate authority within one year of the closing of the Conference that adopted same.

STRUCTURE AND ORGANIZATION

UNESCO is operated by a General Conference, an Executive Board, the Director-General, and the Secretariat.

The General Conference

The General Conference is the governing body of UNESCO and is composed of one representative from each member state. Each nation has one vote in the General Conference, which meets at least once every two years. The General Conference reviews the work of UNESCO and approves the budget for the next financial period.

The Executive Board

The Executive Board consists of twenty-four members elected by the General Conference for a term of three years. Six new members are elected each year.

The Secretariat

The program decided upon by the General Conference is carried out by an international Secretariat with its headquarters in Paris. Head of the Secretariat is the Director-General, nominated by the Executive Board and appointed by the General Conference.

ACTIVITIES

The main departments of the UNESCO Secretariat indicate the areas with which this workshop deals: Education, Natural Sciences, Social Sciences, Cultural Activities, Exchange of Persons, Mass Communication.

The priority program for education approved at the 1960 UNESCO General Conference includes aid to Asia, Africa and the Arab states, as well as continuing Latin American aid. An emergency two-year program for tropical Africa, supported by voluntary governmental pledges, including $1 million from the United States, will concentrate on school construction, production of teaching aids, provision of teachers from abroad for secondary, technical, and higher education institutions and fellowships. In

Children attending the Miraflores Pilot School at La Paz, Bolivia, benefit from new teaching methods introduced by a UNESCO team of experts.

the Arab states, UNESCO will help to create a network of teacher-training colleges, and in Asia UNESCO will concentrate on helping school planning and training school administrators.

Technical schools and management training centers in fifteen countries are being established by UNESCO, under U.N. Special Fund allocations.

An International Convention on Discrimination in Education was adopted by the 1960 General Conference. States becoming parties to the agreement pledge themselves to take immediate steps to eliminate and prevent all discrimination in education.

One of UNESCO's functions is to serve as a clearing house for knowledge so that it may be shared among nations. A clearing house will function best if publications and other materials of information can circulate freely between nations. To accomplish this purpose, the General Conference in 1950 unanimously adopted an agreement aimed at reducing the tariff and trade barriers to the free international exchange of knowledge. On May 21, 1952, this treaty became effective upon its ratification by the tenth nation—Sweden. By April 1, 1961, thirty-three nations had approved the agreement. As of that date the United States Senate had ratified this treaty, but implementing legislation had not been completed.

The agreement ends import duties on books, magazines, paintings, sculpture, travel literature, maps, musical scores, museum materials, and articles for the blind. It also provides for the duty-free import of educational films and other audio-visual materials consigned to recognized cultural institutions. This was the first treaty to become effective under UNESCO sponsorship.

A second international treaty sponsored by UNESCO protects the rights of those who produce the world's books as well as its art and entertainment. By April 1, 1961, the Universal Copyright Convention had been ratified by thirty-five nations, including the United States.

This rural school at Sitio del Nino, El Salvador, has adopted a curriculum proposed by a UNESCO expert.

UNESCO has taken the initiative in forming international organizations responsible for cultural exchanges among nations. Typical of these are the International Theatre Institute, the International Council of Museums and the International Music Council. Meetings of experts are convened by UNESCO for the purpose of sharing educational, scientific and cultural knowledge. Papers prepared by these specialists are distributed from Paris and by national commissions interested in UNESCO's work.

An important cultural project at present is UNESCO's leadership of the campaign to preserve ancient monuments in Egypt which would be destroyed by construction of the Aswan Dam. UNESCO's cultural activities also include continued support of a Southeast Asian program for mass distribution of reading materials' aid to the establishment of public libraries, and publication of catalogues of color reproductions of art treasures and albums of little-known art.

For a number of years UNESCO has spearheaded scientific research on arid-zone problems. This project is nearing completion and the organization will emphasize oceanographic research. An International Oceanographic Commission will foster scientific research through the resources of member nations. UNESCO will also act as a sponsor of international exploration of the Indian Ocean to begin in 1963.

Field Science Cooperation Offices are a means to aid the underdeveloped areas. These UNESCO offices serve as clearing houses for scientific exchange. Social science programs include study of the problems arising from economic and social development, promotion of human rights, particularly in the field of race relations, and study of the causes and remedies of juvenile delinquency.

CHAPTER NINE

Bank

**The International Bank for
Reconstruction and Development**

The Road From Addis Ababa

On the morning of June 25, 1946, the most unusual bank in the world opened its offices for business.

One of the unique features of this bank was that its stock was owned by *governments*. These governments realized that the poverty of a few countries could be a serious threat to the peace of all. They also realized that the best way to eliminate poverty is by helping people help themselves through productive effort. But creating tools, plants, and jobs that make productive effort possible takes money. So the governments agreed that providing the capital necessary for such projects — either through new enterprise or through replacing and rebuilding enterprises devastated during World War II — should be the aim of this new bank.

Thus the International Bank for Reconstruction and Development (Bank) became unique in another respect: its dedication to raising the standard of living of the peoples who lived in its member nations. This was to be done by making loans to member countries that had plans for productive enterprise but could not get money either at home or from private investors in other lands.

This latter point is most important. The Bank was not designed to compete with private investors. The Bank was to make loans only when member states could prove that private financing was not to be had. On the other hand, the Bank was designed to cooperate with private investors by making it possible for them to buy bonds guaranteed by the Bank. Private investors could participate in the development of productive enterprises by relying upon the Bank's good judgment in making loans.

This is an account of how one Bank member — Ethiopia — utilized the Bank's resources to build a better life for her people.

For generations there had been very little change in the economic life of Ethiopia. The economy was almost entirely agricultural, with over ninety-five per cent of the people engaged in primitive farming or livestock raising. Surrounded by desert on three sides and by equatorial highlands on the fourth, the Ethiopian people knew little of the outside world, and foreign capital had been but rarely attracted to the country.

Ethiopia recognized that it would have to turn to outside sources to overcome economic stagnation and to start the country on the road of progress. Even before the end of World War II, it had invited a group of foreign consultants to prepare a development plan for the country. Having a plan, however, was only a first step. How was it to be carried out? While the country had achieved a satisfactory trade balance, mainly because of the export of coffee, it was not in a position to finance all the imports needed for development. But Ethiopia had joined the new International Bank for Reconstruction and Development, and here was a source of help to which the country could turn.

In 1948, Ethiopia therefore began discussions with the World Bank about its development plans and needs. Members do not merely approach this institution and ask for a loan. Like any other bank, the World Bank expects its borrowers to have a sound plan worked out for the use of its money. In Ethiopia's case, the preliminary discussions with the Bank were followed in the spring of 1950 by the visit of a mission of seven Bank officials, headed by Mr. Orvis A. Schmidt, Assistant to the Loan Director. Among the specialists included on the mission staff were economists and a transportation specialist. The purpose of the mission was to consult with the government about its development program and to assist in selecting projects within that program which might be suitable for Bank financing.

Now, in addition to lending money for economic development purposes, the Bank performs another valuable service for a member: it provides good advice. This supplementary function arises naturally from the careful study which the Bank must make of development projects. It must assess the technical and financial justification for the project,the economic prospects of the country where the loan is to be made and the country's ability to repay the loan.

The World Bank mission to Ethiopia, after study, decided that improved transportation was one of the country's most urgent needs, that good road transport was vital to both the internal and foreign trade of the country. Ethiopia had only one short railway line from Addis Ababa, the capital, to Djibouti on the Red Sea, and most of the country's export goods were moved by truck all or part of the way to the seaports. At that time, Ethiopia (which is more than five times the size of the New England States) had only about 3800 miles of all-weather roads. The balance of the nation's roads included some that were passable by truck in the dry season, but most of them were no more than pack trails for donkeys, mules or camels. The road system had been built during the Italian occupation of the country. Lack of funds and a shortage of experienced personnel to supervise highway maintenance had led to such serious deterioration that freight could move from

Ancient and modern transportation share use of one of Ethiopia's new highways, built with the aid of a five-million-dollar loan from the World Bank.

Assab, the major Red sea port, to Addis Ababa only in the dry season, and the travel time was several weeks, even though the distance was only about 500 miles.

The Bank mission found also that transportation costs were high and deliveries slow. Better roads not only would help to remedy this economic drag, but would also bring improvements in health, education and governmental administration by making government services available to outlying communities.

The findings of the mission thus formed the basis for negotiation of the terms of a loan for $5 million to be used to rehabilitate and maintain Ethiopia's road system. During the following months the details of the loan plan were worked out as follows.

In order that repair and maintenance be conducted efficiently, the terms of the loan provided that the Ethiopian Government should establish an autonomous highway authority. Management of the authority was to be composed of experienced administrators, an important part of whose duties was to train Ethiopian personnel. It was further agreed that the highway management would be selected in consultation with the World Bank. While the Bank would provide $5 million to finance the foreign exchange cost of equipment, supplies and services, the Ethiopian Government was to be responsible for all local currency costs, estimated at two to three times the amount of the Bank loan. Specifically, the Government was to provide the highway authority immediately with Eth. $5 million (one Ethiopian dollar equals 40 cents in U. S. currency); additionally for the first three years it was to provide a minimum amount of Eth. $6 million annually, and thereafter, throughout the life of the loan, a minimum of Eth. $5 million annually.

The road program involved the complete rebuilding of three key roads, totaling 900 miles, and leading from Addis Ababa to Assab, to Lekempti and to Jimma. The latter two places are important coffee-growing centers. It also provided for maintenance work on another 1600 miles of roads.

It was decided that the loan would run for a term of twenty years and carry interest at the rate of three per cent, plus commission at the rate of one per cent. (This commission, in accordance with the Bank's Articles of Agreement, is allocated to its special reserve fund.) Amortization payments, calculated to retire the loan by maturity, were to begin on March 1, 1956 and were to be made semiannually through March 1, 1971.

Following these negotiations, which for the first time in the Bank's history were conducted in the borrowing country, the terms were reviewed at Bank headquarters. After approval by the Staff Loan Committee, made up of senior officers, the President of the Bank recommended the loan to the Executive Directors, who approved it. On September 13, 1950, the loan was signed in Paris where the Bank was holding its Fifth Annual Meeting.

This particular loan had the distinction of being the first World Bank loan to an African country. (As of April 1, 1961, ten and one-half years later, the Bank had loaned $780.7 million to fourteen African countries or territories.)

As with all projects for which the World Bank lends money, there was regular check on progress. The difficulties and delays that are inherent in any new program of this kind were encountered and some changes had to be made in the original plan, but it was carried out successfully and all the main objectives were achieved. The advice of Bank experts was found valuable in many aspects of the project. For example, it was the practice in the country to use twenty-ton trucks. As fast as the roads were restored, these trucks were causing fresh damage. At the Bank's suggestion, the Government took steps to have these trucks gradually removed from service and put a nine-ton axle load on all imported trucks.

Funds received from the loan were spent to buy $3 million worth of roadmaking equipment and $1 million worth of fuel and materials. The balance was used to pay for the services of the foreign experts engaged to carry out the work. During the period of the road-building project, Ethiopia itself spent far more than the Bank regarded as a minimum, to a total of $20.4 million. Twentynine hundred miles of roads were rebuilt and improved. The originally-planned 900 miles of main roads, plus 750 miles of other roads were rebuilt; the balance was improved for all-weather use.

This investment in highways brought swift and wide-ranging results. The last disbursement from the loan was made in May, 1954. By 1956, the total number of motor vehicles in operation had risen by 50 per cent. That one-time two-week run from Assab to Addis Ababa had been cut to two days. Export figures speak for the effect of this improvement in transportation. During the period 1949-57, coffee exports increased more than twice in volume and five times in value, while those of oilseeds rose by 90 per cent in volume and doubled in value. As traffic moved more freely, there was a sharp drop in road and rail freight rates, thus reducing the cost of imports, such as gasoline and salt, as well as increasing the profit on exports. Truck rates on a ton of freight from Addis Ababa to Jimma (200 miles) decreased from $28 to $12. To meet truck competition, the railroad also reduced its charges, on some items as much as 50 per cent. In consequence, rail freight traffic also rose.

In a related development, bus transporattion has been established in the country. A fleet of several hundred buses now travels the network of new highways, which is regarded as quite an improvement by Ethiopians who, as late as 1951, had to travel perched on bales or sacks atop trucks.

Substantial increases in domestic and foreign investment, personal income and public revenues have been by-products of the changes wrought by the establishment of this transportation network. Higher production of coffee and oilseeds, for example, has

Construction equipment was imported to rebuild three key roads leading from Addis Ababa to Assab, the main port for Ethiopia, and to two coffee-growing centers, Jimma and Lekempti.

brought more business to all those who deal with processing.

Gauging these results, both the Ethiopian Government and the Bank agreed that the economic potential of the country was only beginning to be realized, that work had just begun. Expansion of the highway system to important agricultural areas in western and southern Ethiopia would open new areas to cultivation, and would, as did the first project, facilitate government services and administration in isolated communities.

Accordingly, a second loan to Ethiopia for highway improvement was made by the Bank on June 28, 1957. This loan, also for a twenty-year term, was for the sum of $15 million to cover the foreign exchange cost of extension and further improvement of the highway system. At the time the loan was made, the total cost of the project was estimated at the equivalent of $37.8 million.

The First National City Bank of New York participated in this second loan, without the World Bank's guarantee, to the extent of $1,491,000, representing the first five payments falling due from September 1, 1961 to September 1, 1963. This participation speaks for the confidence of the financial community in the judgment of the Bank, as well as in the economic potential of Ethiopia.

Roads under construction in this expanded program will open up areas with a large potential for commercial agriculture. Three of them branch out of Jimma, the heart of the coffee district, where coffee is said to have originated and still grows wild. At present only a small fraction of this crop is picked because of the difficulty of transporting it to market. Another road will open a densely populated area in the region of Lake Tana, the source of the Blue Nile. In all, it is estimated that the new roads will make it possible to increase the production of cash crops by the equivalent of $25 million annually.

The Bank's original loan to Ethiopia graphically demonstrates the effectiveness of wisely planned development aid. Careful study of the country's basic needs and skilled advice throughout the duration of the project are characteristic of the Bank's approach and assure that the project is sound. In Ethiopia, this aid, coupled with an emphatic government commitment, sparked economic improvement of proportions far beyond the value of the original investment. By the establishment of a reliable communications and transport system, opportunity for economic and social progress has been opened to the Ethiopian people.

INTERNATIONAL BANK FOR
RECONSTRUCTION AND DEVELOPMENT: BANK

International Headquarters: 1818 H Street, N.W., Washington 25, D.C.

ORIGIN

The Articles of Agreement of the Bank were drawn by the United Nations Monetary and Financial Conference at Bretton Woods, N.H., in July, 1944. The Bank came into existence on December 27, 1945, when its Articles of Agreement were signed by twenty-eight governments. The inaugural meeting of its Board of Governors was held at Savannah, Ga., in March 1946; the Bank officially began operations in Washington, D.C., on June 25, 1946. The Bank has an office in New York City from which its marketing operations are directed and an office at 4, avenue d' Iéna, Paris 16e, France. On November 15, 1947, the Bank became a Specialized Agency cooperating with the United Nations.

PURPOSES

The purposes of the Bank are stated in Article I of the Articles of Agreement:

I.   To assist in the reconstruction and development of territories of members by facilitating the investment of capital for productive purposes, including the restoration of economies destroyed or disrupted by war, the reconversion of productive facilities to peacetime needs and the encouragement of the development of productive facilities and resources in less developed countries.

II.   To promote private foreign investment by means of guarantees or participations in loans and other investments made by private investors; and when private capital is not available on reasonable terms, to supplement private investment by providing on suitable conditions, finance for productive purposes out of its own capital, funds raised by it and its other resources.

III.   To promote the long-range balanced growth of international trade and the maintenance of equilibrium in balances of payments by encouraging international investment for the development of the productive resources of members, thereby as-

Ethiopia's first motel, shown here, borders one of the new first-class roads and speaks for the modernization of the nation's transportation.

sisting in raising productivity, the standard of living and conditions of labor in their territories.

IV.   To arrange the loans made or guaranteed by it in relation to international loans through other channels so that the more useful and urgent projects, large and small alike, will be dealt with first.

V.   To conduct its operations with due regard to the effect of international investment on business conditions in the territories of members and, in the immediate post-war years, to assist in bringing about a smooth transition from a wartime to a peacetime economy.

FUNCTIONS

The major functions of the Bank are included in various Articles of the Articles of Agreement:

• The resources and the facilities of the Bank shall be used exclusively for the benefit of members with equitable consideration to projects for development and projects for reconstruction alike. . . .

• When the member in whose territories the project is located is not itself the borrower, the member or the central bank or some comparable agency of the member which is acceptable to the Bank, fully guarantees the repayment of the principal and the payment of interest and other charges on the loan.

• The Bank is satisfied that in the prevailing market conditions the borrower would be unable otherwise to obtain the loan under conditions which in the opinion of the Bank are reasonable for the borrower.

• A competent committee, as provided for in Article V, Section 7, has submitted a written report recommending the project after a careful study of the merits of the proposal.

• In the opinion of the Bank the rate of interest and other charges are reasonable and such rate, charges and the schedule for repayment of principal are appropriate to the project. . . .

The Bank may make or facilitate loans which satisify the general conditions of Article III in any of the following ways:

• By making or participating in direct loans out of its own funds corresponding to its unimpaired paid-up capital and surplus and, subject to Section 6 of this Article, to its reserves.

• By making or participating in direct loans out of funds raised in the market of a member, or otherwise borrowed by the Bank.

• By guaranteeing in whole or in part loans made by private investors through the usual investment channels.

MEMBERS AND CAPITAL

The original members of the Bank were members of the International Monetary Fund which accepted membership in the Bank before January 1, 1946. Subsequent membership required a nation to be a member of the Fund, and at such terms as the Bank might prescribe. On February 1, 1961, the Bank had sixty-six members. A complete list of members is included in the Appendix.

The authorized capital stock of the Bank is $21,000,000,000 in terms of United States dollars of the weight and fineness in effect on July 1, 1944. This stock is divided into shares of $100,000 each, available only to members.

Trade figures, reserves, national income, and other considerations determine a nation's subscription. As of January, 1961, subscribed capital totaled $19,902,200,000.

The Bank's operating expenses are met from earnings. As a result, there is no need to assess each member for a proportion of the annual budget. By December 31, 1960, the Bank's net earnings aggregated $377.4 million, which is placed in a Supplemental Reserve Against Losses on Loans and Guarantees. A commission of one per cent charged on all loans is placed in a Special Reserve which amounted to $179.1 million at the end of December, 1960. Total reserves on that date thus amounted to $556.5 million.

Members may be suspended from the Bank by a majority vote of the Governors. Any nation that ceases to be a member of the International Monetary Fund automatically ceases to be a member of the Bank after three months, unless permitted to remain a member by three-fourths of the total voting power.

Members may withdraw from the Bank. After satisfying certain conditions established in the Articles of Agreement, members who withdraw receive back their original subscription plus a share of the Bank's earnings during their membership. Poland withdrew from the Bank in 1950; Cuba and the Dominican Republic in 1960.

STRUCTURE AND ORGANIZATION

The Bank has a Board of Governors, Executive Directors, a President and staff.

The Board of Governors

All powers of the Bank are vested in a Board of Governors consisting of a Governor appointed by each member country. Each Governor has an Alternate who may act in his absence. The Board elects its Chairman annually. Each member has 250 votes, plus one additional vote for each share of capital stock held by the nation he represents.

The Executive Directors

The Board of Governors has delegated most of its powers to the Executive Directors. Each Executive Director also has an Alternate. Five Executive Directors are appointed by the five largest stockholders. The other thirteen Executive Directors are elected by the Governors of the remaining members, so that each of the elected Directors usually represents a number of countries. Executive Directors are appointed or elected every two years. The voting power of each is proportionate to the capital subscription of the country or countries he represents. The Executive Directors are responsible for matters of policy and must approve all the loans made by the Bank.

The President

The President is *ex officio* Chairman of the Executive Directors without vote except in case of a tie. He is selected by the Executive Directors and is the chief executive officer of the Bank. He is responsible for the conduct of the business of the Bank and for the organization, appointment, and dismissal of its officers and staff.

ACTIVITIES

The Bank's loans are financed from two sources: the stock subscriptions of member governments and the sale of bonds and other borrowings in the private markets of the world. As one of the Bank's aims is to encourage private funds in international investment, the marketing of bonds is an important activity. The Bank has sold over $2,000,000,000 of bonds and notes outstanding. Although over $1,700,000,000 of this total represents United States dollar bonds, the Bank has also sold issues in Canadian dollars, Belgian francs, Swiss francs, Deutsche marks, Netherlands guilders and pounds sterling.

By the end of March, 1961, the Bank had lent over $5,500,000,000 in fifty-five countries and territories throughout the world for general reconstruction and development; for the generation and distribution of electric power; for transportation, including railroads, roads, shipping, ports and waterways, airlines and airports and pipelines; for telephone, telegraph and radio communications; for agriculture and forestry including farm mechanization, irrigation and flood control, land clearance and improvement, processing and storage, and livestock production; and for a variety of industries including iron and steel, pulp and paper, fertilizer and other chemicals and for mining. Countries of Asia and the Middle East have received $1,851,000,000 in loans; Europe, $1,425,-000,000; Latin America, $1,186,000,000; Africa, $780,000,000; and Australia, $318,000,000.

In addition to making loans, the Bank also provides its member governments with a wide variety of technical assistance not directly connected with lending. This ranges from a full-scale economic survey of the development potential of a country — twenty such surveys have been made — to advice on a single project. Bank staff members have served as advisers to member governments and the Bank has often helped to find suitable persons to staff economic planning organizations and development banks. The Bank has also been called on to contribute its good offices towards the settlement of international economic problems, such as the sharing of the waters of the Indus Basin between India and Pakistan and settlement of the compensation to be paid by the United Arab Republic for the nationalization of the Suez Canal.

The Bank aims to help the neighborhoods of the world help themselves to a higher production of goods and services — which in turn will lead to a higher standard of living and provide a firm basis for peace.

CHAPTER TEN

IFC

International Finance Corporation

Noel

When a businessman in the United States decides to start a new enterprise or expand a going business, he will probably need more money — capital — than he has on hand. If his credit and business reputation are good, getting that capital will be relatively simple, for in the United States as in other highly developed countries, there are number of sources of investment capital. Our business man might borrow the money from a bank at a reasonable and standard rate of interest. Or he might raise the money by selling stock in his business.

In the underdeveloped countries the situation is quite different. In the Latin American countries, for example, there are few local sources of long-term investment capital available to the private businessman. He may be able to borrow money on a short-term basis, but he will have to pay a very high interest rate. This situation has hampered, and in many instances blocked entirely, initiative by locally-owned private industry in the underdeveloped regions.

The World Bank, as seen in the preceding chapter, is able to provide investment capital to governments or to private enterprises if there is government guarantee of the loan. But it cannot aid private business directly. Out of the recognition that competitive private enterprise could play a dynamic role in promoting economic development, the Bank management therefore worked out plans for the International Finance Corporation (IFC), a unique public international institution. Formed and owned by governments, its purpose is to promote the growth of private investment and enterprise in the developing areas of the world. IFC is an investing, rather than a lending agency, and it judges projects on the basis of their merits as investments for private capital. It invests without government intervention or guarantee. Besides investing its own funds, IFC serves as a clearing house to put willing investors in touch with the businessmen who are looking for funds. Like the World Bank, the IFC does not compete with private capital, but supplements it.

How does our private businessman go about getting capital funds from the International Finance Corporation? He must, of course, be able to prove that his enterprise is sound and that the management is experienced. IFC exercises no management functions. He must also demonstrate that his project will contribute to the economy of the country, and he must have the funds to finance at least half the total cost of the project.

An IFC investment made in the NOEL Company in Medellin, Colombia, will illustrate the operation of the agency. NOEL was — and is — Colombia's largest producer of crackers, biscuits and macaroni products. Founded in 1916 as a limited partnership, it was reorganized in 1933 as a corporation. Business improved and a new factory was built in 1946. Gradually the city grew up around the factory and the company's operations, in turn, outgrew its facilities.

NOEL needed to expand and was itself in a position to finance a part of the cost of expansion. The firm bought a site for a new plant a few miles outside of Medellin. NOEL was able to begin construction at the same time that it sought financing for completion of the project. The company's initial approach to the International Finance Corporation was made in May 1958 at a meeting with Mr. Harry Mallinson, Assistant to the Vice-President of IFC, while he was in Colombia.

After NOEL had provided all the required preliminary information, IFC began its first round of investigation. This indicated that the company's products were good and the market for them was expanding. The financial position of the company was sound, management experienced and efficient, and the directors of the company were local industrialists and professional men of good

IFC investment of one million
dollars helped NOEL Com-
pany complete this new
plant outside Medellin, Colombia.

Sanitary tin containers are
filled with soda crackers.
Production in new NOEL
plant has already increased
by 4,000 tons annually.

reputation. Further, the company was publicly owned by some
500 stockholders, most of whom owned small amounts of stock.
Thus NOEL met the requisites for IFC investment and its application could be considered.

At the same time that IFC began discussion with NOEL of the
terms of investment, IFC staff began to examine the company's

operations in much greater detail. This work continued for many months. IFC Investment Officer Pierre Laporte, and Melvin Lord, a staff engineer, made several trips to Medellin. Meanwhile, an independent audit by a private accounting firm was made for IFC and this confirmed the company's sound financial position.

These studies gave rise to suggestions from the IFC staff that resulted in reducing the cost of completing the plant from the estimated figure of $1,350,000 to $1,000,000. The 'company also agreed to a suggestion that it install a modern accounting system that would enable it to keep closer track of its costs of production and distribution.

On September 1, 1959, IFC announced that it had agreed to invest $1,000,000 in NOEL. The agreement was signed in New York by Robert Garner, President of the IFC and by Mr. T. J. Tighe, representative of NOEL in the United States.

The total cost of Noel's expansion was estimated at $2,400,000. IFC's investment of $1 million was made in U.S. dollar notes, bearing six per cent interest and maturing by 1969. IFC does not have a uniform interest rate for its investments. The fixed rate in each case is set in relation to all relevant circumstances including the risks involved and the prospective overall return on the investment.

The agreement with NOEL also called for the payment of additional interest on a deferment plan related to profits. This participation in profits and the option on shares in the company, further specified in the agreement, are features of IFC investments.

Today, NOEL's new plant is in operation a few miles outside bustling Medellin. It covers nearly three times the area of the older factory and is an entirely modern, air-conditioned building with the most up-to-date equipment. Most of the $800,000 worth of new machinery came from the United States. Production has risen from 7,000 tons of foodstuffs per year in the old factory to about 11,000 tons, and at the same time the efficiency of the new plant is much greater.

NOEL's new factory includes a modern cafeteria where employees pay less than cost for a balanced meal. There is an infirmary and a department of social service. The company provides all the benefits required by Colombian labor laws; and beyond these obligatory provisions, it also offers its employees after-hours classes

NOEL products are shipped by truck to widening markets in Colombia. IFC investment to aid NOEL expansion was made after careful study of the company's operations and prospects.

in reading and writing, transportation to and from the factory and ten scholarships each year for sons of employees. Now under construction is a new building for the commissary that will sell staple foodstuffs at cost to employees.

By this investment, IFC has given private enterprise an opportunity to contribute to the development of Colombia. The governments of developing countries, faced with urgent demands of public funds and personnel for education and health and for basic facilities such as transport, communications and power, cannot readily spare their limited resources for activities which private capital can undertake. IFC's helping hand to private enterprise puts an important and dynamic sector of the community into the battle to raise living standards. And it does this in more ways than one.

The case history described here shows how private business within a developing country can be aided by direct IFC investment. Equally important is the IFC function of stimulating the flow of private capital from the industrialized countries to the developing countries. The agency does this by finding private investors to share in an initial investment and by selling IFC investments. Since IFC's own funds for investment are limited — at present a total of $96.2 million is subscribed — the agency's success in the long run will lie in the extent to which it can encourage the private financial community to channel its resources into productive enterprises in the developing countries. At the present, private investment in the projects approved by IFC are worth three and one-half times the amount the IFC has itself put up!

INTERNATIONAL FINANCE CORPORATION: IFC
International Headquarters: 1818 H Street, N.W., Washington 25, D.C.

ORIGIN

The proposal to create the International Finance Corporation originated with the management of the International Bank for Reconstruction and Development, and the Articles of Agreement were drawn by the Executive Directors of the Bank. The IFC came into existence as an autonomous international institution on July 24, 1956, when thirty-one countries with capital subscriptions totaling $78 million, had fulfilled the membership requirements. The Corporation is closely affiliated with the Bank, although it is a separate legal entity and its funds and operations are entirely separate from those of the Bank. The Corporation has offices in Paris, London and New York City. In February, 1957, IFC became a specialized agency cooperating with the United Nations.

PURPOSES

The purposes of the International Finance Corporation are stated in Article I of the Articles of Agreement:

To further economic development by encouraging the growth of productive private enterprise in member countries, particularly in the less developed areas, thus supplementing the activities of the International Bank for Reconstruction and Development . . . the Corporation shall:

1. in association with private investors, assist in financing the establishment, improvement and expansion of productive private enterprises which would contribute to the development of its member countries by making investments, without guarantee of repayment by the member government concerned, in cases

An IFC investment of $300,000 in Concrete Products and Aggregate Ltd., of Thailand, enabled expansion and diversification of operations. Here, prestressed concrete products are loaded on a barge.

where sufficient private capital is not available on reasonable terms;

2. seek to bring together investment opportunities, domestic and foreign private capital, and experienced management; and

3. seek to stimulate, and to help create conditions conducive to the flow of private capital, domestic and foreign, into productive investment in member countries.

OPERATIONS

The principles guiding the operations of the IFC are contained in sections of Article III:

· the Corporation shall not undertake any financing for which in its opinion sufficient private capital could be obtained on reasonable terms;

• the Corporation shall not finance an enterprise in the territories of any member if the member objects to such financing;

• the Corporation shall impose no conditions that the proceeds of any financing by it shall be spent in the territories of any particular country;

• the Corporation shall not assume responsibility for managing any enterprise in which it has invested;

• the Corporation shall undertake its financing on terms and conditions which it considers appropriate, taking into account the requirements of the enterprise, the risks being undertaken by the Corporation and the terms and conditions normally obtained by private investors for similar financing;

• the Corporation shall seek to revolve its funds by selling its investments to private investors whenever it can appropriately do so on satisfactory terms;

• the Corporation shall seek to maintain a reasonable diversification in its investments.

• Whenever it shall become necessary under this Agreement to value any currency in terms of the value of another currency, such valuation shall be as reasonably determined by the Corporation after consultation with the International Monetary Fund.

• The Corporation and its officers shall not interfere in the political affairs of any member; nor shall they be influenced in their decisions by the political character of the member or members concerned. Only economic considerations shall be relevant to their decisions, and these considerations shall be weighed impartially in order to achieve the purposes stated in this Agreement.

MEMBERS AND CAPITAL

The original members of IFC are members of the International Bank which accepted membership in the Corporation before December 15, 1956. Subsequent membership required membership in the Bank and was open at such times and in accordance with such terms as the Corporation might prescribe. As of February 1, 1961, the IFC had fifty-eight members. A complete list of members is included in the Appendix.

Private investment, coupled with $3.9 million invested by IFC, helped finance FERTISA plant for production of synthetic ammonia in Peru. This ammonium sulfate plant is one unit of the installation.

The authorized capital stock of the IFC is $100,000,000 in terms of United States dollars. The stock is divided into 100,000 shares having a par value of $1,000 each. Shares not initially subscribed by original members are available for subsequent subscription. The amount of capital stock may be increased by decision of the Board of Governors.

A schedule of initial subscriptions to capital stock was established ranging from $2,000 for Panama to $35,168,000 for the United States. At present, a total of $96,207,000 is subscribed.

The IFC's operating expenses are met from earnings, and consequently there are no assessments on members for a proportion of the annual budget.

Members may be suspended from IFC by a majority vote of the Board of Governors. Any member which is suspended from membership in the Bank or which ceases to be a member of the Bank is automatically suspended, or ceases to be a member of IFC. Thus when Cuba and the Dominican Republic withdraw from the Bank, they ceased to be members of IFC. Members may also withdraw from the IFC. When a government ceases to be a member, the Corporation will repurchase that government's capital stock in accordance with the provisions for the settlement of accounts.

STRUCTURE AND ORGANIZATION

The International Finance Corporation has a Board of Governors, Board of Directors, a Chairman of the Board of Directors, a President and staff.

The Board of Governors

All powers of the Corporation are vested in the Board of Governors. Each Governor and Alternate Governor of the Bank appointed by a member of the Bank which is also a member of IFC is *ex officio* a Governor or Alternate Governor of the IFC. Alternates vote only in the absence of the Governor. The Board of Governors selects one of its members as Chairman. It meets annually in conjunction with the annual meeting of the Bank. Each member of the IFC has 250 votes plus one additional vote for each share of stock held.

The Board of Directors

The Board of Governors has delegated to the Directors responsibility for the conduct of general operations of the Corporation.

The Board of Directors is composed *ex officio* of each Executive Director of the Bank who has been either appointed by a member of the Bank which is also a member of the Corporation, or elected in an election in which the vote of at least one member of the Bank also a member of the Corporation shall have counted toward his election. The Alternates to each such Executive Director of the Bank also serve *ex officio* as Alternate Directors of the IFC.

The Chairman

The President of the Bank is *ex officio* Chairman of the Board of Directors of the Corporation, but does not vote except in case of a tie.

The President

The President of the IFC is appointed by the Board of Directors on the recommendation of the Chairman. He is the chief executive officer of the IFC responsible for the conduct of business and for the appointment and organization of the staff. All officers of IFC owe their duty in the performance of their functions entirely to the Corporation and to no other authority.

ACTIVITIES

The International Finance Corporation's investments are made primarily in industrial enterprises which are located within a member country or in the territory of a member. These enterprises may include such phases of industry as manufacturing, processing or mining. Electric power, transportation, housing, irrigation or reclamation projects are excluded from consideration. The investment may be made in association with either nationals of the country in which the project is located or with private foreign investors or both. The IFC is prepared actively to seek private capital to supplement its own investment in an enterprise.

The range of enterprises aided to date includes firms producing lumber and rubber products, cement and prestressed concrete, steel, cotton, textiles, twist drills, electrical equipment and automotive parts. In the first four years of operation, the IFC made investment commitments to thirty-five enterprises in seventeen countries to a total of over $41 million.

Twenty-five of these commitments were in Latin American countries, six in Asia and the Middle East, three in Europe (Finland and Italy), two in Australia and one in Africa. The African project aided is one of the more recent investments and is to the Kilombero Sugar Company, Ltd., a Tanganyikan firm newly organized to grow and refine sugar for the local market. The firm will clear and irrigate some 7,000 acres for sugar cane and will construct a sugar mill and refinery, with production expected to begin in 1962. The project is a major step in the development of the fertile and thinly populated Kilombero Valley. Three private firms have also invested in the project and a public issue of preferred shares in the company is to be made to residents of Tanganyika.

At the present time the management of the IFC has proposed to the Board of Governors an amendment to the Articles of Agreement to permit the Corporation to make investments in capital stock. The organization is now prohibited from doing so, and the Directors have concluded that this restriction is a handicap to the mobilization of private capital for foreign investment as well as to the growth of the IFC's operations.

CHAPTER ELEVEN

IDA
International Development Association

A United Nations Agency in the Making

Mr. Johnson of Texas: *There is on the calendar Senate Resolution 264. Mr. President, I yield the floor to the distinguished Senator from Okalahoma, Mr. Monroney, so that the Senate may consider this important piece of legislation.*

So began the formal process by which one man's idea was to become a reality — a reality in the form of a billion-dollar international organization.

The man was United States Senator Mike Monroney. The place was the floor of the United States Senate and the date was February 24, 1958.

Senator Monroney was about to propose an international organization which would make long-term, low-interest loans supplementing International Bank lending and making possible development projects which could not otherwise be financed.

The organization he proposed was to be named the International Development Association, and it came into existence exactly two years and seven months later, on September 24, 1960. Considering the negotiations required among and inside many nations to bring an international financial institution into existence, this was swift action, and it bespeaks the enthusiasm and hard work which many men devoted to this plan.

Senator Monroney's idea was born during a trip through Asia in 1956. He observed a fact mentioned earlier in this book: Unit-

ed Nations aid is more popular among the less developed nations
than bilateral aid. Thus a nation, he noted, took pride in a project
completed with an International Bank loan, but there was no enthusiasm for another project built with U.S. defense support funds.
Senator Monroney was also aware of the amounts of local currencies being amassed by the United States through the sale of
surplus agricultural products, and he envisioned the possibility of
putting that money to work through an international lending
agency.

Prior to introducing his proposal in the Senate, Senator Monroney discussed it at length with Eugene R. Black, President of
the International Bank, who had long been aware of the need for
an international lending agency that could operate with more
flexibility than could the Bank.

Duly introduced, Senate Resolution 264 was referred to the Committee on Banking and Currency which reported favorably on it
in early July. On July 23 the Senate adopted Resolution 264. It
thereby called upon the National Advisory Council on International Monetary and Financial Problems to give "prompt study"
to the establishment of an International Development Association
as an affiliate of the International Bank. The National Advisory
Council had been set up by Congress at the time it approved the
Articles of Agreement of the Bank and the IMF. Its members are
the Secretaries of the Treasury (Chairman), the State Department and the Commerce Department, the Chairman of the Board
of Governors of the Federal Reserve System and the Chairman of
the Board of Directors of the Export-Import Bank of Washington.

The Secretary of the Treasury also serves as the United States
Governor on the Board of Governors of the International Bank.
At the request of President Eisenhower, he and the Under Secretary of State, serving as Alternate U.S. Governor, informally discussed the proposal for IDA with representatives of other member
governments of the Bank at the annual meeting in the fall in 1958.
During the following months, while the Council continued its studies of the proposal, it had additional and frequent informal discussions with other governments, in effect laying the groundwork
for the formal proposal for IDA which the United States government was later to make. Informal consultations were also held
with the Executive Directors of the International Bank.

On August 16, 1959, the Council reported to the President and to the Senate Foreign Relations Committee that IDA was "feasible and desirable" and it presented a plan for the agency, including financing and operations.

Several factors were significant in bringing about approval and enthusiastic support for the Monroney proposal by the National Advisory Council. First was the recognition, already mentioned, of the desirability of multilateral development aid as opposed to bilateral aid; and second was the change in the world economic scene. Japan and the industrialized nations of Western Europe, particularly West Germany, had recovered from World War II. They now had strong economies and were in a position to aid the underdeveloped areas, whereas the United States now faced balance-of-payment difficulties. The proposed IDA would utilize their resources as well as those of the United States.

At the same time that it reported to the President and to the Senate, the Chairman of the National Advisory Council, acting as the U.S. Governor of the International Bank, advised the President of the Bank that the U.S. would introduce a resolution concerning IDA at the annual meeting of the Bank in September. The Council's outline for the organization was sent to the Bank with the suggestion that it serve as the basis on which the Executive Directors could formulate Articles of Agreement for IDA.

The United States proposal was approved at the Bank's annual meeting and the Executive Directors were instructed to prepare Articles of Agreement for submission to the Bank's member states. By January 26, 1960, the Executive Directors had completed this assignment and the Articles of Agreement were submitted to sixty-eight governments for approval.

Within the following month, President Eisenhower sent the Articles of Agreement to the Congress, recommending legislation to authorize U.S. membership in IDA and to provide for payment of the U.S. subscription. Hearings were held by the Senate Foreign Relations Committee and the House Banking and Currency Committee with both reporting favorably. Congressional action was completed on June 29, and the President signed the enabling legislation, Public Law 85-565. This approved U.S. membership and authorized the U.S. subscription of $320,290,000. An appropriation for the first installment of the U.S. subscription was approved by

Congress on July 1. The United States government deposited its instrument of acceptance with the International Bank on August 9, 1960.

Pakistan, meanwhile, had been the first nation to complete governmental action and had become a member of IDA on June 9. Canada deposited its instrument of acceptance on the same day as the United States. By September 24, the required sixty-five per cent ($686,000,000) of authorized initial subscription of $1,000,000,000 had been subscribed and IDA came into being. Fifteen nations had subscribed this amount. They were: Australia, Canada, China, Germany, India, Italy, Malaya, Norway, Pakistan, Sudan, Sweden, Thailand, United Kingdom, United States and Vietnam.

A good measure of credit for this swift ratification action on the part of governments may be attributed to the great confidence in the International Bank which is felt among the world community. Though a separate entity with its own funds, IDA is administered by the Boards and the management of the Bank, whose successful operations lead to an expectation of maximum results from this new organization. IDA loans will further the developmental objectives of the Bank and supplement its activities; it is empowered to finance projects excluded from Bank consideration and to make loans on terms which are more flexible and which bear less heavily on the balance of payments than conventional loans. Balance-of-payments crises have endangered development in a number of countries by limiting their ability to service external loans. IDA may help meet this problem by providing for lenient terms of repayment, by lending free of interest or at a low rate of interest, or by a combination of both. Lenient terms could even include loans repayable in local currencies.

The needs of the less developed nations for financial assistance make the prospect for IDA lending almost boundless. However its present resources impose limits on the number of projects which it can aid. The Articles of Agreement provide for a review of the adequacy of IDA resources at the end of five years and allow for an increase in subscriptions. The success of its operations in the intervening period will undoubtedly determine whether this new venture in development aid will be enlarged. Since March 27, 1961, when IDA officially affiliated itself with the United Nations, the international community has a new workshop in which to shape a better future — a workshop designed by a United States Senator and erected under the leadership of the United States by the many nations of the community.

INTERNATIONAL DEVELOPMENT ASSOCIATION: IDA
International Headquarters: 1818 H Street, N.W., Washington 25, D.C.

PURPOSES

The statement of IDA's purposes in the Articles of Agreement is preceded by a Preamble setting the framework:

The Governments on whose behalf this Agreement is signed, Considering:

• That mutual cooperation for constructive economic purposes, healthy development of the world economy and balanced growth of international trade foster international relationships conducive to the maintenance of peace and world prosperity;

• That an acceleration of economic development which will promote higher standards of living and economic and social progress in the less-developed countries is desirable not only in the interests of those countries but also in the interests of the international community as a whole;

• That achievement of these objectives would be facilitated by an increase in the international flow of capital, public and private, to assist in the development of the resources of the less-developed countries,

do hereby agree as follows.

The purposes are stated in Article I:

The purposes of the Association are to promote economic development, increase productivity and thus raise standards of living in the less-developed areas of the world included within the Association's membership, in particular by providing finance to meet their important developmental requirements on terms which are more flexible and bear less heavily on the balance of payments than those of conventional loans, thereby furthering the developmental objectives of the International Bank for Reconstruction and Development and supplementing its activities.

OPERATIONS

The principles guiding the operations of the IDA are contained in sections of Article V:

• The Association shall provide financing to further development in the less-developed areas of the world included within the Association's membership.

• Financing provided by the Association shall be for purposes which in the opinion of the Association are of high developmental priority in the light of the needs of the area or areas concerned and, except in special circumstances, shall be for specific projects.

• The Association shall not provide financing if in its opinion such financing is available from private sources on terms which are reasonable for the recipient or could be provided by a loan of the type made by the Bank.

• Financing by the Association shall take the form of loans. The Association may, however, provide other financing, either

    (i)   out of funds subscribed pursuant to Article III, Section 1 (additional subscriptions) . . . or

    (ii)   in special circumstances, out of supplementary resources furnished to the Association . . .

• Subject to the foregoing paragraph, the Association may provide financing in such forms and on such terms as it may deem appropriate, having regard to the economic position and prospects of the area or areas concerned and to the nature and requirements of the project.

• The Association may provide financing to a member, the government of a territory included within the Association's membership, a political subdivision of any of the foregoing, a public or private entity in the territories of a member or members, or to a public international or regional organization.

• In addition . . . the Association may:

    (i)   borrow funds with the approval of the member in whose currency the loan is denominated;

    (ii)   guarantee securities in which it has invested in order to facilitate their sale;

    (iii)   buy and sell securities it has issued or guaranteed or in which it has invested;

(iv)   in special cases, guarantee loans from other sources for purposes not inconsistent with the provisions of these Articles;

(v)   provide technical assistance and advisory services at the request of a member; and

(vi)   exercise such other powers incidental to its operations as shall be necessary or desirable in furtherance of its purposes.

MEMBERS AND CAPITAL

The original members of IDA are those members of the International Bank which accepted membership in the Association before December 31, 1960. Subsequent membership was open to other members of the International Bank at such times and in accordance with such terms as the Association may determine. As of February 1, 1961, IDA had thirty-eight members. A complete list of members is included in the Appendix.

Members may be suspended from the Association by a majority vote of the Board of Governors. Any member which is suspended from membership in, or ceases to be a member of the Bank is automatically suspended from or ceases to be a member of the IDA. Members may withdraw from IDA and may receive back their subscription.

The capitalization of IDA is $1,000,000,000. Initial subscriptions were established for each member of the Bank based on the member's proportional subscription to the capital of the Bank. The initial subscriptions were expressed in terms of United States dollars of the weight and fineness in effect on January 1, 1960. Subscribing countries were divided into two classes as follows:

Part I countries: all highly developed countries of Western Europe plus the United Kingdom, Australia, Canada, Japan, Union of South Africa and the United States. Subscriptions allowed to Part I countries were payable in gold or convertible currencies.

Part II countries: the less-developed countries where IDA was designed to operate. The subscriptions of Part II countries were payable ten per cent in gold or convertible currencies and ninety per cent in national currencies. These national currencies may be converted by the Association or used by it to finance exports from a contributing member only with that member's consent.

Initial subscriptions are payable over a five-year period.

IDA is also authorized to accept from members additional resources payable in their own currencies, and it may accept additions from a member which are in the currency of another member. Permission of the member whose currency is involved is required in the latter case. This provision makes it theoretically possible for the United States to make available to IDA local currencies which it holds in other countries.

Other means of increasing capital funds are also authorized. These include borrowing funds with the approval of the member in whose currency the loan is denominated and guaranteeing securities in which the Association has invested in order to facilitate their sale.

STRUCTURE AND ORGANIZATION

The International Development Association has a Board of Governors, Executive Directors, a President and staff.

The Board of Governors

All powers of the Association are vested in the Board of Governors. Each Governor and Alternate Governor of the Bank appointed by a member of the Bank which is also a member of the Association is *ex officio* a Governor or Alternate Governor of IDA. The Chairman of the Board of Governors of the Bank is *ex officio* Chairman of the Board of Governors of IDA, unless the nation he represents is not an IDA member, in which case the Board selects a Chairman. The Board of Governors meets annually in conjunction with the annual meeting of the Bannk. Each original member of IDA has 500 votes plus one additional vote for each $5,000 of its initial subscription. Subscriptions other than initial subscriptions carry voting rights to be determined by the Board of Governors.

Executive Directors

The Executive Directors are responsible for the conduct of the general operations of IDA and have delegated authority from the Board of Governors. Executive Directors of the Bank who are appointed or elected by member countries who have taken membership in IDA are also Executive Directors of the Association. Similarly, their Alternates also serve with IDA.

The President

The President of the International Bank is also IDA's President. He is Chairman of the Executive Directors of the Association, but does not vote except in case of a tie. The officers and staff of the Bank serve concurrently for IDA, though provision exists for such separate staffs as may prove necessary.

ACTIVITIES

As this is written IDA has made its first loan — $9,000,000 to Honduras for highway development. This "development credit," as IDA has decided to call its loans, will help finance an extension of the main highway system with feeder roads into an area of western Honduras. By making this area accessible by road, the government hopes to open new land for settlement and increase farm production.

The terms of this "development credit" are illustrative of the flexibility referred to in the Articles of Agreement. The credit is for a period of fifty years. Payments, which can be made in any convertible foreign exchange, will begin after ten years. Thereafter, Honduras will pay one per cent of principal annually for ten years and three per cent for thirty years. The credit is interest-free, but there will be a service charge of three-quarters of one per cent annually on amounts withdrawn and outstanding.

Other projects are presently being examined in Asia, the Middle East and Latin America. Included among them are "social" projects, which refers to such development needs as sanitation or water supply, productive projects to which IDA alone would lend and projects in which the Bank and IDA might invest jointly.

CHAPTER TWELVE

Dollars, Dinars, Dirhams, and Drachma

The terms in the title of this chapter represent the currencies of nations. When most of us think of dollars, we think of United States dollars. It is interesting that this same designation is used in such widely spread areas as Canada, Ethiopa, and Malaya. Although we shall refer to the dinar in this chapter as being Yugoslavian currency, Iraq, Jordan, and Tunisia so name their currency. The dirham is the currency of Morocco, and the drachma that of Greece. We use these as a chapter title because in combination they provide a rhythm of sounds. In actuality, keeping them attuned one to another is one of the most serious problems confronting the world today.

One of the common misconceptions that most of us have is that we pay *money* for goods and services produced by others. Actually, we pay for these goods and services with other goods and services. The money with which we buy things is worth only as much as the goods and services it represents to the person from whom we purchase. When we buy and sell within our own country, we don't give much thought to this "real" value of money. We accept payment in money from others and expect them to accept ours, because we have a common knowledge of what the money is worth in terms of rice or rockets.

But when we carry on transactions outside our national boundaries, new factors enter into our calculations. We must first concern ourselves with the amount of goods and services that we can

purchase with the *foreign currency we accept in payment*, and secondly with what *kinds* of goods and services this foreign currency
will buy. The flow of goods and capital, the movement of tourists,
the transactions in insurance and freight are all on a constantly
growing international scale. A brief example will underscore this
fact. In 1960, tourists from the United States alone spent $1,745
million in foreign countries and paid $460 million to foreign ship,
plane and rail carriers. And yet this represented but a scant fifteen per cent of international tourist exchange. As we travel, it is
imperative that we be able to estimate what our dollars will be
worth in dinars, dirhams, drachma, and dozens of other currencies.

The problem is a knotty one since, in effect, each nation establishes the value of its own currency. Without international monetary cooperation, chaos can result. This was most obvious in the
ten years before World War II. Nations resorted to all sorts of
financial manipulations designed to speed their *own* way out of
the depression of 1929. Among these practices were the manipulations of their own currencies without regard to that of other nations. This attitude of improving oneself by making a beggar of
one's neighbor, along with special trade agreements, contributed
to world economic disorganization.

Out of this unhappy experience emerged a conviction among
statesmen that something had to be done in the postwar world
to curb these disturbances in the international financial field. Their
answer was the Bretton Woods (New Hampshire) Conference,
which negotiated the Articles of Agreement of the International
Monetary Fund (IMF) and the International Bank for Reconstruction and Development (Chapter 9). The Articles of Agreement of IMF may be called a code of fair practice in international
finance.

The needs were obvious. There must be a fund to which all members contributed and from which each member might borrow in
times of difficulty. This, in turn, assumed that there must be a common denominator for determining the value of each member's currency in terms of gold as well as in the currencies of each of the
other member nations. This latter is known as establishing a par
value. It is important that these par values not be drastically
changed other than by mutual agreement among the members.

The ultimate goal was to be one of complete convertibility of currencies. This means that on any given day a person with dollars, dinars, dirhams, or drachma could exchange his own currency for any one of the others and at the same time feel secure as to the value received in terms of goods and services.

Basic to the entire scheme was the establishment of an international pool of currency. In the first year of IMF's operation, the quota subscriptions of individual members amounted to $6.5 billion. Twenty-five per cent of IMF quotas is paid in gold and the balance in national currency. Since that time membership in IMF has increased to sixty-eight, and its resources now total $14.8 billion.

How has this worked in practice?

The Deputy Secretary of the Fund welcomes technical assistance trainees from the Philippines, India, Thailand, and Iran.

A good example of the way in which IMF helps members who find themselves in financial difficulty is that of Mexico. With the election of a new government in 1958 and the prospect of an unbalanced budget, fear spread throughout the international financial community that a devaluation of the Mexican currency — the peso — might occur. Were this to take place, it would mean that the peso would be worth less in terms of the goods and services that it could purchase. Therefore, people, banks, and organizations holding this currency would attempt to unload it at the earliest possible moment. To forestall this, the Mexican Government early in 1959 sought the advice of the IMF and worked out agreements whereby IMF promised to provide $90 million to support the peso, should the need arise. Of this amount $22.5 million was actually drawn. This firmly stopped speculation in the peso. There was a backflow of currency into Mexico, Mexican reserves increased, and by the end of 1959 Mexico had repaid IMF the entire amount which had been drawn. Confidence had been restored, chaos averted.

Confidence in the value of one currency in terms of another is vital to the peaceful flow of people, goods, and services within the world community. This requires a yardstick against which each member's currency can be measured. The IMF measures this value against both gold and the U.S. dollar. This latter currency is used as the United States guarantees to pay $35 in its currency units for each troy ounce of fine gold that comes into the international trade market. We can turn the most recent issue of "Schedule of Par Values," (31st of March, 1961) published periodically by IMF, which establishes such exchange rates. Since the U.S. dollar is one of the yardsticks, we find the currency value in terms of gold is $35 per ounce, and naturally enough, the currency unit is valued at one dollar. The Yugoslavian dinar is rated at 10,500 units for an ounce of gold, and it requires 300 dinars to purchase an American dollar. One needs 177.117 Moroccan dirhams to purchase an ounce of gold and 5.06 dirhams to "buy" a U.S. dollar. Greek drachmas are rated at 1,050 for gold and 30 for the dollar. The IMF is vitally concerned with these — and all other — par values, and members consult with the IMF for changes in the rates.

The foregoing ratio of currencies seems to make a rather simple mathematical problem out of exchanging these monies one for another. Such is not the case. If it were, we would have achieved full convertibility of currencies. This means that any one of us could, among other things, freely buy the other currencies without the approval of the government concerned. To develop this universal convertibility takes time, confidence, and monetary stability. As of July, 1961 this impressive listing of IMF members have made their currency freely convertible:

Belgium	Ireland
Canada	Italy
Cuba	Luxembourg
Dominican Republic	Mexico
El Salvador	Netherlands
France	Panama
Germany	Peru
Federal Republic of	**Saudi Arabia**
Guatemala	Sweden
Haiti	United States
Honduras	United Kingdom

This is a tribute to the nations concerned and their spirit of cooperation through IMF.

As this ease of convertibility expands, IMF will assist in laying the basis for expansion in trade and production within the world neighborhood. The United Nations has proposed an International Trade Organization (ITO) which would draw rules of fair trade and reduce barriers that hinder the flow of goods and services throughout the world. This agency has not come into being. Some of its objectives have been included in an international commercial treaty, known as the General Agreement on Tariffs and Trade (GATT). Thirty-seven governments, accounting for some eighty per cent of world trade, have signed this treaty. The staff appointed to an Interim Commission of ITO became the secretariat of GATT. The U.N. cooperates with the member nations through this secretariat. IMF works closely with this group. Although there are many steps to be taken, considerable advance has been made in eliminating foreign exchange restrictions which hamper the growth of world trade.

The success of IMF as a center for monetary cooperation will always depend upon relationships with other international organizations and close contact with member nations. Nations have learned that achieving stability through manipulation of their own currency does not work. Only through sound development programs and stable exchange conditions can countries hope to create a climate conducive to attracting foreign capital and creating an adequate basis for continuing economic growth.

IMF is helping nations achieve these objectives. In doing so, IMF is not only benefitting member nations, but the entire world community. The establishment of sound monetary conditions is of vital concern to all countries and all world neighborhoods.

INTERNATIONAL MONETARY FUND: IMF
International Headquarters: 19th and H Streets, N.W., Washington 6, D.C.

ORIGIN
In May, 1944, the President of the United States issued invitations to forty-four United and Associated Nations to attend a monetary conference at Bretton Woods, New Hampshire, in July 1944. On June 15, a group of United States financial experts assembled at Atlantic City, New Jersey, and were joined a few days later by representatives of fifteen nations for a preliminary meeting. The Bretton Woods conference of July 1-22 (formally referred to as the United Nations Monetary and Financial Conference) produced the Articles of Agreement for the International Monetary Fund (IMF) and for the International Bank for Reconstruction and Development.

The Fund's actual existence as an international organization began on December 27, 1945, when governments contributing eighty per cent of the monetary quotas set at Bretton Woods signed the Articles of Agreement. The first organizational meeting of the Board of Governors was convened at Savannah, Georgia, on March 8, 1946. On December 18, 1946, IMF announced its agreement to the official par values for the currencies of thirty-two of its members, and it began operations on March 1, 1947, with a public declaration that it was ready to conduct exchange transactions.

PURPOSES

The purposes of IMF are set forth in Article I of the Articles of Agreement, as follows:

i.   To promote international monetary cooperation through a permanent institution which provides the machinery for consultation and collaboration on international monetary problems.

ii.   To facilitate the expansion and balanced growth of international trade, and to contribute thereby to the promotion and maintenance of high levels of employment and real income and to the development of the productive resources of all members as primary objectives of economic policy.

iii.   To promote exchange stability, to maintain orderly exchange arrangements among members, and to avoid competitive exchange depreciation.

iv.   To assist in the establishment of a multilateral system of payments in respect of current transactions between members and in the elimination of foreign exchange restrictions which hamper the growth of world trade.

v.   To give confidence to members by making the Fund's resources available to them under adequate safeguards, thus providing them with opportunity to correct maladjustments in their balance of payments without resorting to measures destructive of national or international prosperity.

vi.   In accordance with the above, to shorten the duration and lessen the degree of disequilibrium in the international balances of payments of members.

FUNCTIONS

The carrying out of IMF's purposes depends chiefly upon agreements made by the members to the Fund and upon the consultations of its Executive Directors.

In ratifying the Articles of Agreement the members commit themselves to the following: to refrain from competitive foreign exchange practices, to work toward eliminating restrictions on the exchange of national currencies, to strive toward establishing consistent rates for currencies in terms of gold and the United States dollar, and to consult with IMF on the proposed national matters in the monetary fields so that these may be studied as to their international impact.

The headquarters of the International Monetary Fund in Washington, D. C.

The Executive Directors function in continuous session at Washington and meet as frequently as the business of IMF demands. In carrying out their responsibilities to IMF the Directors must constantly weigh the world-wide research and statistical data prepared by the staff. Against this information the Directors determine Fund policy with regard to monetary measures proposed by members. These concern changes in par values, exchange restrictions and gold policies, in addition to requests by members to purchase other currencies or gold for equivalent amounts of the member's national currency.

MEMBERSHIP, QUOTAS AND SUBSCRIPTIONS

The original members of IMF were those countries represented at the United Nations Monetary and Financial Conference whose governments deposited instruments of ratification prior to January 1, 1946. Membership is open to other governments under conditions determined by IMF. As of February 1, 1961, IMF had sixty-eight members. A complete list of members appears in the Appendix. Each member is assigned a quota. Quotas for original members were established by the United Nations Monetary and Financial Conference under Schedule "A" of the Articles of Agreement. These initial quotas ranged from $500,000 assigned Panama to $2,750,000,000 assigned the United States. Countries admitted to IMF subsequent to January 1, 1946, are assigned quotas by IMF. Every five years quotas are reviewed by IMF and, if necessary, adjustments are made. On September 15, 1959, quotas were increased, generally by fifty per cent.

Monetary Fund quotas are paid in gold and in the member's own currency. Twenty-five per cent of the quota is paid in gold. The balance is paid in non-interest bearing demand notes, which IMF can cash in the member's currency. The total quotas of members as of April 1, 1961 was, in round figures, $14.8 million.

Members may withdraw from IMF by transmitting such notice in writing. Under certain conditions members may be required to withdraw from IMF.

There are no annual assessments to members. Operating expenses are met from profits. IMF's income arises out of charges on transactions and interest on excess balances of members' currencies held by the IMF.

STRUCTURE AND ORGANIZATION

The IMF has a Board of Governors, a Board of Executive Directors, a Managing Director, and an international staff.

The Board of Governors

All powers of the IMF are vested in the Board of Governors, consisting of one Governor and one Alternate appointed by each member. Their terms are for five years, subject to the pleasure of the individual governments.

The Governors may delegate and, in fact, have delegated to the Executive Directors all of their powers except, as provided in Article XII, Section 2, of the Articles of Agreement, the power to:

i.   Admit new members and determine the conditions of their admission.

ii.   Approve a revision of quotas.

iii.   Approve a uniform change in the par value of the currencies of all members.

iv.   Make arrangements to cooperate with other international organizations.

v.   Determine the distribution of the net income of the Fund.

vi.   Require a member to withdraw.

vii.   Decide to liquidate the Fund.

viii.   Decide appeals from interpretations of this agreement given by the Executive Directors.

ix.   Elect Directors.

The Board of Governors holds an annual meeting and such other meetings as may be called by the Board or by the Executive Directors. The Governors may also vote between meetings by mail or cable. Voting power is approximately proportional to the amount of capital contributed to the IMF by each member.

The Executive Directors

The Executive Directors are responsible for the conduct of the general operations of IMF, for this purpose exercising all the powers delegated to them by the Board of Governors. They are in permanent session, normally at the headquarters of IMF.

Five of the Executive Directors are appointed by the five countries with the largest quotas in IMF. Thirteen others are elected by the remaining countries.

The Board of Governors of IMF, the World Bank and IFC, meeting in Washington, D.C., 1959.

Each Executive Director exercises voting power approximately in proportion to the quota contributed by his country, in the instances of the five appointed Directors, and each elected Director casts as a unit all the votes of the countries that elected him. Each Director appoints an Alternate with full power to act for him in his absence.

The Managing Director

The Chairman of the Board of Executive Directors is also the Managing Director of IMF. He is appointed by the Executive Directors for a term of five years. He acts as Chairman of the Directors' meetings, but has no vote except a deciding vote in case of an equal division. As Managing Director, he is chief of the operating staff of IMF, and conducts, under direction of the Executive Directors, the ordinary business of IMF. The Executive Directors have provided for a Deputy Managing Director to serve as Acting Chairman of their Board when the Managing Director is absent, and to assist him in administrative matters.

The Staff

The staff of IMF is an international body whose members owe their loyalty and obedience only to IMF on IMF matters. They are divided into four offices and seven departments: Office of Managing Director, Office of the Secretary, Office of Administration, Office of the Treasurer, Legal Department, Research and Statistics Department, Exchange Restrictions Department, and four area departments.

ACTIVITIES

IMF has a continuing and extensive program of technical assistance through staff missions to many parts of the world, and provides studies, reports and publications on international financial subjects.

IMF staff have assisted members in establishing or adapting to their needs institutional machinery such as central banking and exchange systems. IMF has helped countries improve their collection and presentation of financial statistics and has advised members on the monetary impact of development programs.

IMF's activities are summarized in the annual report of the Executive Directors to the Board of Governors. The report includes a summary of the world economic situation with observations and recommendations, a statement of the use of IMF's resources and a report on gold production and transactions. The Annual Report on Exchange Restrictions, Balance of Payments Yearbook and the monthly magazine, International Financial Statistics, are other important publications.

CHAPTER THIRTEEN

WMO
World Meteorological Organization

Winds and Storms

SS *Irish Oak* 30476 49918 82709 95555 15142 86200 24620 05640 149//

Upon such code messages as this, human life and safety depend. Thousands of similar code messages are the stuff out of which the weatherman builds his daily forecasts.

The above message originated on the vessel *Irish Oak*, owned by Irish Shipping Limited and operating on the North Atlantic routes. The *Irish Oak* is one of the more than 3,000 vessels serving as voluntary observing ships in the World Meteorological Organization (WMO) "Selected Ship Scheme." These ships, operating under the Commission for Maritime Meteorology of the WMO, send out each day thousands of observations which provide invaluable synoptic (broadview) weather data when they are coordinated.

All maritime nations are asked to recruit selected ships, not only to make observations of the weather but to transmit them by radio to various collecting centers. By early 1961 there were some 3,500 such selected ships recruited by the national meteorological services of WMO member countries. The United States has over 600 such selected ships, among them the *United States*, the *America*, the *Constitution*, and the *Independence*.

If a ship's owner agrees to join the weather reporting program, the meteorological service of the country in which the ship is regis-

A weather balloon is inflated and equipped with a radiosonde, in the white box at right.

An international comparison of balloon-borne radiosondes is organized by WMO. The three balloons are linked and carry four different national models of these weather-observing instruments, enabling comparision of performance under similar conditions.

tered lends tested instruments, as recommended by WMO. When the Meteorological Service of Ireland notified WMO in 1952 that the *Irish Oak* had entered the program, they indicated that a mercurial barometer, a sling psychrometer, a sea temperature thermometer, a canvas bucket, and a barograph had been placed aboard the vessel.

No special staff is carried for the purpose of making observations. The work is entirely voluntary and is accomplished by the ships' officers. To insure uniformity in reporting, the Commission for Maritime Meteorology requests that the observations be made at 0001, 0600, 1200, and 1800 Greenwich Mean Time (G.M.T.). If unusual conditions exist, such as a vessel being on the fringes of a hurricane where information may prove invaluable, ships are requested to report each hour.

An analysis of the *Irish Oak* code message indicates the elements that are included in each report.

SS *Irish Oak* 30476 49918 82709 95555 15142 86200 24620 05640 149//

Decode: Observation at 1800 GCT (Greenwich Civil Time) Tuesday. Position 47.6 N. latitude, 49.9 W. longitude. Sky overcast. Wind direction 270 (W), speed 9 knots. Visibility 1 mile. Weather, drizzle, continuous and thick but not freezing. Weather during the preceding six hours, mostly drizzle. Barometric pressure 1015.1 millibars. Temperature 42 degrees. Eight-eighths of the sky covered by low clouds. Type of low clouds, stratus or fractostratus, but not fractostratus of the type usually associated with bad weather. Height of cloud layer 300 to 600 feet. Direc-

The Indian model of a radiosonde is examined.

Soil temperature observations are taken at the Gezira Research Station, Wad Medani, Sudan, where WMO has helped set up an agricultural meteorology station.

tion of ship, eastward at 10 to 12 knots. The barometer has been falling, then steady with a net change of -2.0 millibars during the past three hours. Sea temperature 6 degrees warmer than the air. Dew point temperature 40 degrees. Direction of waves indeterminate.

This code has been in use since January 1, 1949, and is known as the Washington Synoptic Code. Because of mutual understanding among nations through the WMO, this numerical code of seven groups consisting of five figures each can be decoded by thousands of collecting centers throughout the world.

The collecting centers to which the *Irish Oak* and other ships report depends upon their location. The Commission for Maritime Meteorology has constructed world areas for shipping forecasts. These not only designate the centers to which ships report but indicate the range of forecasting areas for which individual WMO members are responsible.

The *Irish Oak*, for example, is at present on the North Atlantic run. Her officers will direct their reports to "Observer Washington" when West of 40W. and to "Weatherdun Wire London" when East of 40W. The messages of the *Irish Oak* may be received at any of several coast radio stations in the New England area. Her reports are then relayed to the Weather Bureau Communications Center at Washington, D.C., either by commercial telegraph circuits or by special teletypewriter line.

At the Weather Bureau Communications Center, hundreds of such reports are being received from ships at sea. Along with these are about 750 others from weather stations in North America and the West Indies, plus 2,000 more from stations in Europe, Asia, North Africa, and northern South America. From this weather picture taken by almost 3,000 pairs of eyes, the Synoptic Reports and Forecasts Division of the Weather Bureau constructs reports of the weather situation around the hemisphere.

These reports are then transmitted throughout the WMO area of responsibility for the United States. Bulletins containing North American weather data are broadcast by Radio Stations WSY,. New York, and WEK, New Orleans, to other meteorological services throughout the world. Some seventy low-power government and commercial shore radio stations broadcast at least twice daily bulletins to ships in coastal waters. Special weather bulletins for shipping in eastern North Pacific waters are made by Radio Stations KPH, Bolinas, California, and KTK, San Francisco, California. Similar bulletin broadcasts for shipping in western North Atlantic waters are broadcast by Radio Station NSS, Washington, D.C. It is from this latter station that the radio operator aboard the *Irish Oak* receives the marine forecasts, storm warnings, and reports for which his ship had been partially responsible.

The "selected ships" are a vital link in today's world-wide meteorological network, and the information they provide is perhaps most valuable to aircraft flying over the seas. For while weather forecasting can rely on several land stations making observations several times a day, over the seas there may be nothing but this voluntary service. The addition to the "selected ships scheme" in recent years of a number of Antarctic whaling ships has been a signal achievement for WMO. These ships, engaged in a highly competitive activity, wish to keep their whereabouts a secret. They have been persuaded to supply vital weather date from this area where no other source is available by an agreement which enables them to transmit their position in a code known only to the receiving station.

If problems arise in regard to weather observations and reports on shipboard the director of one of the meteorological services may refer the matter to the President of the Commission for Maritime Meteorology, WMO. Technical experts in the working groups of this Commission study such reports and make recommendations to member nations through the WMO. Sessions of this Commission are constantly striving to improve the collecting, coordination, and distribution of data in the field of maritime meteorology.

The "Selected Ship Scheme" of the Commission for Maritime Meteorology is a practical example of the way in which the neighborhoods of the world may help themselves by helping one another. The WMO weather workshop forecasts an impressive way toward world peace.

The significance of this intergovernmental cooperation was described by the late Mr. I. R. Tannehill, U.S. Weather Bureau staff member who served on the WMO Commission for Synoptic Meteorology:

The weather is not influenced by national boundaries. It is true in many countries that the people are much more concerned with the weather which originates in other countries than with that which originates in their own country. Hurricanes pass over or near to the countries of the Caribbean area. They may devastate sections of the United States. A storm off the coast of France may be of little concern, but subsequently it may develop and be destructive in the Netherlands. Dust storms of Africa sometimes invade southern Italy. Cold waves from Can-

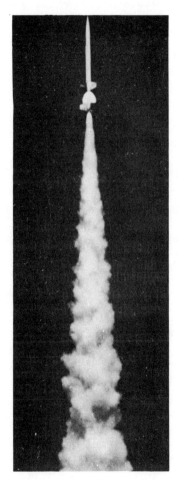

Reading the water temperature at the surface of the sea. Change of temperature is prevented by the use of insulated bucket. A network of some 3500 merchant ships makes regular observations in a voluntary program arranged by WMO.

Research benefits from upper-air observations provided by rockets like this one. During the International Geophysical Year a special program of such observations was conducted.

ada cause misery and sometimes loss of life and property in the United States. Typhoons in the Philippines strike China and Japan. The bitterly cold weather of Central Europe comes from European Russia. It is obvious that the exchange of weather information is absolutely necessary. This requires world uniformity, and an efficient universal means of communication, that is, a weather language which is understood equally well in every country in the world. Surface ships and aircraft of all countries need to know about the weather in other parts of the world, across the national boundaries and beyond continental and oceanic limitations.

WORLD METEOROLOGICAL ORGANIZATION: WMO

International Headquarters: Avenue Guiseppe Motta, Geneva, Switzerland

ORIGIN

International cooperation in meteorology had its beginnings in Brussels, Belgium, in 1853, when representatives from ten nations met to work out a program for collecting certain meteorological observations made at sea. This meeting was inspired by Matthew Fontaine Maury (1806-1873) of the United States Navy.

Matthew Maury had become lame through an accident in 1839. As a result, the Navy Department had relieved him of duties with the fleet and in 1841 had put him in charge of Navy charts and instruments. Out of this responsiblilty Commander Maury developed an organization from which grew the Naval Observatory and the Hydrographic Office. Matthew Maury sensed the importance of international cooperation in maritime meteorology. Commenting upon what was probably one of the first international scientific conferences ever held, Maury later wrote: "The Conference, having brought to a close its labors with respect to the facts to be collected, and the means to be employed for that purpose, has now only to express a hope that whatever observations may be made will be turned to useful account when received and not be suffered to lie dormant for want of a department to discuss them."

Commander Maury's hopes were to be realized. Other meetings followed and at Leipzig, Germany, in 1872, the International Meteorological Organization was formed. The International Meteorological Organization made many constructive contributions to the techniques and standardization of meteorological reporting. However, rapid developments in aviation and marine navigation gave rise to new and complicated problems in applied meteorology. In addition, meteorology was becoming increasingly important to the proper functioning of other activities, such as international telecommunications.

The Directors of the International Meteorological Organization, having cognizance of these developments through long years of experience, felt that their organization should be strengthened by becoming intergovernmental. A most natural second step would be an affiliation with the United Nations as a Specialized Agency for efficient and close cooperation with other international organizations. As a result, the Directors drew up the terms for the Convention of the World Meteorological Organization, WMO, at Washington, D.C., in 1947.

The Convention of the WMO became effective on March 23, 1950, thirty days after the thirtieth government had ratified its provisions. The functions, activities, assets, and obligations of the International Meteorological Organization were transferred to WMO. The First Congress of the WMO met at Paris on March 19, 1951. A United Nations-World Meteorological Organization Agreement was approved by the UN General Assembly on December 20, 1951.

PURPOSE AND FUNCTIONS

Article 2 of the WMO Convention states the purpose and functions of the Organization as follows:

a.   To facilitate world-wide cooperation in the establishment of networks of stations for the making of meteorological observations or other geophysical observations related to meteorology and to promote the establishment and maintenance of meteorological centers charged with the provision of meteorological services;

b.   To promote the establishment and maintenance of systems for the rapid exchange of weather information;

c.   To promote standardization of meteorological observations and to ensure the uniform publication of observations and statistics;

d.   To further the application of meteorology to aviation, shipping, agriculture, and other human activities; and

e.   To encourage research and training in meteorology and to assist in coordinating the international aspects of such research and training.

MEMBERSHIP

As of February 1, 1961, WMO had 108 members. Membership is open to any state or territory which administers a meteorological service of its own and all members, whether states or territories, have equal technical rights within the organization. A complete listing of these members appears in the Appendix.

STRUCTURE AND ORGANIZATION

The constituent bodies of the WMO are the Congress, the Executive Committee, the Regional Associations, the Technical Commissions, Ad Hoc Working Groups and Panels of Experts, and the Secretariat.

Congress

The governing body of the Organization is the Congress. Members of the WMO Congress are the heads of the meteorological services in their respective countries or territories. The Congress is convened at least every four years. As the policy-making body, the Congress adopts technical regulations on meteorological practices and procedures, establishes financial and staff regulations, and elects the Secretary-General.

Executive Committee

The Executive Committee is composed of eighteen members, including the three officers (President and two Vice-Presidents) of the Organization, the Presidents of the Six Regional Associations, and nine Directors of meteorological services of member states or territories who are elected by the Congress. This body meets annually to carry out the policies of the Congress.

Regional Associations

The WMO Congress established six Regional Associations composed of member states and territories whose meteorological networks lie in or extend into one of these areas. The regions are Africa, Asia, South America, North and Central America, the Southwest Pacific, and Europe. Regional Associations meet once every four years, but in the interim may set up working groups on subjects of regional interest. These are operational rather than technical groups and act to coordinate meteorological and associated activities in their own regions as well as to make recommendations to the Congress and the Executive Committee.

Technical Commissions

Eight Technical Commissions have been established by the Congress. They are composed of technical experts in their respective fields of pure and applied meteorology. They advise other international organizations on meteorological questions, make recommendations to the Congress and Executive Committee, and maintain close touch with one another through the WMO Secretariat. Technical Commissions are established in the following fields: aerology, aeronautical meteorology, agricultural meteorology, hydrological meteorology, climatology, instruments and methods of observation, maritime meteorology, and synoptic meteorology. In practice the Technical Commissions operate largely through working groups.

Working Groups and Panels of Experts

Working Groups and Panels of Experts may be convened by the Executive Committee on an *ad hoc* basis to study a particular problem. Such groups are an additional means of providing the organization with expert knowledge on special questions. Currently, there are panels or groups on the meteorological aspects of atomic energy, artificial satellites and the International Geophysical Year.

Secretariat

Besides providing the central administrative machinery for the organization, the Secretariat is responsible for production of the

World map of WMO Regions.

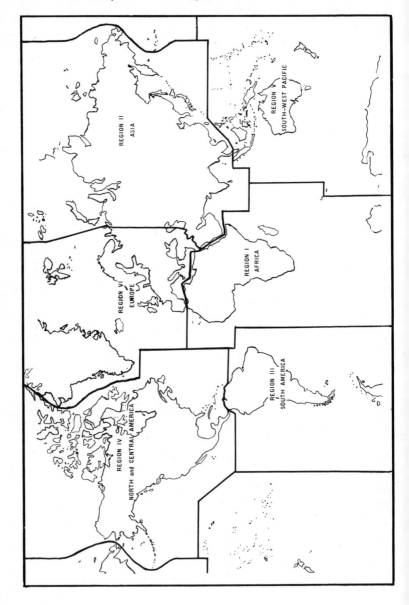

technical material, including a considerable number of special-ized publications, some of which are basic to the maintenance of the international meteorological network.

ACTIVITIES

In order that the world-wide weather network, presently num-bering around 8,500 stations, may continue to work effectively, WMO must continuously keep up-to-date the many-volume docu-ment known as "Publication No. 9, Weather Reports — Stations, Codes, Transmissions." The information provided in this document makes it possible for the several million observations taken each year to be standardized, and it is the foundation of the weather map in the daily newspaper, the forecast heard on the radio.

Other basic publications include the technical regulations for the operation of meteorological services, which are unusual in that they have, in effect, the force of law following their adoption by the World Meteorological Congress. Among technical publications is the "International Cloud Atlas," which classifies clouds in great detail for the use of meteorologists. Publications connected with the International Geophysical Year have been a special WMO job. Chief among these is the series of microcards containing all of the observations — totalling some thirteen million — taken during the Geophysical Year by 3,000 participating stations. It is expected that the data contained on these cards will be under study for the next thirty years.

Through the technical assistance program, WMO is helping its members to expand the network of observing stations. The even-tual goal is to cover the whole of the world's surface, both land and sea, with suitably placed stations well enough equipped to give effective information. Gaps in the network in the Near East are now being filled as the result of technical aid to Syria, Jordan and Saudi Arabia. A recent aspect of expert assistance involves helping countries develop the system of high-level observations so necessary to the operations of jet aircraft. In South America, oddly, the assignment to Chile of an expert on potato blight, a disease closely related to weather conditions, started a chain of meteorological advances which have now brought U.N. Special Fund aid, including equipment, to a regional hydrometeorological program aimed at efficient water resource development.

In Yugoslavia and the Sudan, both of which have experienced meteorological services, WMO experts have helped start research into the application of meteorology to local agricultural problems. In the Sudan, this has tied in with WMO's role in the arid zone international research program led by UNESCO. Desert locust control and the preparation of a Climatic Atlas for Africa are other projects of concern to Arid Zones which WMO had aided.

Training programs and fellowships figure importantly in WMO technical aid. Meteorological assistants have been trained in a number of countries, such as Morocco and Tunisia, in the latter in cooperation with ICAO.

WMO's Panel on Artificial Satellites has urged international exchange of meteorological information obtained from satellites and in particular asked consideration of the most effective way to circulate storm warnings based on this information. Tiros, the United States meteorological satellite, has already shown the possibility of a scheme, outlined in a WMO publication, for covering the whole of the earth's surface continuously with six meteorological satellites.

Problems of the future with which WMO is concerned include the high-speed transmission of weather information and the use of computer-type machines to undertake the calculations required by the forecaster. As the science of meteorology advances, the "weatherman" may also he able to forecast floods sufficiently in advance to prevent disaster or to determine the conditions of vegetation related to weather which lead to forest fires.

This intergovernmental workshop, which grew out of the advantages nations gained from cooperating on meteorological matters, offers many promises to the nations of the world as it extends the benefits of meteorological knowledge to human activities — safer transportation, better communications and improved control over agriculture, water resources and health.

CHAPTER FOURTEEN

IMCO

Inter-Governmental Maritime Consultative Organization

Abu Ail and Jabal at Tair

In this age of the missile and electronic communication, lighthouses are likely to be overlooked. Yet for centuries ships have relied on them to give warning of danger. This remains as true today as it was when the ships of the Phoenician traders sailed the Mediterranean in ancient times and the light was provided by wood fires.

Usually lighthouses are operated by the country on whose soil they are located. But occasionally a lighthouse may be so important to many nations that its maintenance becomes the subject of an international agreement. Such a case is the Cape Spartel light, located on the African side of the approaches to the Straits of Gibraltar. Under the terms of a treaty signed by eleven nations, including the United States, the International Commission of the Cape Spartel Light was established in 1865 to guarantee the management, maintenance and permanent neutrality of the Light.

Sometimes the question of running lighthouses used by the ships of many nations may give rise to problems not easily solved between those nations. A situation of this kind involves lights in the Red Sea. The lights are located on the islands of Abu Ail and Jabal at Tair. Small, rocky, and uninhabited but for lighthouse staff, the islands are north of the straits through which ships pass from the Gulf of Aden to the Red Sea on their way to the Suez Canal. Jabal at Tair is north of the port of Hodeida in Yemen and Abu Ail is to the south. There is heavy traffic on this shipping lane and the combination of weather conditions and navigational hazards make these lighthouses particularly vital to seafarers.

Abu Ail and Jabal at Tair were once part of the Ottoman Empire and were built in 1901 and 1902 by a French company, known as the Ottoman Lighthouse Company, under an agreement with the Turkish government. On the outbreak of World War I, they were occupied and maintained by British forces. Under the treaty of peace signed with Turkey at Lausanne in 1923, Turkey renounced all rights and title over the islands and over the territory of Mocha where another light was located. Turkish property situated in those territories was to pass without payment to the state in whose favor the territories were detached from the Ottoman Empire. While the territory of Mocha passed into the possession of Yemen under this treaty, the future of these islands has never been settled, and they have never become the possession of any other nation. Sovereignty over them is in doubt even today.

In 1927, the first scheme for maintaining the lighthouses on the islands was proposed by the British, who had been keeping the lighthouses in operation. It provided that the nations whose shipping used the Red Sea would collectively agree to employ the Ottoman Lighthouse Company to maintain the lights. The Company would be paid a fixed sum contributed by governments in proportion to the amount of their shipping passing through the Suez Canal. These proposals were set down in an International Convention which further provided that ships of all nations would eventually pay dues in support of the lights.

While the Convention was signed in 1930 by six governments, it never came into force. Before the needed ratifications were received, the Ottoman Company demanded, with the support of the French government, that its fee be stabilized on the basis of its gold value at the time the Convention was signed. The British government felt it would be impractical to revise the Convention and therefore suggested new temporary arrangements under which it would continue to maintain the lights on a cost-sharing basis with the French, German, Italian, Dutch and Japanese governments. Contributions were to be based on the proportion of each nation's shipping passing through the Suez Canal. Germany, Italy and the Netherlands paid their contribution until 1939, but the French and Japanese governments refused to participate. Dur-

The light which keeps vigil for shipping of every nation. The maintenance of lighthouses is essential to the safety of seafarers and a matter of concern to members of IMCO.

ing World War II, the British again bore the full cost of running the lights, but after the war the Netherlands resumed its contribution.

In 1951, the British once more proposed a cost-sharing arrangement, assessments to be made on the countries whose ships were the principal users of the lights, that is, those whose tonnage passing through the Suez Canal amounted to three per cent or more of the total. These governments were the United Kingdom, Norway, France, Panama, Liberia, Italy, the Netherlands, the United States and Sweden. The Italian, Dutch and U.S. governments indicated their willingness to accept this arrangement in 1956, but it was not brought into operation as other governments did not approve it.

In January, 1960, the British government decided to take this problem to the International Maritime Consultative Organization (IMCO). IMCO is the first international agency of its kind in the field of shipping. A consultative and advisory organization, it is charged with securing the highest practicable standards of maritime safety and efficient navigation, and it provides machinery for cooperation among governments in technical matters affecting shipping engaged in international trade.

Britain requested the Council of IMCO to consider what arrangements could be made for sharing the cost of running these lighthouses. The Council accepted the request and suggested that the British prepare a new draft agreement and make background technical studies on such points as the condition of the lighthouses, needed improvements and costs. In November, 1960, the Maritime Safety Committee of IMCO discussed the navigational importance of the lights and having agreed that they were needed, it was decided that the matter should be placed before all the members of the agency at the 1961 Assembly.

Extensive technical studies were carried out for the British government by Mr. K. C. Sutton-Jones of the London engineering firm of Messrs. Stone-Chance Ltd. Mr. Sutton-Jones prepared detailed estimates of the cost of renovating the lighthouses and, following a suggestion of the Maritime Safety Committee, also studied the need for additional lighthouses on the same shipping lane. The future operating costs of the two stations were estimated by Mr. Sutton-Jones at £27,000 yearly ($75,600).

The new draft agreement prepared by the British government for IMCO's consideration was substantially the same as that of 1956. It provides for sharing of the cost by any government whose tonnage passing through Suez is three per cent or more of the total.

The IMCO Assembly in April, 1961, decided that the agency could properly assist in solving this particular problem and directed the Secretariat to study the proposed financing arrangements and help find an equitable solution. Such studies are now underway.

Thus the advisory and consultative functions of IMCO have been brought to bear on a problem which thirty-four years of negotiation among governments have failed to solve, and it may be anticipated that the persuasive powers and moral influence of an international organization will lead to satisfactory resolution of this long-standing impasse.

With IMCO's establishment, the group of international organizations that the United Nations considered important in coordinating technical and economic problems of transport and communication was completed. IMCO already has close working relations with ICAO, ITU and WMO, and these four agencies together with UPU provide a well-balanced team to deal with every facet of international transport and communications.

INTER-GOVERNMENTAL MARITIME
CONSULTATIVE ORGANIZATION: IMCO
International Headquarters: Chancery House, Chancery Lane, London W.C. 2., England

ORIGIN
The proposal for an intergovernmental organization in the field of maritime shipping originated with the Transport and Communications Commission of the United Nations Economic and Social Council at its first meeting in May, 1946. This proposal was endorsed by the United Maritime Consultative Council, a temporary wartime agency, which at its final meeting drafted an agreement for the proposed new agency.

The United Nations Maritime Conference was held in Geneva in February-March, 1948 and a Convention for IMCO drafted. A Preparatory Committee of twelve members was also established to prepare for the first Assembly of the agency. Ratification by twenty-one governments of which seven must have at least one million gross tons of shipping, was required to bring IMCO into existence. These ratifications were slow in coming, and the requirements were not met until March 17, 1958. The first Assembly of the organization was held in January, 1959 and the secretariat of the agency established.

PURPOSES
IMCO's purposes are established in Part I of the Convention.
Article 1
a. to provide machinery for cooperation among Governments in the field of governmental regulation and practices relating

to technical matters of all kinds affecting shipping engaged in
international trade, and to encourage the general adoption of
the highest practicable standards in matters concerning maritime safety and efficiency of navigation;

b.   to encourage the removal of discriminatory action and un-
necessary restrictions by Governments affecting shipping engaged in international trade so as to promote the availability
of shipping services to the commerce of the world without discrimination; assistance and encouragement given by a Government for the development of its national shipping and for purposes of security does not in itself constitute discrimination, provided that such assistance and encourgement is not based on
measures designed to restrict the freedom of shipping of all flags
to take part in international trade;

c.   to provide for the consideration by the Organization of matters concerning unfair restrictive practices by shipping concerns
in accordance with Part II;

Measures to prevent pollution of the sea by oil and other
wastes will be sought by IMCO. In Rotterdam harbor a private company runs a cleaning service for ships such as this
one.

Rules for collision prevention have been laid down by international agreement. Standard fog signals enable ships to pass each other despite poor visibility.

d.   to provide for the consideration by the Organization of any matter concerning shipping that may be referred to it by any organ or specialized agency of the United Nations.
e.   to provide for the exchange of information among Governments on matters under consideration by the Organization.

FUNCTIONS
IMCO's functions are established in Part II of the Convention.
Article 2
The functions of the Organization shall be consultative and advisory.
Article 3
In order to achieve the purposes set out in Part I, the functions of the Organization shall be:
a.   subject to the provisions of Article 4, to consider and make recommendations upon matters arising under Article 1 (a.), (b.) and (c.) that may be remitted to it by Members, by any organ or Specialized Agency of the United Nations or by any

other intergovernmental organization or upon matters referred to it under Article 1 (d.)

b. to provide for the drafting of conventions, agreements, or other suitable instruments, and to recommend these to Governments and to intergovernmental organizations, and to convene such conferences as may be necessary;

c. to provide machinery for consultation among Members and the exchange of information among Governments.

Article 4

In those matters which appear to the Organization capable of settlement through the normal processes of international shipping business the Organization shall so recommend. When, in the opinion of the Organization, any matter concerning unfair restrictive practices by shipping concerns is incapable of settlement through the normal processes of international shipping business, or has in fact so proved, and provided it shall first have been the subject of direct negotiations between the Members concerned, the Organization shall, at the request of one of those Members, consider the matter.

MEMBERSHIP

As of February 1, 1961, IMCO had forty-five members and one associate member. Members of the United Nations may become members of IMCO by depositing instruments of ratification. Other states may become members upon recommendation of the Council and approval by two-thirds of the members. Territories whose international affairs are the responsibility of a member or of the United Nations may become associate members through communication of this desire by the member or by the United Nations to the Secretary-General of the United Nations.

STRUCTURE AND ORGANIZATION

IMCO's Convention provides for an Assembly, a Council, a Maritime Safety Committee, and a Secretariat.

Assembly

The Assembly consists of all members and meets every two years. The Assembly elects four members of the Council and the members of the Maritime Safety Committee. It considers and reviews reports of the Council and votes the budget of the Organization. The Assembly recommends to members for adoption regulations concerning maritime safety which have been referred to it by the Maritime Safety Committee through the Council.

Council

The Council consists of sixteen members: six represent governments with the largest interest in providing international shipping services; six represent other governments with the largest interest in seaborne trade; and four are elected by the Assembly from governments having a substantial interest in providing international shipping services, or in international seaborne trade.

The Council meets at least twice a year between Assembly Sessions. The Council receives reports from the Maritime Safety Committee and transmits them to the Assembly. The Council submits reports to the Assembly reviewing IMCO's activities between Assembly sessions. It submits budget estimates, with recommendations, to the Assembly. The Council appoints the Secretary-General with the approval of the Assembly and makes provisions for staff appointments and conditions of employment.

Maritime Safety Committee

The Maritime Safety Committee consists of fourteen members elected by the Assembly from among nations with an important interest in maritime safety. Not fewer than eight members shall represent the largest ship-owning nations. Members are elected for a term of four years and may be eligible for re-election. The Committee meets regularly once a year, and at other times upon the request of five members.

The Committee considers such matters as aids to navigation, construction and equipment of vessels, rules for the prevention of collisions, the handling of dangerous cargoes, and other matters. The Committee may perform whatever duties are assigned it by the Assembly. The Committee is charged with maintaining close relationships with other intergovernmental bodies concerned with transport and communication in promoting maritime safety and rescue.

Secretariat

The Secretariat includes the Secretary-General, a Secretary of the Maritime Safety Committee, and such staff as the Council may determine necessary for the proper administration of the Organization.

ACTIVITIES

At its first session the IMCO Assembly agreed to accept duties related to two important international conventions — one on the safety of life at sea and the other intended to prevent pollution of the sea by oil.

The former convention is the main international agreement on rules and recommendations for maritime safety. Dating from 1948, it needed revision to take into account technical and scientific advances. IMCO's first task was to organize a revision conference. This was held in June, 1960. Of the new safety recommendations included in the revised convention, about half call for action on the part of IMCO. For example, IMCO and the International Labor Organization are asked to cooperate in training seafarers in the use of aids to navigation, life-saving appliances and other equipment. IMCO is asked to consult with ITU on technical radio recommendations dealing with distress calls, radio equipment and similar problems. IMCO is requested to look into such questions as standards of watertight subdivision in passenger ships and test procedures for fire protection. The new convention and the collision regulations — revised at the same time — also include recommendations for safety of nuclear-powered vessels, new provisions on the use of radar in reduced visibility and approval of modern types of life-saving equipment. Life-saving signals have been made more precise and signals used by aircraft in search and rescue operations have been incorporated.

The problem of pollution of the sea by oil is difficult and enduring. National laws now regulate disposal of waste by ships to a certain extent. However, lack of conformity in such laws and irregular application lead to an increasing pollution of the sea and damage to the valuable resources it provides to man. IMCO will seek agreement among nations on practical measures to control pollution.

IMCO has tackled another problem which has caused complications in maritime transport — the widely varying systems of measuring the tonnage of a ship. The agency will attempt to bring about a uniform system of measurement. In a further step aimed at simplifying shipping by sea, the Assembly has instructed the Secretariat to investigate ways of reducing the voluminous paperwork now required for ships entering or leaving a port.

IMCO has not taken part in the United Nations Expanded Program of Technical Assistance to date. However, at its 1961 session, the Assembly decided to inform the United Nations that the organization was now in a position to give the technical assistance program advice and guidance on questions in its jurisdiction.

CHAPTER FIFTEEN

IAEA
International Atomic Energy Agency

Tracers in Thailand

Radioiodine . . . . radiochromium . . . . radiopotassium . . . . radioiron . . . . radiosodium . . . . Curious terms? Today these raradio-active elements, commonly known as tracers, are in regular use in hospitals and medical research institutions in the scientifically advanced nations. They have become valuable tools of the medical profession—in therapy, research and diagnosis. In this last field especially, they have made a most significant contribution to medical progress.

A mere five years ago it would have been unlikely that these new tools of medical science could be put into regular use in the underdeveloped regions of the world. Five years ago, in fact, there was not yet a United Nations agency concerned with the peaceful uses of atomic energy. Now the people of the world have such an organization, the International Atomic Energy Agency (IAEA), and the prospects for the underdeveloped nations have undergone a change. IAEA is pledged "to accelerate and enlarge the contribution of atomic energy to peace, health and prosperity throughout the world." One of its important tasks is to give technical assistance to its member nations in introducing and developing the peaceful uses of atomic energy.

Thailand was one of the first members of IAEA to ask for such assistance. A Thai Atomic Energy Commission for Peace had been established in 1954 composed of representatives of the Ministries of Defense and Industry, universities, agriculture and medical institutions. Under bilateral aid programs, a number of Thai scientists had taken advanced training in the United States and other countries. With the help of the Thai Atomic Energy Commission, work with radioisotopes had begun at Siriraj Hospital. However, working conditions in Bangkok, as well as the types of patients and diseases there differed greatly from those in the areas where the Thai doctors had trained. It was felt that having an IAEA expert on the spot would advance their work.

Accordingly, application was made by the Thai government to IAEA for an expert to help develop the diagnostic and research uses of radioisotopes. In February, 1959, Mr. Normal Veall, of Guy's Hospital, London, was sent to Thailand by the IAEA on this mission. Mr. Veall was the first long-term technical assistance expert provided to a member state by the agency. Following a series of lectures before Thai medical workers on the application of radioisotopes in medicine, Mr. Veall began work with the staff at the Radiology Department of Siriraj Hospital and at the School of Medical Technology, which trains laboratory technicians for both Siriraj and Chulalongkorn Hospitals.

Mr. Veall found that Thai medical workers were particularly interested in diagnostic techniques using radioactive chromium (radiochromium). One of the factors leading to this particular interest was the widespread incidence of blood-cell disorders in Thailand. Diagnosis and research in this field was an important practical problem. These particular disorders lead to a type of anemia which can be aided by removal of the spleen. Medical researchers felt that radioactivity measurements would indicate whether the spleen was the cause of the anemia, thus indicating in advance of an operation whether a patient might benefit. To take these measurements, red blood cells of a patient are labeled with radioactive chromium and reinjected in the body. The IAEA expert set up training procedures and arranged for IAEA to provide the essential parts of a scintillation counter to be used for training purpose. A second counter was later secured, and this diagnostic technique soon became routine procedure at Siriraj and Chulalongkorn Hospitals.

Meanwhile, Mr. Veall was assisting the authorities of Chulalongkorn Hospital in establishing a radioisotope measurement laboratory where several new types of work were initiated. Among these

Radioactive meat is fed a snake in experiment concerned with production of anti-venom serum. Thai medical research teams are working under the guidance of an IAEA expert provided under the UN technical assistance program.

was an experimental study of the use of radiophosphorous for diagnosing certain types of lung ailments.

Thai researchers had still another problem to put to Mr. Veall: Could snake venom be labeled with radioisotopes to advance research? These researchers had theorized that venom labeled with radioiodine would be useful in basic studies on immunity as well as in the routine production of anti-venom serums. With the aid of the Pasteur Institute in Bangkok, radioactive cobra venom, labeled with radioiodine, was prepared and some preliminary tests carried out with promising results. Mr. Veall subsequently reported to IAEA that he felt advances in the field of snake venom research would be facilitated by this new technique. He suggested that a stock of uniformly labelled venom be prepared and stored by IAEA for supply to research workers in countries particularly concerned with this problem. This development — a new idea or an advanced technique originating in a less developed country —

was no surprise to officials concerned with the technical assistance program of the United Nations Family of Agencies. Many improved methods or solutions to problems have been worked out first in these countries, and some twenty-five per cent of all technical assistance experts are themselves nationals of the less developed nations.

In the course of Mr. Veall's work in Thailand, he noted several subjects suitable for continued research projects which he felt would be of particular interest to many of the less developed countries. These lines of inquiry included blood disorders, nutritional disorders, and cholera. With the advanced training they have received in the use of radioactive tracers, Thai scientists are now in a much better position to pursue this research. IAEA procedures that foster the exchange of scientific information will channel the results of this research to other nations for use in their own research programs.

Training of atomic energy specialists and scientists is a no less important function of the IAEA's aid to member nations. The fellowship program is financed in part by the agency and in part directly by member governments that have offered facilities to the agency. Among these governments is the United States, which has provided generous training opportunities. In 1960, the United States made provision for IAEA fellows to participate in the first class of graduate scientists and engineers at the new International Institute of Nuclear Science and Engineering at the Argonne National Laboratory. One of the fellows was Dr. Panpit Pansuwana, a young woman who is Assistant Director of the School of Medical Technology at Siriraj Hospital, Dhonburi, Thailand. Dr. Pansuwana was accepted at the Institute on an advanced level as her qualifications indicated that she would be able to contribute significantly to the overall Argonne research program. She specialized in biological research during her fellowship.

IAEA aid to Thailand has not concluded with this one technical assistance expert and fellowship. An agreement between the agency and the government calls for the provision of an expert in the use of tracers in agriculture, a health physicist, an expert in nuclear instrumentation, an expert in prospecting and another in the analysis of nuclear raw materials. Equipment necessary to these projects was also to be provided. As for fellowships, forty-

Radioactivity measurements help to diagnose cause of this child's anemia in Bangkok hospital. Dr. T. Chomnijarakij works with Mr. Norman Veall, IAEA expert.

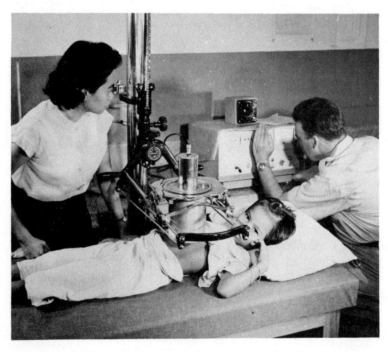

three more have already been awarded to Thai scientists and specialists.

These aid plans arose from the visit of a preliminary assistance mission which studied the requirements of the country with respect to nuclear physics, raw materials, reactors, the agricultural and medical use of isotopes and the training of nuclear personnel. Such a mission is the first step in helping a member nation develop atomic energy. As seen in this report of aid to Thailand, specific needs can be worked out and priorities established on the basis of the mission's survey. Aid can be given where it is most needed and can be best used. Similar missions have now visited more than half of the member nations which have requested such a survey. Specific plans for many of these countries are getting under way in 1961.

Research on the uses of atomic energy in medicine, in agriculture, in the production of electric power, suggests revolutionary improvements to man's way of life on this planet. In setting up an international agency to foster such research, the nations have made clear their intent that these improvements are to be shared by all mankind. Thus the same energy which keeps the world in motion will, in time, bring light to its every surface.

INTERNATIONAL ATOMIC ENERGY AGENCY: IAEA

International Headquarters: Karntnerring, Vienna 1, Austria

ORIGIN

In the now famous "Atoms for Peace" proposal, President Dwight D. Eisenhower, on December 8, 1953, urged the General Assembly of the United Nations to establish an international organization through which the atom might be made "to serve the peaceful pursuits of mankind." In December, 1954, the General Assembly unanimously adopted the "Atoms for Peace" resolution calling for the establishment of such an agency. Eighty-one nations took part in a Statute Conference held at United Nations Headquarters in the fall of 1956, unanimously approving the draft statutes. The Agency came into existence on July 29, 1957 and held its first General Conference in October, 1957.

An agreement bringing the organization into relationship with the United Nations went into effect on approval by the First General Conference. This agreement does not refer to IAEA as a "Specialized Agency," as do the agreements with the other agencies. As an agency established "under the aegis of the United Nations," IAEA is recognized by the U.N. as "responsible for international activities concerned with the peaceful uses of atomic energy" and is accorded a "leading position" in this field.

PURPOSE

The purpose of the International Atomic Energy Agency is set forth in Article II of the Statutes:

The Agency shall seek to accelerate and enlarge the contribu-

Dr. Ranpit Pansuwana, seated, Assistant Director at the School of Medical Technology, Siriraj Hospital, Dhonburi, Thailand, undertakes advanced research at Argonne National Laboratory in the United States on a fellowship grant from the IAEA. Here, equipment used for biology studies is being examined.

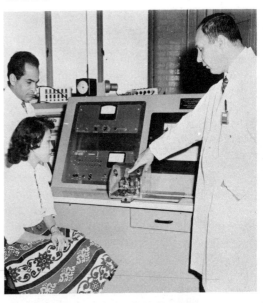

tion of atomic energy to peace, health and prosperity throughout the world. It shall ensure, so far as it is able, that assistance provided by it or at its request or under its supervision or control is not used in such a way as to further any military purpose.

FUNCTIONS

The functions of the Agency are contained in sections of Article III:

To encourage and assist research on, and development and practical application of, atomic energy for peaceful uses throughout the world; and, if requested to do so, to act as an intermediary for the purposes of securing the performance of

services or the supplying of materials, equipment, or facilities by one member of the Agency for another; and to perform any operation or service useful in research on, or development or practical application of, atomic energy for peaceful purposes;
• To make provision, in accordance with this Statute, for materials, services, equipment, and facilities to meet the needs of research on, and development and practical application of, atomic energy for peaceful purposes, including the production of electric power, with due consideration for the needs of the under-developed areas of the world;
• To foster the exchange of scientific and technical information on peaceful uses of atomic energy;
• To encourage the exchange and training of scientists and experts in the field of peaceful uses of atomic energy;
• To establish and administer safeguards designed to ensure that special fissionable and other materials, services, equipment facilities, and information made available by the Agency or at its request or under its supervision or control are not used in

One of two mobile isotope laboratories donated by the United States to the IAEA is presented at a ceremony in Vienna.

such a way as to further any military purpose; and to apply safeguards, at the request of the parties, to any bilateral or multilateral arrangement, or, at the request of a State, to any of that State's activities in the field of atomic energy;

• To establish or adopt, in consultation and, where appropriate, in collaboration with the competent organs of the United Nations and with the specialized agencies concerned, standards of safety for protection of health and minimization of danger of life and property (including such standards for labour conditions), and to provide for the application of these standards to its own operations as well as to the operations making use of materials, services, equipment, facilities, and information made available by the Agency or at its request or under its control or supervision; and to provide for the application of these standards, at the request of the parties, to operations under any bilateral or multilateral arrangement, or, at the request of a State, to any of that State's activities in the field of atomic energy;

• To acquire or establish any facilities, plant and equipment useful in carrying out its authorized functions, whenever the facilities, plant, and equipment otherwise available to it in the area concerned are inadequate or available only on terms it deems unsatisfactory.

Bearing in mind the destructive power of the atom, the Statutes include the following among the Agency's responsibilities listed in Article III:

.... the Agency shall:

• Conduct its activities in accordance with the purposes and principles of the United Nations to promote peace and international cooperation, and in conformity with policies of the United Nations furthering the establishment of safeguarded worldwide disarmament and in conformity with any international agreements entered into pursuant to such policies;

• Establish control over the use of special fissionable materials received by the Agency, in order to ensure that these materials are used only for peaceful purposes;

• Allocate its resources in such a manner as to secure efficient utilization and the greatest possible general benefit in all areas

IAEA mobile training laboratory en route to a Mexican university. Professors use this laboratory to instruct in the techniques and applications of radioactive isotopes.

of the world, bearing in mind the special needs of the under-developed areas of the world;

· Submit reports on its activities annually to the General Assembly of the United Nations and, when appropriate, to the Security Council: if in connexion with the activities of the Agency there should arise questions that are within the competence of the Security Council, the Agency shall notify the Security Council, as the organ bearing the main responsiblility for the maintenance of international peace and security, and may also take the measures open to it under this Statute. . . .

To assist the Agency in safeguarding fissionable materials, its rights and responsibilities are set forth in detail in Article XXII. In part, these are:

· To examine the design of specialized equipment and facilities, including nuclear reactors, and to approve it only from the viewpoint of assuring that it will not further any military purpose, that it complies with applicable health and safety standards, and that it will permit effective application of the safeguards provided for in this article;

· To require the observance of any health and safety measures prescribed by the Agency;

· To approve the means to be used for the chemical processing of irradiated materials solely to insure that this chemical processing will not lend itself to diversion of materials for military purposes and will comply with applicable health and safety standards;

... to require deposit with the Agency of any excess of any special fissionable materials recovered or produced as a by-product over what is needed for the above-stated uses in order to prevent stockpiling of these materials. . . .

· To send into the territory of the recipient State or States inspectors, designated by the Agency after consultation with the State or States concerned, who shall have access at all times to all places and data and to any person who by reason of his occupation deals with materials, equipment, or facilities which are required by this Statute to be safeguarded, as necessary to account for source and special fissionable materials supplied and fissionable products and to determine whether there is compliance with the undertaking against use in furtherance of any military purpose . . . (and) with the health and safety measures referred to in . . . this article;

· In the event of non-compliance and failure by the recipient State or States to take requested corrective steps within a reasonable time, to suspend or terminate assistance and withdraw any materials and equipment made available by the Agency or a member . . .

· The Agency shall, as necessary, establish a staff of inspectors . . .

Continuing, the Statutes call for reports of non-compliance with Agency regulations to be made by the Board of Governors to all members and to the Security Council and General Assembly of the United Nations.

MEMBERSHIP

Initial membership in IAEA was open to any state which was a member of the United Nations or one of the agencies and which signed the Statute within ninety days of its opening date. Subsequent membership required approval of the General Conference upon recommendation of the Board of Governors. Members may be suspended for persistent violations of the Statute or of agreements entered into under the Statute.

As of February 1, 1961, seventy-four states were members of IAEA.

STRUCTURE AND ORGANIZATION

The IAEA has three main organs, the General Conference, the Governing Body and the Secretariat, headed by a Director-General. It is further served by a Scientific Advisory Committee.

The General Conference

The General Conference consists of all members, each having one vote. It meets normally once a year and takes decisions by majority vote, except for financial questions, amendments to the Statute and suspension from membership, which require a two-thirds majority.

The General Conference elects ten members of the Board of Governors, approves membership applications, considers the annual report of the Board, approves the budget recommended by the Board and the appointment of the Director General and approves reports for submission to the United Nations.

The Board of Governors

The Board of Governors consists of members designated or elected on a technological and regional basis. The outgoing Board of Directors designates for membership on the Board the five members most advanced in the technology of atomic energy, including the production of source materials, and the member similarly most advanced in each of the following areas not represented by the aforesaid five: North America, Latin America, Western Europe, Eastern Europe, Africa and the Middle East, South Asia, South East Asia and the Pacific, Far East. Also designated are two

Students of the Guadalajara School of Medicine line up for a session in the IAEA mobile laboratory touring Mexican training establishments at the government's request.

members from among the following other producers of source materials: Belgium, Czechoslovakia, Poland and Portugal, and one other member as a supplier of technical assistance. Ten members are elected by the General Conference with due regard to geographical representation.

The Board of Governors carries out the functions of the Agency. It takes decisions by simple majority except on certain specific matters, such as budget, which require a two-thirds majority. It normally meets every three months. The Board is authorized to establish such committees as it feels necessary.

The Secretariat

The Secretariat is headed by a Director-General, who is the chief administrative officer of the Agency under the authority of and subject to the control of the Board of Governors. There are five departments in the Secretariat: Training and Technical Information; Technical Operations; Research and Isotopes; Safeguard and Inspection; Administration, Liaison and Secretariat.

Scientific Advisory Committee

The Agency has appointed seven eminent scientists to serve as a Scientific Advisory Committee, whose function is to advise on scientific and technical questions arising out of the Agency's program.

ACTIVITIES

As seen earlier in this chapter, IAEA provides a number of types of technical aid to its members. Already referred to are the general survey mission, provision of technical experts and the fellowship. By late 1960, the agency had awarded 1,000 fellowships to scientists from forty-five countries. Another means by which the agency furthers peaceful uses of atomic energy is the training course. These are conducted on several levels. Regional training courses, such as one held in early 1961 in Cairo on the use of radioisotopes, are intended primarily to assist the less developed countries. Others, such as that held at IAEA headquarters in February, 1959, on the techniques of medical radioisotope scanning further the work of scientists in even the most technologically advanced nations. This particular meeting was held in cooperation with the World Health Organization.

Many of IAEA's scientific training courses and seminars are held in collaboration with other United Nations agencies. Special agreements covering all phases of working relationships have been concluded by IAEA with most of the other agencies.

IAEA helps member nations develop uses of atomic energy in still another way — by assisting them to obtain nuclear fuel. The first request — for three tons of natural uranium for use in a research reactor — came from Japan. The uranium requested was given to IAEA by Canada free of charge and was then sold to Japan by the agency for $35.50 per kilogram, a price which covered only the cost of handling. IAEA has also helped Finland to secure enriched uranium.

Research is a major function of the agency. Over 100 scientific research contracts have now been made with institutions and laboratories in member countries. Reports made on conclusion of the research are published and made available to all member states. The agency has now built its own research laboratory near Vienna—the first truly international laboratory—and will conduct many studies there as well.

The publications program of IAEA is yet another significant means of promoting "atoms for peace." Such publications as the "International Directory of Radioisotopes" and "The World Directory of Nuclear Reactors" bring together information never before available from one source. Technical series and reports of scientific meetings make new information widely available.

The agency has also been active in furthering the establishment of safeguards for the atomic age. A conference held with UNESCO in 1959 brought together scientists from thirty-one nations to explore the problem of disposal of radioactive wastes at sea. Further research on this subject is now being undertaken by the government of Monaco for IAEA. Recommendations for the safe handling of isotopes have been published. Studies are underway on the establishment of standards for the safe transport of radioactive materials, the licensing of reactor operations and other aspects of safety and health protection.

One of the major studies being made by IAEA concerns the use of nuclear energy to provide power. This problem is of special importance to nations which anticipate depletion of conventional power resources in the not-too-distant future.

CHAPTER SIXTEEN

Teamwork: The United Nations Family in Action

In 1951, when Libya became independent, the country had scarcely even a postman who could read an address on a letter. There was one Libyan lawyer and no Libyan doctors.

The United Nations, which had unanimously voted independence for this former Italian colony, knew that the country would need help not only in the immediate problem of establishing government services, but in the formidable and long-range task of developing an impoverished economy and educating an unlettered people. Accordingly, the Assembly urged the Economic and Social Council and the United Nations agencies to give Libya all possible technical and financial assistance.

Since that time, just about every member of the United Nations Family has been called on to give expert help to a coordinated development program for Libya. The need for coordination and teamwork in "promoting a higher standard of living" was recognized at the outset. It would not, for example, actually help a nation to improve health and reduce the death rate if there were not a corresponding improvement in food production. U.N. aid to Libya well illustrates the teamwork idea underlying the entire technical aid program.

In Libya, as in other aided countries, technical assistance and U.N. Special Fund programs are administered and coordinated by a resident representative of the Technical Assistance Board. The resident representative has a particularly important role to play in

Typing class at the ILO-aided Technical and Clerical Training Center in Tripoli, Libya. Graduates help fill the country's need for skilled workers.

helping governments to shape specific aid requests. In his on-the-spot office a host of inter-agency problems, which would take months to resolve between headquarters, can be dealt with quickly and effectively.

Chief among the agencies helping Libya are the United Nations Bureau of Technical Assistance Operations, the ILO, UNESCO, FAO and WHO. Each of these organizations has had major programs under way in the country for a number of years. Progress has been marked and encouraging. The Technical and Clerical Training Center, for example, which was established by the government in late 1950, had graduated 460 young men by the end of 1959. At the beginning this project was aided by UNESCO and shortly thereafter was turned over to ILO. The school began in an abandoned barracks with no textbooks and only a few typewriters. ILO provided basic equipment and thirty instructors. Today the school has a well-equipped building and teaching has been turned over to Libyans. In a further step, an Institute of Higher Technology is now being established by the government with U.N. Special Fund aid. ILO also helped Libya draft and put into practice a social security law.

UNESCO's attention has been given to the establishment of a school system. During the four years of war, from 1942 to 1946, all schools were closed, and thereafter only a small fraction of school-age children attended the few elementary schools. UNESCO has concentrated on training primary and secondary school teachers and helping to produce textbooks. This task has been approached in several ways: setting up model schools in the cities and combining teacher training with fundamental education in the rural areas. Gradually these projects, too, are being turned over to Libyans.

Libya is an agricultural country, nearly twice the size of Texas. Ninety-seven per cent of its area is desert sand. FAO has sent technical experts to help create a self-supporting economy from this difficult land. Special equipment has been designed, such as a multi-purpose plough which can be used by peasant farmers. Horticulturists have helped develop non-irrigated nurseries; basic crops have been improved, new crops tested and animal production expanded through government livestock centers. Movement of the sand to growing areas is being checked with plantings. Olive and fruit orchards abandoned when the Italian settlers left are being reestablished.

WHO has helped the government set up public health services. The first Libyan sanitarians and nurses were graduated in 1958 and 1959. UNICEF has been in the picture as well, providing equipment for training schools and for maternal and child health projects, and aiding in tuberculosis control, among other projects.

The roster of U.N. agencies working in Libya continues with ICAO helping to establish civil aviation services; WMO aiding new meteorological services; ITU assisting in the communications field. Some of the projects undertaken by the United Nations Bureau of Technical Assistance Operations illustrate the scope of the activities of this member of the UN team: Libyan officials have been trained in public administration techniques; U.N. experts helped the government take the first census of the country; low-cost housing projects were designed (the first village based on the design was started in 1959); surveys of ports, harbors, electric

Students at this new Tripoli Nursing School, set up with aid from UNICEF and WHO, will staff health centers and hospitals. Nurses are critically needed, as many Libyan women observing Moslem purdah rules cannot be cared for by male personnel.

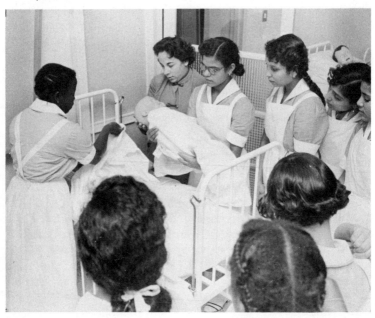

power production and distribution made; advice given on the setting up of a tax system and the establishment of national statistics. A total of fifty-nine experts from UN agencies was working in Libya on January 1, 1961.

Libya is but one example of a region where the multiplicity of skills available through the U.N. agencies are being applied to the problems of underdevelopment. The same type of effort is being made, for example, to help the governments concerned bring a better life to the Indians of the Andean Mountains. In Central America, U.N. aid aims not only to raise the living standards of the people, but to help these republics achieve economic integration. One of the most exciting and comprehensive projects is the regionally-sponsored development of the Mekong River, which flows from the Himalayas to the South China Sea. Still in the early stage, this bold program, initiated by the members of the United Nations Economic Commission for Asia and the Far East, has already drawn in many of the U.N. team members and is receiving aid from the member governments of the Colombo Plan as well. It envisions control and use of a great and untamed river for the benefit of the four lower-basin countries — Thailand, Vietnam, Cambodia and Laos — whose economies center on the Mekong's water.

How does this technical assistance program operate? It is, first of all, a completely voluntary operation. Government contributions to it are freely made. Aid is given only on request. Secondly, it is a multilateral operation. Many nations contribute funds, experts and training facilities and an equally large number of countries benefit. Most of the recipient countries are also donors of skills and funds. About one-quarter of the experts come from countries which are themselves receiving aid.

The program has now completed a decade of operation and

Small multi-purpose plough, developed by FAO expert especially for use by Libyan peasant farmers, is being demonstrated.

some figures indicate its extent: 135 countries or territories received technical assistance in the form of experts or fellowships;
18,000 fellowships were granted and served in 114 countries; experts recruited from 80 countries numbered some 9,000. With the
volume of requests growing — especially from the newly independent countries of Africa — and financial support from governments increasing, the Technical Assistance Board was able to report in the spring in 1961 that "the outlook for international technical assistance has never been as promising as it is today." This
increased financial support — pledges rose from $34 million from
85 governments for 1960 to $42 million from 103 governments and
territories for 1961 — has enabled the Technical Assistance Board
to step up aid to African countries without reducing the share of
assistance to other areas of the world.

Certain guiding principles are followed by the T.A.B. in deciding on a particular aid project. The aid must be requested by the
government; the government must meet local costs and provide
matching personnel and facilities so that work will be carried on
after aid ends; the project must contribute to the economic development of the country, and the aid must be free of political consideration. Recently the T.A.B. was authorized by the Economic
and Social Council to plan aid on a "project" basis, which means
that the T.A.B. will approve a program for its duration whether
that be five years or one. This new system will reduce administrative burdens and ensure continuity of longer-term activities.

A new type of technical assistance administered by the United
Nations has brought a new word into the international vocabulary:
OPEX. This abbreviation stands for the program of providing
operational, executive and administrative personnel to perform,
rather than to advise on, a specific job for a government. OPEX
appointments have included, for example, the chief of the Libyan
Olive Oil Bureau, the Director of Ports and Telecommunications
in Libya, the technical director of a water plant in Paraguay, the
manager of a jute mill in Nepal and an air traffic controller in
Tunisia. Part of the job of an OPEX officer is to train local personnel to take over as quickly as possible. OPEX is particularly
well suited to help the newly independent states by giving them
expert staff who can fill gaps in their services until their own nationals are trained to take over.

An experimental plot of barley for seed improvement, shown here, is one aspect of FAO technical aid to Libya.

Sand dune fixation and reforestation are underway in Libya with FAO advice. Sand dunes are anchored with live plants in the grid system planting near Tripoli, shown here. Trees are set in the center of each grid.

The Libyan government has had the help of UNESCO expert, G. S. Thomas, left, in setting up a national broadcasting system. Technical aspects have been organized and Libyan personnel are being trained at the Broadcast School in Tripoli.

Technical assistance laid the groundwork and pointed up the need for the type of aid given by the United Nations Special Fund. Carrying technical assistance one step farther, the Special Fund aims at helping countries create conditions which will attract development capital and use it well. It concentrates on three types of projects: surveys of natural resources, training of people, and research concerning the uses of local materials and products. As with technical assistance projects, the request for aid must be submitted by a government. The Special Fund contributes only to relatively large-scale projects and requires that the requesting government make a large contribution itself and also accept a long-term obligation to follow up. Most Special Fund projects are aided only for an average of three and one-half years, the intention being to get these essential economic programs started and on solid footing.

Training programs have been emphasized among the 157 projects authorized to the spring of 1961 by the Governing Council, as education at all levels is vitally needed to enable the underdeveloped countries to better utilize technical aid. The variety of aid given by the Special Fund within its three general fields is reflected in the following approved projects: national forestry school (Brazil); instructor and foreman training center (Chile); institute of public administration (Ghana); telecommunications training center (Malaya); institute for petroleum exploration (India); secondary school teacher training institute (Ivory Coast); geological survey institute (Iran); building materials research laboratory (Indonesia); engineering school (Morocco) and soil survey (Pakistan).

Even a brief index of Special Fund projects sheds light on the needs which exist among underdeveloped countries. Virtually every area of economic and social development calls for new knowledge among the people who seek to improve their lives. The underdeveloped nations of the world look to the United Nations Family of Agencies to bring this knowledge to their people. They have learned that the U.N. aid program belongs to everyone; every neighborhood of the world has something to give to it and something to gain from it.

CHAPTER SEVENTEEN

The United States in the United Nations Agencies

Following World War II, there was a marked change in the foreign policy of the United States. This was in keeping with the nation's assumption of a leading role in international affairs. One result of this change has been our active participation in virtually every international organization in the postwar period.

The basic objective of this participation is to forward the nation's interest in world affairs. The national interests of the United States coincide to a great degree with those of other nations. As we strive toward our goals of peace, freedom, and security, we have joined together with other nations to achieve these goals through democratic participation in intergovernmental organizations. In no field of non-political international activity has this cooperation shown more constructive results than those growing out of the conventions, treaties, recommendations and field operations of the Agencies.

The United States is an active member of each of the Agencies. Our participation, first of all, requires authorization by Congress. This authorization has taken various forms. We participate in the International Civil Aviation Organization, the International Telecommunication Union, the World Meteorological Organization, the International Labor Organization (revised Constitution), the Inter-governmental Maritime Consultative Organization and the International Atomic Energy Agency, under the regular treaty-making provisions of the Constitution of the United States. Our

Robert L. Garner, First President of the International Finance Corporation, Washington, D.C.

Paul G. Hoffman, Managing Director, United Nations Special Fund.

membership in the Food and Agriculture Organization, the World Health Organization, and UNESCO is authorized by joint resolutions of Congress which have the effect of sanction for actions of the President. Our participation in the IMF, the Bank, the International Finance Corporation, the International Development Association and the Universal Postal Union is under the mandate of Acts of Congress.

The action taken by the government of the United States in the ratification of the Convention on the Maritime Consultative Organization *(Chapter 14)* serves as an example of general procedure.

The final document of the Conference of Geneva was signed for the United States by Mr. Garrison Norton and Mr. Huntington T. Morse of the U.S. delegation to this Conference on March 6, 1948. Mr. Norton, who headed the delegation, noted after his signature that his approval was "subject to acceptance" by his government.

On June 17, 1948, the Secretary of State transmitted a copy of the Convention to the President for his consideration. In a covering letter, the Secretary of State outined the historical background of the Convention and indicated that the Department of State supported the document with the concurrence of the Department of Commerce, the United States Coast Guard, and the United States Maritime Commission. The Secretary further advised the President that representatives of the National Federation of American Shipping and of the Shipbuilders Council of America had been members of the U.S. delegation to the Conference, and that they too concurred in acceptance.

The Secretary of State further suggested a reservation in regard to the Convention. Article 4 of the IMCO Convention relates to the making of recommendations by the Organization in matters relating to unfair restrictive practices by shipping concerns. As alleged practices of this kind come under the review of the antitrust laws of the United States, the Secretary suggested the Senate insure that if the treaty were ratified it would not have the effect of altering the antitrust laws.

On June 18, 1948, the President transmitted the Convention to the Senate of the United States for its advice and consent, as required in Section 2, Article II, of the Constitution of the United States. The President recommended approval of the Convention with the reservation described by the Secretary of State.

The Convention was referred to the Committee on Foreign Relations in the Senate. Hearings were held on the Convention. Following approval by the Committee, its Chairman transmitted a report to the Senate urging consent to the ratification of the Convention subject to the reservation and understanding suggested by the President. On June 27, 1950, the Senate ratified this treaty and in a resolution set forth its reservations.

The Convention was signed by the President and transmitted by the Department of State to the United States Representative to the United Nations. On August 21, 1950, Ambassador Warren R. Austin transmitted the instrument of ratification to the Secretary-General of the United Nations. In his letter of transmittal, Ambassador Austin conveyed the text of the Senate reservation and added that the statement was "merely a clarification of the intended meaning of the Convention and a safeguard against any possible misinterpretation."

Upon authorization by Congress, and the coming into existence

Mr. C. P. Vasudevan of India, left, studied all aspects of long distance and trunk telephone systems with the American Telephone and Telegraph Company in New York City under the United Nations technical assistance fellowship program.

of a United Nations Agency, the major responsibility for our participation falls to the Department of State. There are some Agencies, however, in which the Department of State does not assume primary responsibility, and these exceptions are worth noting.

United States relations with the Universal Postal Union and the World Meteorological Organization are the responsibility, respectively, of the Post Office Department and the Department of Commerce through the United States Weather Bureau. Our relations with the IMF and the Bank are authorized by the Bretton Woods Agreements Act, which establishes a National Advisory Council on International Monetary and Financial Problems to advise the President on major problems arising out of the administration of these two Agencies. This Council consists of the Secretary of Treasury (Chairman), the Secretary of State, the Secretary of Commerce, the Chairman of the Board of Governors of the Federal Reserve Board and the Chairman of the Board of Directors of the Export-Import Bank of Washington. The Acts of Congress authorizing U.S. participation in the IFC and IDA directed that the Council also handle relations with these new agencies.

The official channel between the United States and the Agencies, other than those mentioned above, is the Bureau of International Organization Affairs in the Department of State. Within this Bureau, the Office of Economic and Social Affairs is responsible for the development of United States policies and activities within the Agencies. This Office insures that spokesmen for United States policy speak with one voice in the international organizations, and that the policy will represent the best possible judgment.

The Offices of International Administration and of Conferences handle the Bureau's many administrative problems arising from assembling and instructing delegates to international conferences. Two other offices in this Bureau concentrate on affairs directly related to United States participation in political-security and dependent-area questions of the United Nations.

The Bureau is headed by the Assistant Secretary for International Organization Affairs, who is responsible to the Secretary of State. He gives approval to policies prepared by the various Offices within the Bureau, which are in turn transmitted to United States representatives at conferences of the Agencies

The Assistant Secretary also maintains close relations with the Congress through hearings before Congressional Committees and in meetings with subcommittees of the Senate Foreign Relations Committee. These meetings not only serve the purpose of keeping the Congress posted on State Department activity in the Agencies, and other United Nations affairs, but they are also important in implementing decisions made by the Agencies that must at all times receive government approval before they become operative in the United States.

Public organizations, groups, and individuals communicate their opinions regarding United States participation in the Agencies, and other international organs, to the Department of State through the Office of Public Services in the Bureau of Public Affairs. This Office in turn may, upon request of organizations or of the Bureau for International Organization Affairs, invite public groups to participate as consultants in policy matters.

The interest of public groups is of vital concern in the cause of international cooperation. The National Citizens' Committee for the World Health Organization may be cited as one of the many examples of organized public interest in Specialized Agency matters. Its purpose is to acquaint the American public with the relationship of public health to the general welfare and peace of the entire world, and to underscore the importance of international health programs.

American citizens are directly influencing the course of Specialized Agency affairs through the high offices they hold in the organizations. These individuals are carrying on the American tradition of international cooperation and good will as it was established by such figures as Postmaster General Blair, Samuel Gompers, and Matthew Maury.

Among the officials active in the organization of U.N. Agencies was Dr. Francis W. Reichelderfer, Chief of the United States Weather Bureau, who has long been prominent in international meteorological organizations, and was named the first President of the World Meteorological Organization in 1951. Dr. Edward Pearson Warner dates his first active participation in aviation back to 1910 when, at the age of sixteen, he entered a glider he had built himself in a meet sponsored by the Intercollegiate Aviation Society. His career since that date has touched virtually every phase of aviation, and was climaxed in May 1947, when the first Council of the International Civil Aviation Organization chose Dr. Warner as its new President.

Americans now holding important posts in the Agencies include Mr. Eugene R. Black, President of the International Bank for Reconstruction and Development, who was formerly senior Vice-President of the Chase National Bank, and has enjoyed a distinguished career in banking.

The International Finance Corporation, an affiliate of the Bank, was first headed by Robert L. Garner, another American experienced in the investment field. Sterling Cole, former chairman of

Mr. Montgomery Blair (1813-1883) who as Postmaster General of the United States was responsibile for the first international postal conference in 1863.

W. Sterling Cole, first Director-General of the International Atomic Energy Agency.

the Joint Congressional Committee on Atomic Energy, was elected the first Director-General of the International Atomic Energy Agency in 1957, while David A. Morse, a skilled administrator, is now serving his third consecutive term as Director-General of ILO. The Managing Director of the United Nations Special Fund, partner of the agencies in development programs, is Paul Hoffman, an American distinguished in international economic affairs.

Standing behind these leaders are hundreds of government officials who are contributing to the work of the Agencies. Hundreds more of our citizens are members of the international civil service, contributing their talents to the effective operation of individual Agencies in dozens of varying capacities.

Individual citizens are contributing to the Agencies in many constructive ways. Private citizens have served as delegates to international conferences called by the Agencies. Others are serving on national commissions and organizations dedicated to furthering public interest in the organizations. International Bank dollar bond issues have been heavily subscribed in the United States financial market. Local groups are underwriting UNESCO gift coupon sales, and other groups are increasing their knowledge of international affairs through studies of the Agencies.

A review of the purposes of the United Nations Agencies shows them to be democratic and humanitarian. These are ideals which Americans have demonstrated they are willing to support — so that the concept of democracy may be maintained, improved, and expanded throughout the neighborhoods of the world. The United Nations Agencies are workshops for the world — a world of peace, freedom, and friendship.

THE UNITED STATES IN THE
UNITED NATIONS AGENCIES

FOOD AND AGRICULTURE ORGANIZATION: FAO

Authorization. The United States participates in FAO pursuant to a joint resolution approved July 31, 1945. On February 19, 1946, the President designated FAO as a public international organization entitled to enjoy the benefits of the International Organizations Immunities Act.

Payments. The United States contribution is paid from funds appropriated to the Department of State for this purpose. Its contribution for 1960 was $2,999,210.

Agencies Chiefly Concerned. The Departments of State, Agriculture, and Interior are primarily concerned with the work of FAO, but there is an Inter-Agency Committee, under the chairmanship of the Under Secretary of Agriculture, composed of representatives of the Departments of State, Agriculture, Army, Interior, Commerce, Labor, Treasury, HEW (Health, Education and Welfare), ICA (International Cooperation Administration) and Bureau of the Budget, which advises the Secretary of State concerning United States policy in FAO and implementation of its recommendations.

Participation. The United States participates in sessions of the Conference by an official voting member designated annually by the President, assisted by alternates and advisers. Participation in the Council is through a member, alternate, and associate members designated by the President.

INTERNATIONAL CIVIL AVIATION ORGANIZATION: ICAO

Authorization. The President ratified the Convention on International Civil Aviation on August 6, 1946, upon the advice and consent of the Senate. The instrument of ratification was deposited August 9, 1946. On May 31, 1947, the President designated the International Civil Aviation Organization as a public international organization entitled to enjoy the benefits of the International Organizations Immunities Act.

Payments. The United States contribution to ICAO is paid from funds appropriated to the Department of State for this purpose. The United States assessment for the calendar year 1960 was $1,307,518.

Agencies Chiefly Concerned. The Agencies concerned are the Civil Aeronautics Board, the Bureau of the Budget, the Federal Communications Commission, the Department of Commerce, the Post Office Department, the Army, the Navy, the Air Force, the Office of Defense Mobilization, the Treasury, and the Department of State. Coordination of U.S. participation in ICAO is handled through the Air Coordinating Committee.

Participation. The United States is the depository government for instruments of ratification of the ICAO treaty. The United States has been represented on the Council of ICAO since its beginning and in addition has representatives in Montreal specifically charged with representing this government on the Air Transport Committee and the Air Navigation Commission. The United States maintains a permanent representative at the seat of ICAO in Montreal.

WORLD HEALTH ORGANIZATION: WHO

Authorization. United States participation in WHO was authorized by a joint resolution approved by the President on June 14, 1948. On December 30, 1948, the President designated WHO as a public international organization entitled to enjoy the benefits of the International Organizations Immunities Act.

Eugene R. Black, President of International Bank for Reconstruction and Development.

David A. Morse, Director-General of the International Labor Organization.

Payments. The United States pays its contribution out of funds appropriated to the Department of State for this purpose. Its contribution for the financial year 1960 was $5,355,110.

Agencies Chiefly Concerned. The Public Health Service of the Department of Health, Education and Welfare, and the Department of State are the United States agencies principally concerned with the United States participation in WHO.

Participation. The United States played a leading part in the movement that led to the establishment of WHO.

UNIVERSAL POSTAL UNION: UPU

Authorization. Authorization for the making of postal arrangements with foreign states rests currently upon the Act of June 12, 1934, which provides that the Postmaster General, by and with the advice and consent of the President, may negotiate and conclude postal treaties or conventions. The Universal Postal Convention of Paris of July 5, 1947, was signed by the Postmaster General, "by virtue of the powers vested by law in the Postmaster General, hereby ratified and approved, by and with the advice and consent of the President of the United States of America," on June 1, 1948; and the President approved the convention on June 9, 1948.

Payments. The United States contribution is paid from funds appropriated for the Post Office Department. Its contribution for 1960 was $26,238.

Agencies Chiefly Concerned. Delegates from the United States to the Universal Postal Congress are appointed by the Postmaster General.

Participation. The United States does not subscribe to the international parcel post, money order, C.O.D., and insurance services on the basis of Union agreements. Individual arrangements are made with each nation concerned, except in the case of the Parcel Post Agreement of the Postal Union of the Americas and Spain.

INTERNATIONAL LABOR ORGANIZATION: ILO

Authorization. By a joint resolution approved June 19, 1934, effective August 20, 1934, the Congress authorized the President on behalf of the United States to accept an invitation for membership in the International Labor Organization. The United States acceptance of the instrument of amendment of the ILO Constitution was deposited August 2, 1948, having been signed by the President pursuant to a joint resolution approved by Congress June 30, 1948. On February 19, 1946, the President designated the ILO as a public international organization entitled to enjoy the benefits of the International Organizations Immunities Act.

Payments. The United States contribution is paid from funds appropriated to the Department of State. The United States net assessment for 1960 was $1,975,364.

Agencies Chiefly Concerned. The determination of U.S. policy toward ILO is the responsibility of the Department of State. This responsibility is exercised in collaboration with the Department of Labor and other interested agencies of the Government through the medium of an Interdepartmental Committee on International Labor Policy on which the Departments of Commerce, Health, Education and Welfare (HEW), Justice, and the International Cooperation Administration (ICA) are also represented.

Participation. Representatives of the Government, workers, and employers have all held seats on ILO's Governing Body.

Delegates from the United States to the annual Conference are appointed by the President. Members of United States Delegations to other ILO meetings are usually appointed by the Department of State.

Under the amended ILO Constitution, additional responsibilities are placed on federal states, including the United States. Conventions and recommendations on questions falling within the jurisdiction of state and territorial governments rather than within the federal jurisdiction must now be submitted to the states and territories by the federal government.

INTERNATIONAL TELECOMMUNICATION UNION: ITU

Authorization. The United States participates in the reorganized ITU through ratification, deposited July 17, 1948, of the International Telecommunication Convention, signed at Atlantic City on October 2, 1947. This convention entered into force on January 1, 1949. Subsequently Congress authorized U.S. ratification of the amended Convention signed at Buenos Aires on December 22, 1952.

On May 31, 1947, the President designated the International Telecommunication Union as a public international organization entitled to enjoy the benefits of the International Organizations Immunities Act.

Payments. Contributions of the United States are paid from funds appropriated to the Department of State for this purpose. The contribution for 1960 was $225,000.

Agencies Chiefly Concerned. The Department of State is responsible for coordinating the interests of various other government agencies in connection with all matters pertaining to international telecommunications. This coordination is generally effected through the Telecommunications Coordinating Committee, which advises the Secretary of State and which consists of representatives of the following interested agencies: the Federal Communications Commission, the Department of the Treasury, Army, Navy, Air Force, Department of Commerce (Civil Aeronautics Administration), and the Department of State.

Participation. Since World War II, the United States has played an active role in bringing about a reorganization of the Union and in revising the radio regulations. It took the initiative in convening the Atlantic City Conferences for these purposes. Because of

the provisions of Article 13 of the Atlantic City Convention stip-
ulating that the telegraph regulations, telephone regulations, radio regulations, and additional radio regulations will be binding
on all members, the United States formally declared in the final
protocol adopted by the Conference that it did not, by signature
of the convention, accept any obligation in respect of the telegraph regulations, the telephone regulations, or the additional radio regulations.

UNITED NATIONS EDUCATIONAL, SCIENTIFIC AND CULTURAL ORGANIZATION: UNESCO

Authorization. A joint resolution, approved July 30, 1946, provided for membership and participation by the United States in
UNESCO and authorized an appropriation therefor. In fulfill-
ment of Article VII of the UNESCO Constitution, this resolution
also authorized the establishment of a U.S. National Commission
for UNESCO. On September 30, 1946, the UNESCO Constitution
was signed for the United States and the instrument of acceptance was deposited with the British government. On May 31, 1947,
the President designated UNESCO as a public international organization entitled to enjoy the benefits of the International Organizations Immunities Act.

Payments. The annual United States contribution is paid from
funds appropriated to the Department of State for this purpose.
The United States contribution for 1960 was $3,832,952.

Agencies Chiefly Concerned. The Department of State is the
agency charged with primary responsibility in relation to UNES-
CO. The Library of Congress also participates in the work of the
organization. Additionally, there is an Interdepartmental Committee on Education Activities in International Organizations
consisting of the Departments of Health, Education and Welfare
(HEW), Agriculture, Labor, State and the International Cooperation Administration (ICA).

Participation. Within the United States, the National Commission for UNESCO was established in September, 1946, and is composed of members named by selected national organizations, officers of certain federal agencies, of state and local educational
authorities, and members-at-large. It works with organizations and

individuals in the development of UNESCO's work.

The UNESCO Relations Staff, provided by the Department of State, serves a dual function as the agency of liaison between UNESCO and the United States Government and as the secretariat for the United States National Commission.

INTERNATIONAL BANK FOR RECONSTRUCTION AND DEVELOPMENT: BANK

INTERNATIONAL MONETARY FUND: IMF

Authorization. United States membership in both the Bank and the Fund was authorized by an act of Congress approved July 31, 1945. The United States signed the Articles of Agreement of the Bank on December 27, 1945, and of the Fund on December 20, 1945. This act also authorized the extension of certain immunities and privileges to the Bank and Fund and their members, authorized the payment of the subscription of the United States to the Bank, and set up, as the body to deal with Bank and Fund matters, a National Advisory Council on International Monetary and Financial Problems. Members of this Council are the Secretaries of Treasury (chairman), State, and Commerce; the chairman of the Board of Governors of the Federal Reserve Board; and the chairman of the Board of Directors of the Export-Import Bank of Washington.

On July 11, 1946, the President designated the Bank and Fund as public international organizations entitled to enjoy the benefits of the International Organizations Immunities Act.

Payments. The United States share in the subscribed capital of the Bank is $6,350,000,000 (20 per cent of which has been paid in), and its quota in the Fund is $4,725,000,000. There are no annual assessments for the Bank or Fund. The Bank meets expenses from income. The Fund meets expenses from earnings.

Agencies Chiefly Concerned. Note *Authorization* above.

Participation. The United States has the right to appoint an Executive Director to the Bank in addition to the United States Governor. As a result of the subscription referred to above, this Director exercises 30.35 per cent of the voting power of all the directors.

The United States has the right to appoint an Executive Director to the Fund, in addition to the United States Governor. As a result of the quota referred to above, the United States Director at the present time exercises approximately 25 per cent of the total voting power of all Directors.

INTERNATIONAL FINANCE CORPORATION: IFC

Authorization: United States membership in the International Finance Corporation was authorized by an Act of Congress approved August 11, 1955. By this same Act Congress authorized the payment of the U.S. subscription and authorized the extension of privileges and immunities to the IFC. The National Advisory Council on International Monetary and Financial Problems was designated as the body to deal with IFC relations, as it does with Bank and Fund relations.

Payments. The United States share in the subscribed capital of the IFC is $35,168,000. As with the Bank and the Fund, there are no annual assessments as expenses are met from income.

Agencies Chiefly Concerned. Note *Authorization* under Bank and Fund.

Participation. The United States has the right to membership on the Board of Directors of IFC, in addition to its membership on the Board of Governors. The U.S. Governor and Director appointed to the Bank serve *ex-officio* on IFC Boards. As a result of the subscription referred to above, the United States Director at the present time exercises 33.99 per cent of the voting power of all the Directors.

INTERNATIONAL DEVELOPMENT ASSOCIATION: IDA

Authorization. The United States membership in the International Development Association was authorized by an Act of Congress approved June 29, 1960. By this same Act Congress authorized the payment of the U.S. subscription. The same privileges and immunities granted to the International Bank were extended to IDA by this legislation and the National Advisory Council on International Monetary and Financial Problems was designated as the body to deal with IDA relations. The United States signed the Articles of Agreement of IDA on August 9, 1960.

Payments. The United States share in the subscribed capital of the IDA is $320,290,000. There are no annual assessments, as expenses are met from income.

Agencies Chiefly Concerned. Note *Authorization* under Bank and Fund.

Participation. The United States led the movement for establishment of IDA, the original proposal for the organization having been made by U.S. Senator Mike Monroney, of Oklahoma. The U.S. Governor appointed to the International Bank serves *ex officio* on the IDA Board of Governors. Similarly, the Executive Director appointed by the U.S. to the Bank serves in the same capacity with IDA. As a result of the subscription referred to above, the United States Director will exercise approximately 28 per cent of the total voting power when the capital of IDA is fully subscribed.

WORLD METEOROLOGICAL ORGANIZATION: WMO

Authorization. Following the consent of the Senate, the United States participation in WMO was authorized by certification of the WMO Convention on May 4, 1949.

Payments. The United States contribution to WMO is paid from funds appropriated to the Department of Commerce (Weather Bureau) for this purpose. The United States contributed $125,913 to WMO in 1960.

Agencies Chiefly Concerned. The United States Weather Bureau of the Department of Commerce is the agency of the United States Government bearing chief responsibilities for our relations with and participation in WMO.

Participation. The United States Government is the depository for instruments of ratification to the WMO Convention. Members of the WMO Congress are represented by the heads of their meteorological services.

INTERGOVERNMENTAL MARITIME CONSULTATIVE ORGANIZATION: IMCO

Authorization. The United States instrument of ratification to the Convention on IMCO was transmitted to the Secretary-General of the United Nations on August 21, 1950. The Convention had been approved by the United States Senate on June 27, 1950.

International Bank bonds are brought to the attention of the investing market.

This advertisement is neither an offer to sell nor a solicitation of offers to buy any of these securities. The offering is made only by the Prospectus.

NEW ISSUE

January 25, 1962

$100,000,000

International Bank for Reconstruction and Development

Twenty Year Bonds of 1962, Due February 1, 1982

Interest Rate 4½%

Price 100%

Plus accrued interest from February 1, 1962

Copies of the Prospectus may be obtained from any of the several underwriters, including the undersigned, only in States in which such underwriters are qualified to act as dealers in securities and in which the Prospectus may legally be distributed.

The First Boston Corporation · Morgan Stanley & Co.

The Chase Manhattan Bank · Bankers Trust Company · First National City Bank New York

Morgan Guaranty Trust Company of New York · The First National Bank of Chicago · Manufacturers Hanover Trust Company

Chemical Bank New York Trust Company · Bank of America N.T.&S.A. · The Northern Trust Company

Continental Illinois National Bank and Trust Company of Chicago · Harris Trust and Savings Bank

Dillon, Read & Co. Inc. · Kuhn, Loeb & Co. Incorporated

Blyth & Co., Inc. · Drexel & Co. · Eastman Dillon, Union Securities & Co. · Glore, Forgan & Co.

Goldman, Sachs & Co. · Harriman Ripley & Co. Incorporated · Kidder, Peabody & Co. · Lazard Frères & Co.

Lehman Brothers · Merrill Lynch, Pierce, Fenner & Smith Incorporated · Salomon Brothers & Hutzler

Smith, Barney & Co. Incorporated · Stone & Webster Securities Corporation · White, Weld & Co.

Payments. The United States contribution is paid from funds appropriated to the Department of State. The United States contributed $49,776, to IMCO in 1960.

Agencies Chiefly Concerned. The Department of State is the agency charged with primary responsibility for relations with IMCO. Coordination with other interested agencies is effected through an interdepartmental committee, the Shipping Coordinating Committee, whose membership consists of the Department of State, the Maritime Administration, Department of Defense and the Treasury Department.

Participation. The United States is represented on the IMCO Council and has been elected to the Maritime Safety Committee.

INTERNATIONAL ATOMIC ENERGY AGENCY: IAEA

Authorization. The President ratified the Statute of the International Atomic Energy Agency on July 29, 1957, upon the advice and consent of the Senate.

Payments. The annual United States contribution to the regular budget of the IAEA is paid from funds appropriated to the Department of State for this purpose. The United States contribution for 1960 was $1,899,560. The United States has also made voluntary contributions to the IAEA General Fund and to the fellowship program.

Agencies Chiefly Concerned. The Department of State and the Atomic Energy Commission share responsibility for United States relations with IAEA. The Atomic Energy Agency implements technical aspects of U.S. participation, including special projects such as fellowships.

Participation. The proposal for a United Nations Atomic Energy Agency was made by President Eisenhower in an address to the General Assembly in December, 1953 and the U.S. is the depository government for instruments of ratification of the Statutes. In addition to contributing to the IAEA General Fund and fellowship program, the United States has given the Agency two mobile laboratories, equipped for teaching use. One of these is visiting Latin American countries, the other is in use in Asia.

APPENDIX

Aims and Purposes of the United Nations

The aims and purposes of the United Nations are contained in the Preamble and Article I of the Charter, which read as follows:

WE THE PEOPLE OF THE UNITED NATIONS DETERMINED
to save succeeding generations from the scourge of war, which twice in our lifetime has brought untold sorrow to mankind, and to reaffirm faith in fundamental human rights, in the dignity and worth of the human person, in the equal rights of men and women and of nations large and small, and to establish conditions under which justice and respect for the obligations arising from treaties and other sources of international law can be maintained, and to promote social progress and better standards of life in larger freedom.

AND FOR THESE ENDS
to practice tolerance and live together in peace with one another as good neighbors, and to unite our strength to maintain international peace and security, and to ensure, by the acceptance of principles and the institution of methods, that armed force shall not be used, save in the common interest, and to employ international machinery for the promotion of the economic and social advancement of all peoples.

HAVE RESOLVED TO COMBINE OUR EFFORTS
TO ACCOMPLISH THESE AIMS,
Accordingly, our respective Governments, through representatives

assembled in the city of San Franciso, who have exhibited their full powers found to be in good and due form, have agreed to the present Charter of the United Nations and do hereby establish an international organization to be known as the United Nations. . . . The Purposes of the United Nations are:

1. To maintain international peace and security, and to that end: to take effective collective measures for the prevention and removal of threats to the peace, and for the suppression of acts of aggression or other breaches of the peace, and to bring about by peaceful means, and in conformity with the principles of justice and international law, adjustment or settlement of international disputes or situations which might lead to a breach of the peace;

2. To develop friendly relations among nations based on respect for the principle of equal rights and self-determination of peoples, and to take other appropriate measures to strengthen universal peace;

3. To achieve international cooperation in solving international problems of an economic, social, cultural, or humanitarian character, and in promoting and encouraging respect for human rights and for fundamental freedoms for all without distinction as to race, sex, language, or religion; and

4. To be a center for harmonizing the actions of nations in the attainment of these common ends.

CHARTER OF THE UNITED NATIONS, CHAPTER IX
International Economic and Social Cooperation

Article 55
With a view to the creation of conditions of stability and well-being which are necessary for peaceful and friendly relations among nations based on respect for the principle of equal rights and self-determination of peoples, the United Nations shall promote:

a. Higher standards of living, full employment, and conditions of economic and social progress and development;

b. Solutions of international economic, social, health, and related problems; and international cultural and educational cooperation; and

c. Universal respect for, and observance of, human rights and fundamental freedoms for all without distinction as to race, sex, language or religion.

Article 56

All members pledge themselves to take joint and separate action in cooperation with the organization for the achievement of the purposes set forth in Article 55.

Article 57

1. The various specialized agencies, established by intergovernmental agreement and having wide international responsibilities, as defined in their basic instruments, in economic, social, cultural, educational, health, and related fields, shall be brought into relationship with the United Nations in accordance with the provisions of Article 63.

2. Such agencies thus brought into relationship with the United Nations are hereinafter referred to as specialized agencies.

Article 58

The organization shall make recommendations for the coordination of the policies and activities of the specialized agencies.

Article 59

The organization shall, where appropriate, initiate negotiations among the states concerned for the creation of any new specialized agencies required for the accomplishment of the purposes set forth in Article 55.

Article 60

Responsibility for the discharge of the functions of the organization set forth in this chapter shall be vested in the General Assembly and, under the authority of the General Assembly, in the Economic and Social Council, which shall have for this purpose the powers set forth in Chapter X.

CHARTER OF THE UNITED NATIONS, CHAPTER X

THE ECONOMIC AND SOCIAL COUNCIL

Composition

Article 61

1. The Economic and Social Council shall consist of eighteen Members of the United Nations elected by the General Assembly.

2. Subject to the provisions of paragraph 3, six members of the Economic and Social Council shall be elected each year for a term of three years. A retiring member shall be eligible for immediate re-election.

3. At the first election, eighteen members of the Economic and Social Council shall be chosen. The term of office of six members so chosen shall expire at the end of one year, and of six other members at the end of two years, in accordance with arrangements made by the General Assembly.

4. Each member of the Economic and Social Council shall have one representative.

Functions and Powers

Article 62

1. The Economic and Social Council may make or initiate studies and reports with respect to international economic, social, cultural, educational, health, and related matters and may make recommendations with respect to any such matters to the General Assembly, to the Members of the United Nations, and to the specialized agencies concerned.

2. It may make recommendations for the purpose of promoting respect for, and observance of, human rights and fundamental freedoms for all.

3. It may prepare draft conventions for submission to the General Assembly, with respect to matters falling within its competence.

4. It may call, in accordance with the rules prescribed by the United Nations, international conferences on matters falling within its competence.

Article 63

1. The Economic and Social Council may enter into agreements with any of the agencies referred to in Article 57, defining the terms on which the agency concerned shall be brought into relationship with the United Nations. Such agreements shall be subject to approval by the General Assembly.

2. It may coordinate the activities of the specialized agencies through consultation with and recommendations to such agencies and through recommendations to the General Assembly and to the members of the United Nations.

Article 64

1. The Economic and Social Council may take appropriate steps to obtain regular reports from the specialized agencies. It may make arrangements with the Members of the United Nations and with the specialized agencies to obtain reports on the steps taken to give effect to its own recommendations and to recommendations on matters falling within its competence made by the General Assembly.

2. It may communicate its observations on these reports to the General Assembly.

Article 65

The Economic and Social Council may furnish information to the Security Council and shall assist the Security Council upon its request.

Article 66

1. The Economic and Social Council shall perform such functions as fall within its competence in connection with the carrying out of the recommendations of the General Assembly.

2. It may, with the approval of the General Assembly, perform services at the request of Members of the United Nations and at the request of specialized agencies.

3. It shall perform such other functions as are specified elsewhere in the present Charter or as may be assigned to it by the General Assembly.

Voting

Article 67

1. Each member of the Economic and Social Council shall have one vote.

2. Decisions of the Economic and Social Council shall be made by a majority of the members present and voting.

Procedure

Article 68

The Economic and Social Council shall set up commissions in economic and social fields and for the promotion of human rights, and such other commissions as may be required for the performance of its functions.

Article 69

The Economic and Social Council shall invite any Member of the United Nations to participate, without vote, in its deliberations on any matter of particular concern to that Member.

Article 70

The Economic and Social Council may make arrangements for representatives of the specialized agencies to participate, without vote, in its deliberations and in those of the commissions established by it, and for its representatives to participate in deliberations of the specialized agencies.

Article 71

The Economic and Social Council may make suitable arrangements for consultation with non-governmental organizations which are concerned with matters within its competence. Such arrangements may be made with international organizations and, where appropriate, with national organizations after consultation with the Member of the United Nations concerned.

Article 72

1. The Economic and Social Council shall adopt its own rules of procedure, including the method of selecting its President.

2. The Economic and Social Council shall meet as required in accordance with its rules, which shall include provision for the convening of meetings on request of a majority of its members.

MEMBERS OF THE UNITED NATIONS AND THEIR MEMBERSHIP IN THE RELATED AGENCIES

COUNTRY	IAEA	ILO	FAO	UNESCO	WHO	IMF	BANK	IDA	IFC	ICAO	UPU	ITU	WMO	IMCO
Afghanistan	x	x	x	x	x	x	x	x	x	x	x	x	x	
Albania	x	x		x	x						x	x	x	
Argentina	x	x	x	x	x	x	x	x	x	x	x	x	x	x
Australia	x	x	x	x	x	x	x	x	x	x	x	x	x	x
Austria	x	x	x	x	x	x	x			x	x	x	x	x
Belgium	x	x	x	x	x	x	x			x	x	x	x	x
Bolivia		x	x	x	x	x	x			x	x	x	x	x
Brazil	x	x	x	x	x	x	x	x		x	x	x	x	x
Bulgaria	x	x			x	x						x	x	x	x
Burma	x	x	x	x	x	x	x			x	x	x	x	x

COUNTRY	IAEA	ILO	FAO	UNESCO	WHO	IMF	BANK	IDA	IFC	ICAO	UPU	ITU	WMO	IMCO
Byelorussia	x	x		x	x						x	x	x	
Cambodia	x		x	x	x					x	x	x	x	x
Cameroun		x	x	x	x					x	x	x	x	
Canada	x	x	x	x	x	x	x	x	x	x	x	x	x	x
Central African Republic		x		x	x							x		
Ceylon	x	x	x	x	x	x	x			x	x	x	x	
Chad		x		x	x							x		
Chile	x	x	x	x	x	x	x	x	x	x	x	x	x	
China	x	x		x	x	x	x	x		x	x	x	x	x
Colombia	x	x	x	x	x	x	x			x	x	x	x	
Congo (capital: Brazzaville)		x		x	x							x	x	
Congo (capital: Lepoldville)		x		x							x		x	
Costa Rica		x	x	x	x	x	x			x	x	x	x	
Cuba	x	x	x	x	x	x				x	x	x	x	
Cyprus		x	x		x					x				
Czechoslovakia	x	x		x	x					x	x	x	x	
Dahomey		x		x	x							x		
Denmark	x	x	x	x	x	x	x	x	x	x	x	x	x	x
Dominican Republic	x	x	x	x	x	x				x	x	x	x	x
Ecuador	x	x	x	x	x	x	x		x	x	x	x	x	x
El Salvador	x	x	x	x	x	x	x		x	x	x	x	x	
Ethiopia	x	x	x	x	x	x	x		x	x	x	x	x	
Federation of Malaya		x	x	x	x	x	x	x	x	x	x	x	x	
Finland	x	x	x	x	x	x	x	x	x	x	x	x	x	x
France	x	x	x	x	x	x	x	x	x	x	x	x	x	x
Gabon		x		x	x							x		
Ghana	x	x	x	x	x	x	x	x	x	x	x	x	x	x
Greece	x	x	x	x	x	x	x		x	x	x	x	x	x
Guatemala	x	x	x	x	x	x	x		x	x	x	x	x	
Guinea		x	x	x	x					x	x	x	x	
Haiti	x	x	x	x	x	x	x		x	x	x	x	x	x

COUNTRY	IAEA	ILO	FAO	UNESCO	WHO	IMF	BANK	IDA	IFC	ICAO	UPU	ITU	WMO	IMCO
Honduras	x	x	x	x	x	x	x	x	x	x	x	x	x	x
Hungary	x	x		x	x						x	x	x	
Iceland	x	x	x		x	x	x		x	x	x	x	x	x
India	x	x	x	x	x	x	x	x	x	x	x	x	x	x
Indonesia	x	x	x	x	x	x	x		x	x	x	x	x	x
Iran	x	x	x	x	x	x	x	x	x	x	x	x	x	x
Iraq	x	x	x	x	x	x	x	x	x	x	x	x	x	
Ireland		x	x		x	x	x	x	x	x	x	x	x	x
Israel	x	x	x	x	x	x	x	x	x	x	x	x	x	x
Italy	x	x	x	x	x	x	x	x	x	x	x	x	x	x
Ivory Coast		x		x	x					x		x	x	x
Japan	x	x	x	x	x	x	x	x	x	x	x	x	x	x
Jordan		x	x	x	x	x	x	x	x	x	x	x	x	
Laos		x	x	x						x	x	x	x	
Lebanon		x	x	x	x	x	x		x	x	x	x	x	
Liberia		x	x	x						x	x	x		x
Libya		x	x	x	x	x	x		x	x	x	x	x	
Luxembourg	x	x	x	x	x	x	x		x	x	x	x	x	
Madagascar (Malagasy Republic)		x		x	x								x	
Mali		x		x	x					x		x	x	
Mexico	x	x	x	x	x	x	x		x	x	x	x	x	x
Morocco	x	x	x	x	x	x	x	x		x	x	x	x	
Nepal			x	x	x					x	x	x		
Netherlands	x	x	x	x	x	x	x		x	x	x	x	x	x
New Zealand	x	x	x	x	x					x	x	x	x	x
Nicaragua	x	x	x	x	x	x	x	x	x	x	x	x	x	
Niger				x	x							x	x	
Nigeria		x	x	x	x					x			x	
Norway	x	x	x	x	x	x	x	x	x	x	x	x	x	x
Pakistan	x	x	x	x	x	x	x	x	x	x	x	x	x	x
Panama		x	x	x	x	x	x		x	x	x	x		x
Paraguay	x	x	x	x	x	x	x		x	x	x	x	x	
Peru	x	x	x	x	x	x	x		x	x	x	x	x	
Philippines	x	x	x	x	x	x	x	x	x	x	x	x	x	
Poland	x	x	x	x	x					x	x	x	x	x

COUNTRY	IAEA	ILO	FAO	UNESCO	WHO	IMF	BANK	IDA	IFC	ICAO	UPU	ITU	WMO	IMCO
Portugal	x	x	x		x					x	x	x	x	
Romania	x	x		x	x						x	x	x	
Saudi Arabia			x	x	x	x	x	x			x	x	x	
Senegal	x	x		x	x					x		x	x	x
Somalia		x	x	x	x						x			
Spain	x	x	x	x	x	x	x	x	x	x	x	x	x	
Sudan	x	x	x	x	x	x	x	x	x	x	x	x	x	
Sweden	x	x	x	x	x	x	x	x	x	x	x	x	x	x
Thailand	x	x	x	x	x	x	x	x	x	x	x	x	x	
Togo		x	x	x	x								x	
Tunisia	x	x	x	x	x	x	x	x		x	x	x	x	
Turkey	x	x	x	x	x	x	x	x	x	x	x	x	x	x
Ukraine	x	x		x	x						x	x	x	
Union of South Africa	x	x	x		x	x	x	x	x	x	x	x	x	
USSR	x	x		x	x						x	x	x	x
United Arab Republic	x	x	x	x	x	x	x	x	x	x	x	x	x	x
United Kindgom	x	x	x	x	x	x	x	x	x	x	x	x	x	x
United States	x	x	x	x	x	x	x	x	x	x	x	x	x	x
Upper Volta		x		x	x								x	
Uruguay		x	x	x	x	x	x			x	x	x	x	
Venezuela	x	x	x	x	x	x	x			x	x	x	x	
Yemen		x		x							x	x		
Yugoslavia	x	x	x	x	x	x	x	x	x	x	x	x	x	x
Total UN Members (99):	68	93	78	93	98	65	63	36	57	79	85	92	88	42
Total Agency Membership:	74	96	82	99	104	68	66	38	58	84	102	105	108	45

See following pages for additional members and associate members.

• UPU *lists separate memberships for UAR (Egypt) and UAR (Syria). However, as of October, 1961, Syria has withdrawn from the UAR and has separate membership in the United Nations. No membership changes have yet been made in the Agencies.*

NON-MEMBERS OF THE UNITED NATIONS AND THEIR MEMBERSHIP IN THE AGENCIES
(February 1, 1961)

COUNTRY	IAEA	ILO	FAO	UNESCO	WHO	IMF	BANK	IDA	IFC	ICAO	UPU	ITU	WMO	IMCO
German Federal Republic	x	x	x	x	x	x	x	x	x	x	x	x	x	x
Holy See	x										x	x		
Korea, Republic of	x		x	x	x	x	x			x	x	x	x	
Kuwait				x	x					x	x	x		x
Monaco	x			x	x						x	x		
San Marino											x			
Switzerland	x	x	x	x	x					x	x	x	x	x
Vietnam	x	x	x	x	x	x	x	x		x	x	x	x	

SUMMARY OF MEMBERSHIP OF UNITED NATIONS AGENCIES
(February 1, 1961)

	UN Member Countries	Non-Member Countries	Territories	Total	Associate Members
IAEA	68	6		74	
ILO	93	3		96	
FAO	78	4		82	6
UNESCO	93	6		99	6
WHO	98	6		104	2
IMF	65	3		68	
BANK	63	3		66	
IDA	36	2		38	
IFC	57	1		58	
ICAO	79	5		84	
UPU	85[1]	8	8	102	
ITU	92	7	6	105	5
WMO	88	4	16	108	
IMCO	42	3		45	1

[1] *Egypt and Syria have formed the United Arab Republic, but are still listed under the former designations by UPU. UPU's count in this category is therefore 86, totaling a membership of 102.*
See footnote • preceding page

ADDITIONAL MEMBERS OF THE UNITED NATIONS AGENCIES
(February 1, 1961)

In addition to the members listed on the foregoing charts, the total memberships of the United Nations Agencies include the following:

FAO:

Associate Members: 6

    Chad
    Gabon Republic
    Malagasy Republic
    Rhodesia and Nyasaland, Federation of
    Senegal
    Sudan

UNESCO:

Associate Members: 6

    Mauritius
    Ruanda-Urundi
    Sierra Leone
    Singapore
    Tanganyika
    West Indies, Federation of the

WHO:

Associate Members: 2

    Rhodesia and Nyasaland, Federation of
    Sierra Leone

UPU:

UPU's 102 members include the following not listed on the charts:

    Algeria
    Netherlands Antilles and Surinam
    Portuguese Provinces in West Africa
    Portuguese Provinces in East Africa, Asia and Oceania
    Spanish Territories in Africa
    Whole of the British Overseas Territories, including the Colonies, Protectorates and Territories under Trusteeship exercised by the United Kingdom
    Whole of the Territories represented by the French Office of Posts and Telecommunications
    Whole of the Territories of the United States, including the Trust Territory of the Pacific Islands

ITU:

ITU's 105 members include the following not listed on the charts:
Overseas States of the French Community and French Overseas Territories
Overseas Territories for the international relations of which the United Kingdom is responsible
Portuguese Overseas Provinces
Rhodesia and Nyasaland, Federation of
Spanish Provinces in Africa
Territories of the United States of America

ITU:

Associate Members: 5
Bermuda-British Caribbean Group
British East Africa
British West Africa
Ruanda-Urundi, Territories of
Singapore-British Borneo Group

WMO:

WMO's 108 members include the following not listed on the charts:
British East African Territories including the Seychelles
French Polynesia
French Somaliland
Hong Kong
Mauritius
Netherlands Antilles
Netherlands New Guinea
New Caledonia
Portuguese East Africa
Portuguese West Africa
Rhodesia and Nyasaland, Federation of
Ruanda-Urundi
Singapore and the British Territories in Borneo
Spanish Territories of Guinea
Surinam
West Indies and other British Caribbean Territories

IMCO:

Associate Members: 1
Nigeria

BUDGETS OF THE UNITED NATIONS AGENCIES
(Including Contributions by the United States)

AGENCY	1959 BUDGET	U.S. SHARE	1960 BUDGET	U.S. SHARE	1961 BUDGET	U.S. SHARE
International Atomic Energy Agency: IAEA	$ 5,225,000	$ 1,698,648	$ 5,843,000	$ 1,899,560	$ 6,168,000	
International Labor Organization: ILO	8,529,857	2,132,464	9,300,909	1,975,364	9,857,110	
Food and Agriculture Organization: FAO	8,500,000	2,712,494	18,800,000 (for 1960-61)	2,999,210 (for 1960)		
United Nations Educational, Scientific and Cultural Organization: UNESCO	12,807,377	3,789,810	13,163,086	3,832,952	16,015,382	
World Health Organization: WHO	14,287,600	4,744,090	16,918,700	5,355,110	19,800,000	
International Monetary Fund: IMF	Meets expenses from earnings. (Administrative budget 1958-59 $6,210,000)		Meets expenses from earnings. (Administrative budget 1959-60 $6,700,000)		Meets expenses from earnings. (Administrative budget 1960-61 $7,385,000)	
International Bank for Reconstruction and Development: Bank	Meets expenses from income. (Administrative budget 1958-59 $9,475,500)		Meets expenses from income. (Administrative budget 1959-60 $10,006,500)		Meets expenses from income. (Administrative budget 1960-61 $11,432,300)	

AGENCY	1959 BUDGET	U.S. SHARE	1960 BUDGET	U.S. SHARE	1961 BUDGET	U.S. SHARE
International Development Association: IDA	(came into existence Sept. 24, 1960)		Meets expenses from income. (Administrative budget 1960-61 $600,000)			
International Finance Corporation: IFC	Meets expenses from earnings. (Administrative expenses 1958-59 $1,413,319)		Meets expenses from earnings (Administrative expenses 1959-60 $1,702,898)			
International Civil Aviation Organization: ICAO	3,672,000 (Canadian)	1,515,771	4,057,000 (Canadian)	1,307,518		
Universal Postal Union: UPU	615,187	22,243	596,977	26,238	681,567 (estimate)	
International Telecommunication Union: ITU	1,587,313	213,200	1,766,198	225,000	2,073,525	
World Meteorological Organization: WMO	498,107	70,710	655,105	125,918	671,379	
Intergovernmental Maritime Consultative Organization: IMCO	726,000 (for 1959-61)	100,000		49,776		

Suggestions for Teachers

Perhaps the one serious objection that can be made concerning the teaching about the United Nations and its related agencies is that it lacks perspective. This is understandable — and dangerous.

Understandable because many American teachers who now hold positions of authority in educational institutions were in the vanguard of those who favored U.S. membership in the League of Nations and the World Court. Having seen their hopes realized in the United Nations, they then proceeded to give this new organization and its agencies a prominent place in school curricula. They prepared numerous "unit studies" and added them to courses of study. Unfortunately there was but little in the way of materials to which the classroom teacher could turn for help. As a result much of the teaching was about the structure of the U.N. rather than its purposes.

Compounding the foregoing is the fact that the headquarters of the United Nations was established in New York. This has given rise to the "tour concept" of world peace. Many students who make a trip through the United Nations complex of buildings come out the other end as "authorities." Teachers have been guilty of fostering this idea. The United Nations has become a popular place to visit rather than an organization to be viewed in perspective.

In addition, we live in a country that can well afford to organize and finance a multitude of private and public institutions designed to foster the idea of world peace. It is indeed lamentable that, with all the resources at their command, only a few of these organizations have produced materials that are useful in the classroom. I hasten to underscore the fact that we should not look to the United Nations and its agencies to supply these materials. They have limited budgets and many people to serve.

Taken all in all, I fear that this combination of eagerness, geographic location, and superficiality have combined to give our students the dangerous idea that the United Nations is the be-all and end-all of world peace. Any student of history knows that the United Nations is but one example of man's will to peace as expressed through many centuries.

This challenge I give to my teaching colleagues — if the United Nations were to come to an end tomorrow, would your students still have faith in the principles underlying international organizations and cooperation?

I list the following examples of approaches to a study of the United Nations and its agencies as ones that may be helpful in meeting this challenge:

1. *The U.N. as an extension of local community services.*

The case studies in this book have a great deal to contribute to this approach. The activities in which the agencies engage have their counterpart in our own neighborhood, no matter how isolated we may feel it to be. Our post office forwards mail to the far corners of the world. Our telephone switchboard links us with millions of people outside our continental limits. We have our local problems of education, health services, working conditions, and transportation. Our banks engage in the financing of local enterprise. Tomorrow's weather is as important to us as it is to the captain of a large ocean-going vessel.

What I am suggesting here is that when teacher and student examine any one of these local services that they then relate them to the Agency concerned. Elementary teachers do an excellent job of explaining how dependent we are on these community services. Many chapters in this book will enable these teachers to relate the local to the international. Ask your students how many problems they can think of that confront a pilot in flying an airplane from New York to Paris. The writer's experience has been that a minimum of fifty will be recorded. Then turn to Chapter 3 in the text and see how the case study replies to these queries. It is relatively unimportant that the ICAO has a headquarters in Montreal, and that it has eighty-four members. The really important thing is that common-sense answers to the original questions demand the cooperation of many nations. When this concept begins to develop in classroom discussion, international cooperation through organization begins to appear in perspective.

I offer several reservations in pursuing this community-services aspect too diligently. One of the writer's graduate students tackled this approach through a flannel-board presentation. She had quite rightly related the local school to UNESCO, the local airport to ICAO, the local bank and post office to their international counterparts. But she had made the very serious error of labeling the local supermarket as FAO and the neighborhood physician as WHO. In fact, the services provided by these agencies are best illustrated by the county farm agent and the local health officer. These agencies did not come into being to distribute food or to minister to illness but rather to raise the quantity and quality of harvests and to lower the incidence of the diseases that beset the human race.

This approach overcomes one of the major difficulties encountered by those interested in education in the field of world affairs — examples of international cooperation seem remote from the everyday life of the average citizen. This problem may best be illustrated by a high school student's remark: "Sure, it's all right to *talk* about this stuff, but what can we *do* about it?"

A well-developed action study in the Agencies lends itself to *action* in the following ways: A thorough study of this kind is a discipline which can have value for the individual as a new source of knowledge, pleasure, and interest; in gathering materials for community groups, schools, and libraries, one is creating resources that may be used by others for study; exhibits reflecting the work of the Agency may be arranged for the school and community; adults may find reasons for interesting themselves in the budgets of the Agencies by communicating their thoughts to their national legislators; young people may participate in the "Trick or Treat" program developed by UNICEF in which 10,000 communities turned Hallowe'en energies into local-information and fund-raising campaigns for UNICEF (details may be had by writing the U.S. Committee for UNICEF, United Nations, New York); together, youth and adults may participate in any one of dozens of working field projects through the UNESCO Gift Coupon Plan (details may be had from UNESCO, United Nations, New York); a study of this kind quickens one's sense of responsibility toward discussion groups, celebrations, and organizations that exist to further an understanding of world affairs.

Action studies within the Agencies will take into account most of those understandings essential to a knowledge of world affairs. It has been the author's experience that such a study tends to lead toward the following goals:

a. A better understanding of global geography.

b. A better understanding of particular regions and areas in the world.

c. A better understanding of the world's supply of natural resources (including food) and their distribution.

d. A better understanding of other peoples, including their race, religion, culture, economic circumstances, and educational opportunities.

e. A better use of current events as reported by the press and other media.

f. An improvement in such basic skills as: map reading; use of globes and charts; use of radio, films, television, pamphlets and other media; acquiring information through research, correspondence, and personal interview.

2. *The U.N. as an extension of local community problems.*

The writer is currently developing a manuscript that includes a series of case studies illustrative of this approach. He suggests particularly to those teachers charged with the responsibility of presenting a course in "Problems of American Democracy" that they may teach the U.N. in perspective by projecting these problems to the international level. This can best be done through the excellent—but unheralded—work of the Economic and Social Council (ECOSOC). This organ of the United Nations deals with the problems of human rights, narcotic drugs, juvenile delinquency, urban redevelopment, housing, unemployment, regional planning, and the like. The case studies are in ECOSOC's archives for the digging. We suggest your class pick up a spade.

3. *An approach through the agenda of the General Assembly.*

A perspective on the workings of the United Nations can be gained by devoting fifteen minutes of class time to a study of the items that appear on the agenda of the General Assembly. This agenda is prepared well in advance, and a copy may be had by writing to the Public Inquiries Unit, United Nations, New York. A good metropolitan newspaper will present the day-to-day debate, and a short daily class review will present the United Nations in perspective. Background information is provided by the Carnegie Endowment for International Peace in their annual September issue of *International Conciliation,* which may be obtained from Taplinger Publishing Co., Inc. 119 West 57th Street, New York 19, New York (price 50 cents).

CLASSROOM MATERIALS

Materials for the development of action studies are readily available. The suggestions that follow are starting points for the building of a resource library.

A.   From the International Documents Service, Columbia University Press, 2960 Broadway, New York 27, New York (Official United Nations Sales Agent):

1. *How to Find Out About the United Nations,* 95 pp., (35c). A valuable handbook that lists resources important to a study of the Agencies.

2. *Everyman's United Nations,* Sixth Edition, 1959 ($3.50). A good basic reference text on the United Nations and its related Agencies.

3. *United Nations Review,* published monthly at the United Nations. Subscription price $6.00 per year. Presents a concise current account of the Agencies and affords good background information on meetings and decisions.

B.   From the UNESCO Publications Center, 801 Third Avenue, New York, New York:

1. *UNESCO Courier,* published monthly by UNESCO. Subscription price $3 per year. An excellent selection of feature articles and photographs, many of which deal with the work of the Agencies. The unusually high caliber of the photographs

in the *Courier* make them particularly useful for bulletin boards and exhibits.

C. Letters should be directed to the Public Information Officer of each Agency explaining the fact that a resource file is being built and requesting catalogues of publications, free materials, sources of films and filmstrips that portray the work of the Agency, and addresses of national commissions or organizations directly concerned with the work of the Agency. *Teachers should request these materials over their own signature and on school stationery. Agency budgets are limited, and their resources are imposed upon when teachers ask students to make broadside requests for information.* Many of the Agencies have done excellent pamphlets concerning particular activities of the organization, some of which are available free of charge and in multiple copies where the purpose of their use is made known. Other Agencies have periodicals that will be sent free of charge to groups expressing interest in the work of the Agency. The Public Information Sections of these Agencies are very cooperative in answering specific questions regarding the Agencies. Address: The Public Information Officer at the following:

FAO, UNESCO, WHO, IAEA and UNICEF have offices at the United Nations, New York

The International Headquarters of the Bank, IDA and IFC are located at 1818 H Street, N.W., Washington, D.C.

The International Monetary Fund is at 19th and H Streets, N.W., Washington, D.C.

ILO: 917 Fifteenth St., N.W., Washington, D.C.

ICAO: International Aviation Building, Montreal, Canada.

UPU: Case, Berne 15, Switzerland.

ITU: Palais Wilson, Geneva, Switzerland.

WMO: Geneva, Switzerland.

IMCO: Chancery House, Chancery Lane, London, W.C.2., England.

D. To supplement these materials the resources of school and community libraries can be used for building a reference bibliography on conditions, activities, countries, and history of the action study decided upon. Articles appearing in newspapers and magazines should be clipped and filed for future reference.

E.   As work progresses on the action study, it is possible to acquire helpful information and literature from the consular offices of the nations concerned as well as from private and public enterprises and organizations that may have an interest in the activity. Most governments have Information Divisions, and a letter addressed to the nation's capital city and directed to the Public Information Officer will establish correspondence.

F.   In no other field is such excellent film and filmstrip work being done. To mention a few of the private concerns, association, organizations, and governmental sources producing and distributing films on international affairs the author has used would be unfair to the dozens of others that could not be listed. Most libraries have standard reference books that review films and filmstrips as well as indicating the sources of supply. As a start, it is suggested that catalogues be requested from the following:

Film and Visual Information Division
Office of Public Information
United Nations, New York

UNESCO Liaison Office
United Nations, New York

G.   The United Nations maintains a Public Inquiries Unit at the United Nations Headquarters in New York. The purpose of the Public Inquiries Unit is to service requests for information about the United Nations and the Agencies. Teachers, students, librarians, and study groups will discover this to be a most valuable resource. From time to time the Office of Public Information of the United Nations issues bulletins on the membership, budgets, and current activities of the Agencies. Copies of these bulletins may be requested of the Public Inquiries Unit. They will prove helpful in supplementing the data included as part of the Appendix to this book.

Index

Mexico: UNESCO Program in, 135; IMF backs currency of, 181

Midwives, India, 75-76

Minimum Time Route (MTR), 49

Monaco, and IAEA, 228

Monroney, Senator Mike, 169-171

Morse, David A., 106, 244

Morse, Huntington T., 239

Morse, Samuel F. B., 117

Moscow, U.S.S.R., postal route to, 92-94

N

National Advisory Council, 170

Naval Observatory, 196

New York City, first international health conference, 79

New York University, 14

Nicaragua, UNESCO Program in, 134

NOEL, IFC investment in, 158-161

Norton, Garrison, 239

O

Oil Pollution, control of, 212

Oldenbroek, J. H., 104

OPEX, 234

Ottoman Empire, 204

Ottoman Lighthouse Company, 204

P

Pakistan, joins IDA, 172

Panel on Artificial Satellites, WMO Agency, 202

Pansuwana, Dr. Panpit, 217

Paris, 197

Paris Peace Conference 1919, air flight agreements, 59-61

Pasteur Institute, Bangkok, 216

Peso, IMF backing of, 181

Phonetic Alphabet, international, 66-67

Postal Conferences: first international, 96-97

Postal Studies, Consultative Committee for, 99-100

Post Office Dept., U.S., cooperation with U.N., 91-94

Provisional International Civil Aviation Organization, 61

Q

Queens College (N.Y.), 14

R

Radioactive Wastes, disposal of, 228

Radio Frequency Allocation Table, 127

Radioisotopes, 215-218, 227

Red Sea, 203-204

Reichelderfer, Dr. Francis W., 243

Rhine Navigation Conference (1946), 103-104

Rhine River, transport on, 101-109

Roads, Bank loans for construction of in Ethiopia, 146-150

Rome, early fish culture, 26-27

Routh, Martin, commercial fishing expert, 34-35

"Trick or Treat" for
UNICEF, 89

U

UNESCO, *see* United Nations
Educational, Scientific and
Cultural Organization

UNICEF, *see* United Nations
Children's Fund

United Nations Children's
Fund (UNICEF): case
study, 70-78; headquarters,
85; origin, 85; purpose,
85-86; Structure and
Organization, 87; activities,
87-88; finances, 88-89

United Nations Educational,
Scientific and Cultural
Organization (UNESCO):
case study of, 131-136;
headquarters, 136; gift-
coupon plan, 136; origin,
136; purpose, 137; functions,
137-138; members, 138-139,
261-266; Structure and
Organization, 140; activities,
140-143; U.S. in, 250-251;
budget, 268

United Nations, establishes
relationship with Agencies,
20

United Nations, High Com-
missioner for Refugees, 21

United Nations, postage
stamps, 91-92

United Nations Relief and
Rehabilitation Administration (UNRRA), 21

United Nations Special Fund,

see Special Fund of United
Nations

United States in United
Nations Agencies: Bank,
251-252; FAO, 245-246;
IAEA, 255; ICAO, 246; IDA,
252-253; IFC, 252; ILO,
248-249; IMCO, 253-254;
IMF, 251-252; ITU, 249-250;
UNESCO, 250-251; UPU,
247-248; WHO, 246-247;
WMO, 253

Universal Postal Congress,
98-99

Universal Postal Union (UPU):
case study, 91-96; head-
quarters, 96; origin, 96-97;
purpose, 97-98; functions,
98; membership, 98, 261-266;
Structure and Organization,
98-100; activities, 100; U.S.
in, 247-248; budget, 268

UNRRA, *see* United Nations
Relief and Rehabilitation
Administration

UPU, *see* Universal Postal
Union

V

Veall, Norman, 215-218

Venezuela, UNESCO
Program in, 134-135

Versailles Peace Conference,
109-110

Vienna, IAEA laboratory
at, 228

W

Warner, Dr. Edward, quoted
purposes ICAO, 68-69, 243